PENGUIN BOOKS

THE VATICAN DIARIES

John Thavis recently retired as the prizewinning chief of the Rome bureau of Catholic News Service, where he had covered the Vatican since 1983. He is the past president of the International Association of Journalists Accredited to the Vatican, and in 2007 the Catholic Press Association awarded him the Saint Francis de Sales Award, the highest honour given by the Catholic press. He divides his time between Minnesota and Rome.

D0993800

John Thavis

THE VATICAN DIARIES

A Behind-the-Scenes Look at the
Power, Personalities and Politics at
the Heart of the Catholic Church

PENGUIN BOOKS

PENGUIN BOOKS

Published by the Penguin Group
Penguin Books Ltd, 80 Strand, London WC2R ORL, England
Penguin Group (USA) Inc., 375 Hudson Street, New York, New York 10014, USA
Penguin Group (Canada), 90 Eglinton Avenue East, Suite 700, Toronto, Ontario, Canada M4P 2Y3
(a division of Pearson Penguin Canada Inc.)
Penguin Ireland, 25 St Stephen's Green, Dublin 2, Ireland (a division of Penguin Books Ltd)
Penguin Group (Australia), 707 Collins Street, Melbourne, Victoria 3008, Australia
(a division of Pearson Australia Group Pty Ltd)
Penguin Books India Pvt Ltd, 11 Community Centre, Panchsheel Park, New Delhi – 110 017, India
Penguin Group (NZ), 67 Apollo Drive, Rosedale, Auckland 0632, New Zealand
(a division of Pearson New Zealand Ltd)
Penguin Books (South Africa) (Pty) Ltd, Block D, Rosebank Office Park,
181 Jan Smuts Avenue, Parktown North, Gauteng 2193, South Africa

Penguin Books Ltd, Registered Offices: 80 Strand, London WC2R ORL, England

www.penguin.com

First published in the United States of America by Viking Penguin,
a member of Penguin Group (USA) Inc. 2013
First published in Great Britain in Penguin Books 2013
001

Copyright © John Thavis, 2013
All rights reserved

The moral right of the author has been asserted

Printed in Great Britain by Clays Ltd, St Ives plc

ISBN: 978-0-241-96741-6

www.greenpenguin.co.uk

Penguin Books is committed to a sustainable
future for our business, our readers and our planet.
This book is made from Forest Stewardship
Council™ certified paper.

ALWAYS LEARNING   **PEARSON**

To Laurie

CONTENTS

This is the very perfection of man, to find out his own imperfections.

—Saint Augustine

THE
VATICAN
DIARIES

INTRODUCTION

To judge by the headlines, the Vatican seemed to be un-
raveling. In the middle of 2012, a series of leaked documents
prompted Pope Benedict to launch an internal investigation. The
documents were embarrassing, if not exactly incriminating; many dealt
with the murky world of Vatican finances, while others revealed details of
security operations, notes from private papal meetings and letters from
high-profile Italian personalities seeking papal audiences—some with an
enclosed check. In the eyes of top Vatican officials, the most scandalous aspect of what the press dubbed "Vatileaks" was not the content of the leaked
material, but the fact that classified documents were being circulated at all.

As someone who has covered the Vatican for thirty years, I know that
"Vatican secrecy" is largely a myth. More than three thousand people work
in the Vatican's administrative machine, and many of them will share information if given the opportunity. But such information is typically
passed on through casual conversation, not purloined documents. It was
that detail that made this scandal so unusual, and that led a triumvirate of
investigating cardinals to aggressively pursue the culprits. The paper trail
led rather easily to Paolo Gabriele, who as the pope's valet was one of the
few people with access to the daily flow of documents in and out of the
papal apartment. The father of three children, a devout Catholic who had
worked since 1998 in the service of two popes, Gabriele seemed an unlikely Vatican mole. The universal assumption was that he was being manipulated by higher-ups. All of which, as explained more fully in this
book's final chapter, pointed to an increasingly open power struggle inside
the Roman Curia.

The news of Paolo Gabriele's arrest generated curiosity and a degree
of derision in the news media. "The butler did it" became the punch line
to a bad joke, and the joke was on the Vatican. To make matters worse, the

aging Pope Benedict seemed painfully unaware of what was going on around him.

Meanwhile, another drama was unfolding: The president of the Vatican bank, Ettore Gotti Tedeschi, once touted as Pope Benedict's financial reformer, was summarily and very publicly fired. Among the reasons listed in a harshly worded memo were Gotti Tedeschi's "progressively erratic" personal behavior and his failure to explain "the dissemination of documents last known to be in the president's possession."

To most outsiders, this was a new Vatican, a Vatican that had gone off the rails. I viewed the events a bit differently. To me, they were the public eruption of a private culture that has long reigned inside the Vatican walls—a culture of miscommunication and miscues, of good intentions and flawed execution, of conflicting agendas and shifting alliances. It is a culture in which clerical careerism often overshadows quiet dedication to the work of the church. It is a culture founded on hierarchical order, but swamped in organizational confusion. It is a culture in which the pope is considered immune from criticism, yet often is kept uninformed about the details of important decisions. It is, in theory, a culture of confidentiality— yet it leaks like a two-thousand-year-old boat.

When I began covering the Vatican for Catholic News Service, or CNS, in the early 1980s, I was stunned by the lack of coordination among Roman Curia offices and the haphazard way information was made public—more often via a maze of rumor and innuendo rather than through official channels. Eventually I came to appreciate the opportunities afforded by such ambiguity. Because the atmosphere within the Vatican is more medieval village than corporate headquarters, I found myself working most effectively through informal encounters and backdoor conversations. My sources ran the gamut from top Vatican diplomats to the ushers in Saint Peter's Basilica—and once they came to know and trust you, they all talked. I soon learned that the restricted communication flow at the Vatican worked in my favor: Given the isolation of many Roman Curia offices, a reporter was often viewed as a necessary pollinating agent, bringing grains of gossip and traces of intelligence from one department to another. Unwittingly, we were part of the Vatican grapevine.

I discovered that, despite its institutional facade, the Vatican remains predominantly a world of individuals, most of whom have a surprising amount of freedom to operate—and, therefore, to make mistakes. It's not only that many cardinals and department heads behave like feudal lords; there's also a significant population of minor officials, consultants, adjuncts and experts who see themselves as protagonists in their own right, bit players who from time to time wander onto center stage.

As endearing as I find this lack of micromanagement, it has undoubtedly brought headaches and embarrassment to the Vatican in recent years. A core element of the Catholic Church's mission, after all, is to convince others of the truth of its faith. Evangelizing is effective communication—yet the Vatican has become a kind of showcase for missteps, distractions and mixed messages, a place where the pope is upstaged by his own gaffes or those of his top aides.

Part of the reason is the oddly parochial attitude that still prevails within the universal nerve center of the Catholic Church. There's a chronic disconnect between what people say and do in Vatican City and the effect that has on the 1.2 billion Catholics around the world. The tale of Sławomir Oder is instructive.

In January 2010 much of the world was surprised to learn that the late Pope John Paul II had for years whipped himself with a leather belt as a form of self-mortification. The news left many Catholics bewildered and a little disappointed; this was the pope, after all, who was known for his "Theology of the Body," a series of 129 talks that described the beauty of the human body as part of God's plan—an approach deemed "revolutionary" by Catholic commentators, particularly for its positive vision of human sexuality. Self-flagellation, in the minds of most people, suggested self-loathing and an unhealthy attitude toward one's own body. The Polish pontiff, it was said, had a belt hanging on a hook in his closet, and the nuns who cooked and cleaned for him would hear the groans when he used it on his own back.

As soon as I heard the news, I wondered why the Vatican was putting out this particular tidbit of information. But it turned out that top people at the Vatican were as blindsided as everyone else by the revelation, which appeared in a book written by the official promoter of John Paul's sainthood cause, Polish Monsignor Sławomir Oder. The enthusiastic monsignor had teamed up with an Italian journalist to draw a portrait of "the real John Paul II," as the cover of the book proclaimed. The book was launched at a press conference at the Hotel Columbus, a few steps from Saint Peter's Square. Strangely, no Vatican official attended. The reason, I learned, was that Oder had had no Vatican authorization for the biography. His book was a personal project and, amazingly, no one had bothered to stop him.

The disclosure of the late pope's penitential practices could not have come at a more awkward time. Nearly five years after his death, the church was preparing to declare John Paul blessed, a major step toward sainthood, and Pope Benedict XVI was expected to set the date of the official ceremony sometime soon. In the hopes of Vatican officials, the beatification Mass would recapture the spiritual intensity that had marked the days of John Paul's funeral and Benedict's election in 2005. Rome would once again be the center of the world, hosting millions of people and thousands of journalists, and the Catholic Church would be given another unparalleled opportunity to get its message across through modern media.

Now a shadow hung over that scenario. Self-mortification practices like fasting had been standard in the Catholic Church for centuries. But whipping oneself with a belt? In the popular imagination, it evoked the bloody scene of self-flagellation by the albino monk in *The Da Vinci Code*, which had been ridiculed by Catholics as a grotesque exaggeration.

"Is this the image we want to give people of the world today? Is this our model of holiness? Flagellation is archaic. It's something from the past, and that's where it belongs," one Vatican official quietly vented to me when I began calling around for reaction.

Another priest who used the legacy of John Paul II in his ministry with the sick was equally distressed. The late pope, he said, was widely respected for his acceptance of the suffering caused by illness, not for self-inflicting pain.

Others began questioning why Monsignor Oder had been allowed to publish a book based on confidential testimony that he, as postulator, or primary manager, of the cause, was supposed to keep private. Polish Father Adam Boniecki, a longtime adviser to Pope John Paul, was incensed, observing, "It's surprising and grave that it was the postulator who wrote something like this. These are episodes, documents and revelations about the private life of Pope John Paul that are covered by pontifical secret." Monsignor Oder was quickly summoned to Poland for talks with Cardinal Stanisław Dziwisz, Pope John Paul's former secretary, who was said to be equally disturbed. In Rome, church officials noted that the Vatican had appointed Oder to shepherd the beatification cause to the finish line—not scoop the Vatican with a tell-all book. Some suggested he be quietly dismissed.

The more I gauged the Vatican's irritation level, the more I realized that Oder's book was a classic example of the fragmented chain of command in what is arguably the world's most hierarchical organization. In theory, the Vatican operates according to a top-down structure of authority; in actual fact, the Vatican is a patchwork of departments, communities and individuals, all loosely bound by a sense of mission but without comprehensive management or rigorous oversight. And, I must admit, I prefer it that way. I appreciate the fact that functionaries often shoot their mouths off when they're not supposed to, that documents are leaked and that, at the end of the day, the Vatican is marked more by human flair and fallibility than ruthless efficiency. I like the fact that even something as supposedly finetuned as a sainthood cause can be fumbled by an overzealous promoter.

The popular image of the Vatican is largely a myth. In the news and entertainment industries, the Vatican is portrayed as an organizational behemoth—monumental, powerful and cloaked in secrecy, a well-oiled machine quietly pursuing a global agenda with a hierarchy that marches in lockstep.

The real Vatican is a place where cardinals crack jokes and lose their tempers, where each agency of the Roman Curia jealously guards its turf, where the little guys and big shots may work at cross-purposes and where slipups and misunderstandings are common. It's a place where the pope's choice of a particular hat can become the raging controversy of the day, and where an American cardinal hell-bent on underground parking can evict a two-thousand-year-old necropolis. It's a place where the carefully orchestrated liturgies and ceremonies sometimes come unglued. It's a place where Paolo Gabriele and Sławomir Oder fit right in.

Over the years, I've also met a number of Vatican employees I would place in the "faithful servant" category. Like most major bureaucracies, the Vatican has its share of quiet heroes, people working silently against the odds to make the church more responsive and more transparent. Their stories rarely surface in news accounts of Vatican crackdowns, scandals and pronouncements, yet they help steady the ship and correct its course.

All of this, I decided, needed to be told. I wanted to accurately depict the culture behind the headlines and explain how things really work at the Vatican—not through the pope's speeches or official texts and declarations, and not through political analysis of Vatican policy, but from the inside, where the business of governing the universal church churns and sputters. I wrote this book because I'm convinced that the backstage reality at the Vatican is infinitely more interesting than the caricature of power and authority that dominates mainstream media. As a reporter and then Rome bureau chief for Catholic News Service from 1983 to 2012, I was able to witness the Vatican's internal dynamics from a privileged vantage point. My job routinely took me into Vatican offices, placed me in the front row of papal ceremonies and even got me a seat on the papal plane.

This is a book of fact, not fiction. The episodes described in its pages actually happened. My narration, which includes some reconstructed dialogue, is based on hundreds of interviews, transcripts, audio and video archives and firsthand observation. The characters, bigger and lesser, are real. And although their stories may occasionally have a through-the-looking-glass quality, know that they are not the product of journalistic imagination, but an accurate chronicle of life and times in a most curious world.

CHAPTER ONE

THE BELLS

THE VATICAN HILL on the west side of Rome has hosted ecclesial drama since the earliest days of the Roman Catholic Church. Saint Peter was believed to have been crucified here under the Emperor Nero, in the middle of a racing circus—a spot that today lies just below the Vatican's duty-free mini-mall. Nero, according to church historians, used to throw nighttime parties in what are now the Vatican Gardens, illuminating the festivities by tying Christians to high poles and setting them on fire. The persecutions eventually ended, and Saint Peter's tomb in the cemetery on the Vatican hill eventually became such a popular pilgrimage site that the Emperor Constantine decided to build a sumptuous basilica there in AD 326. Local tradition says he was so enthused about the project that he took off his royal finery and began digging the foundations with his own hands.

Renaissance popes rebuilt the basilica half a millennium ago on an even more massive scale. It is architecture designed for theater, and the drama is never more intense than when a pope dies and a new one is elected. The dead pope is carried in procession and placed on a bier beneath the basilica dome, where he lies in state before his funeral. If he was much loved, like John Paul II, pilgrims come from around the world to pay their respects. But popes have not always been so popular. In 1559, when Paul IV died, Romans rioted in celebration and broke open the prisons of the Inquisition; in the late 1800s Pope Pius IX's hearse was attacked by an anticlerical mob and his corpse narrowly escaped being thrown into the Tiber River. Only in the last century did popes become widely respected defenders of human rights, peace and social justice. Their funerals nowadays bring kings and queens, premiers and presidents to a kneeling position before the papacy. The pope is buried, usually in the basilica crypt. Some days later, a curtain is pulled aside and a new pope appears on the balcony of the church's central facade, cheered by a passionate crowd of the faithful in Saint Peter's Square. The transition is complete: Sadness has turned to excitement, and the death knell of the basilica bells is replaced by peals of joy.

In April 2005 an estimated two billion people followed those events on television or the Internet following the death of John Paul II. For the first time in history, papal transition became a global experience as Saint Peter's Basilica served as the backdrop for endless TV stand-ups, pilgrim interviews and liturgical play-by-play commentary. As the 115 voting cardinals prepared to enter into conclave, journalists began reporting signs of what appeared, in retrospect, an almost inevitable outcome: the election of German Cardinal Joseph Ratzinger as Pope Benedict XVI. Framed in tradition and colored by ceremony, the announcement of *habemus papam* must have seemed like one of the most choreographed moments of church pageantry to those watching around the world.

Yet what the world saw was one thing; what was actually going on inside the ornate hallways and chambers of the Vatican was quite another.

The papal election was the most fascinating news event I'd covered in many years. But for months afterward I was bothered by a nagging mystery. One day, long after the conclave paraphernalia had been put back in storage and the words "Pope Benedict" no longer sounded strange, I walked over to Saint Peter's Basilica and went looking for a man named Giuseppe. I heard he had a story to tell.

It was day two of the conclave, April 19, 2005, and a faint odor of incense still hung in the air from the morning Mass, wafting from the Chapel of the Most Holy Sacrament across the nave of the great basilica, where it blended with a new and stronger smell, one that rose from an immense crowd of tired and sweaty pilgrims.

Enrico, an usher in Saint Peter's, stood sentrylike in a crisp blue suit and lifted his eyes toward the logjam of visitors. "Ciao, Giuseppe," he said. "Another long day, huh? It's never going to end."

Giuseppe Fiorucci shrugged and kept moving across the patterned floor of the basilica. Enrico was a talker, and Fiorucci didn't have time for a conversation. A short man with a steady gait, he steered a course around the mass of humanity and was glad, today as all days but especially today, that he was not an usher—glad that it was someone else's job to deal with the questions in ten languages and the crying babies and "Where's the bathroom?" and "No flash, please" and "Can we leave flowers?" and "How long before we get to the pope's tomb?" Today he was glad he was only a *sampietrino*, a basilica workman, and that his blue denim outfit exempted him from dealing with all the needs of so many pious and insistent people.

He reached the other side of the church, adjusted the glasses on his broad face and gazed back. The light was stretching across the main aisle now, illuminating the red and white patches of the Polish flags draped across backpacks and shoulders. So many Poles. First to see the body, now to see the tomb. Three million in ten days, the news reported. According to Enrico, never had so many people passed through Saint Peter's. Enrico was just an usher, of course, but he sometimes had coffee with Bishop Lanzani, and Bishop Lanzani knew everything about the basilica. Or so they said.

"Attention, please!" Paolo, who was doing guard duty to the left of the main altar, came up from behind and wrapped his big hands around Fiorucci's neck. He continued his joke in flawed English: "We remind you to please to remain quiet."

Paolo nodded toward a small rear door of the basilica and made a sign that he needed a smoke. Fiorucci shook his head, but Paolo dragged him by the sleeve. The doorway, however, was blocked by a rope barrier attached to brass hooks, and two Vatican gendarmes stood sentry. His cigarette break would have to wait.

"I forgot. The cardinals," Paolo muttered under his breath.

The back door of Saint Peter's led to a parking lot in front of the Domus Sanctae Marthae, the $20 million guesthouse that lodged the cardinals who would elect the new pope. The *Domus* was on the south side of the basilica; the Sistine Chapel, where the voting sessions were held, was on the north. Most cardinals came out to board a bus that took them through the Vatican Gardens to the Sistine, but you could always count on the oddball who would insist on going by foot. Yesterday it was German Cardinal Walter Kasper, who took a route through the Vatican Gardens. This morning a Latin American cardinal was walking the travertine path around the back of Saint Peter's. The Vatican security guards and the basilica staff had to make sure the door was sealed and that no one—not one pilgrim with a flag, not one child with a loud voice, not even a bishop—could in any way communicate with the cardinals as they passed. Not that anyone was trying.

The pilgrims inside the basilica, in fact, had little immediate interest in the Sistine Chapel proceedings. They were all headed downstairs to the crypt where John Paul II lay buried. But when they reached his tomb, after waiting hours in line, they had an unpleasant surprise: They couldn't stop to pray. They were essentially on a conveyor belt, told to keep moving along. They couldn't even take photos. This seemed strange: When the pope had been lying in state, the basilica ushers did nothing to prevent people from taking snapshots or cell phone photos of the dead pontiff; now they would yell at anyone who pulled out a camera. The reason was logistical. Up in the basilica, the main aisle was wide enough to contain a river of pilgrims that flowed at a good speed past the papal bier. Down in the crypt, it was shoulder to shoulder, with barely space for a single-file line. When the line stopped, the ambience turned claustrophobic and people started to panic. So the rule was no photos, no praying, no singing, no placing objects near the tomb. The lucky ones got to toss written messages in a big straw basket.

The brusqueness of the ushers contrasted with the sentiments of the visitors, many of whom were crying. To those who worked at the Vatican, it seemed the pope's death had unleashed so much raw emotion—too much, perhaps. The media had turned it into a personal story about the humanity of John Paul II and the way he had touched people around the globe. Yet many of those who worked here didn't feel the pathos. One basilica official named Alfredo recalled a conversation with a security guard who had served Pope John Paul through his entire pontificate and had traveled with him to more than 130 countries. As the security guard did duty at the foot of the pope's corpse, Alfredo had approached to pay his respects.

The guard looked up and asked with absolute nonchalance: "Alfredo, how you doing?"

He was taken aback by the familiar tone, two feet from the dead pope.

"Well, I'm a little sad."

"Why?" the guard said abruptly.

"Because this man worked very hard for twenty-six years and suffered a lot at the end," he said.

"But, Alfredo, the pope is dead!" the guard rejoined.

In other words, why waste your sentiments? In fact, many Vatican employees—even the ones who knew and respected John Paul—seemed somewhat detached about his passing.

Fiorucci walked back toward the front of the church, turning inside a small vestibule off the side aisle, which housed the elevator to the roof. He placed his hand along a wall panel and gave a little shove. The panel opened, revealing a hidden inner wall hung with all manner of keys. He picked one set from a hook, and then another, and closed the panel quietly.

Riccardo was sitting on his chair next to the lift. "Going up again?" he asked.

Fiorucci nodded. The two men stepped inside the Otis elevator, Riccardo turned a key and it whirred up slowly through a shaft carved out of brick masonry. Riccardo was happy to have some company. He spent most days hauling load after load of tourists back down from the cupola, but the roof had been closed until the conclave was over.

"Drop me off at the *lumaca*," Fiorucci said.

The elevator glided to a stop and Fiorucci walked out into a narrow hallway.

"White smoke today—you'll see," Riccardo said. Then the doors closed and he disappeared. After a few seconds, silence. The heavy silence you find inside walls that are twenty feet thick.

Fiorucci trudged along a dusty, narrow corridor. White smoke? That would be nice. But not likely this morning. It was too early. He walked past dim rooms hidden in the basilica's inner walls, alongside bare brick, kicking up pigeon feathers. The birds came in through air shafts or other holes in the basilica. They were a problem, but you couldn't seal a building like this—it had to breathe. The masonry expanded and contracted like a lung, sometimes as much as five inches in a single day. "Thermal shifting," Bishop Lanzani had called it. Saint Peter's facade, a marble mosaic as big as a soccer field, absorbed the movement the way a body absorbs a good stretch. On the inside of the building, you could see the cracks that ran like varicose veins wherever the plaster was old.

Like others who worked for the Fabbrica of Saint Peter's, Fiorucci knew this roof-level route as well as he knew the layout of his own home. He could have walked it in the dark, and sometimes—when a circuit shorted out, for instance—he had done just that. "Fabbrica" generally means "building" but here it was understood as "workshop." The 150 *sampietrini* in its employ did everything from dusting cornices to replacing roof tiles. A lot of them performed double duty, donning overalls and wielding vacuum cleaners and floor buffers for the first half of their shift, then putting on suits to help with crowd control and lower-level security. All were artisans in the traditional sense, and a number of them were practiced in the ancient skill of "cupola climbing," suspended by ropes whenever outside repairs on the dome were needed. The outside world might look on them as the maintenance men of an architectural landmark, but they saw it differently. They knew that Saint Peter's was more than a relic; it was a living thing, an ever renewing act of construction whose beauty and glory ultimately depended on them, the workers who patched up the plaster, strung electrical wire, repaired water damage and kept the bronze from overtarnishing. As senior electrician, Fiorucci was in charge of the bells, but he spent most days on never-ending fix-up projects. It was like keeping an aging relative in good health.

The Fabbrica was one of the oldest institutions at the Vatican, and it maintained a proud independence from the Vatican's main bureaucracy, the Roman Curia—too much independence, in the eyes of some Vatican prelates. Those who oversaw Vatican finances had long wanted to lift the dome off Saint Peter's and have a good, hard look at what lay underneath. The basilica's organization was divided into two areas: Administration was the responsibility of the Fabbrica, while pastoral services were provided by the Chapter of Saint Peter's. The Chapter had forty or so canons, priests who took care of "spiritual" services in the basilica, hearing confessions, scheduling Masses and participating in papal liturgies. The Chapter had built up considerable financial holdings, and there had been rumors for years about shady dealings. Its reputation wasn't helped when, in 2001, one of the Chapter's former officers was accused of trying to sell artworks falsely attributed to Michelangelo to the Metropolitan Museum of Art in New York. The Fabbrica, meanwhile, was facing its own problems. It, too, was independently financed, relying on the largesse of donors through the centuries to build a substantial patrimony. Recently, however, the Fabbrica had lost money, big money—millions of dollars, according to some sources—by making massive stock investments just before the dollar crashed against the euro in 2003. Pope John Paul had for years listened to complaints about the lack of financial oversight, but even as he centralized budget and management over many Vatican agencies, he never touched the basilica's autonomy. At the Vatican, political ties were always stronger than economic arguments, and the basilica knew how to defend itself. Alliances were forged, influence was wielded and the Fabbrica and the Chapter survived. As one monsignor put it, it was not just a question of protecting one's turf, but of defending hundreds of years of tradition.

These financial affairs were above Fiorucci's pay grade; as long as he drew his monthly paycheck and was served a hot meal in the Fabbrica's cafeteria, he was a happy man. But like all the *sampietrini*, he had witnessed recent standoffs between the basilica's administrators and other Vatican agencies. It was worst when John Paul was lying in state. Suddenly, everyone wanted to be in charge at Saint Peter's: There was a constant parade of *raccomandati*, the privileged ones, who came through the back door and were led to the head of the line by officials of the Secretariat of State or Roman Curia congregations or the Governatorato, which administered Vatican City State. Basilica officials had the right to determine access, and on more than one occasion they had turned away these unexpected backdoor delegations. It was all slightly embarrassing, especially to the VIPs. Ancient resentments bubbled to the surface at times like this, and there was friction between the Fabbrica staff and the Swiss Guards on duty inside the church. In the eyes of the basilica authorities, the Swiss Guards had come to believe they had absolute jurisdiction over every square inch of Vatican City. They, too, sometimes needed to be put in their place.

Fiorucci stopped before a doorway. On the stone lintel was carved *Lumaca della Campana*. He took the big key out of his overalls pocket and turned it twice in the bronze lock. He stooped and ducked inside, closing the door behind him, then turned to climb the narrow winding stairs to the bell tower. The stairway, shaped like a *lumaca*, or snail, was steep, and he took his time. From above a single bell chimed and reverberated down the spiral chamber: nine fifteen a.m. The cardinals would just be finishing morning prayers, and then the voting would begin. He reached a platform and exited the *lumaca*, now moving across a wider wooden stairway. It was like an obstacle course, ending in the tall open room that housed the bells. From below it appeared as if there were just one or two bells, but in fact there were six in all, each with an ancient purpose remembered, sadly, by very few people today. The *rota*, with its well-worn clapper, was the oldest bell, dating to the middle of the fourteenth century. Originally it was used to call to assembly the judges of the Roman Rota, the Vatican's main tribunal. Back then, the judges would have no trouble recognizing the tone and cadence of the chime. That was the remarkable thing: Before telephones or electronics, and before the din of Roman traffic took over, the bells were the Vatican's way of communicating across the city. Another bell, the *predica*, sounded the hours of assembly for prayer. The bells rang out complex chimes for Sundays, feast days, the octave of feast days, ember days, days of fasting and papal anniversaries. It was Rome's ceremonial code language. But today, amid the cacophony of modern life, it was sometimes hard to hear the ringing outside of Saint Peter's Square.

Fiorucci walked to the edge of the tower where the bronze *campanone* stood in all its tarnished majesty. Winding around the bell's main section was a bas-relief depicting a procession of saints. Saints Peter and Paul, the patrons of Rome, were on the side facing the square. They were topped by inscriptions, cherubs and a frieze of strange symbols that included smiling faces, papal crests and the keys of Saint Peter. Above, naked boys holding dolphinlike sea snakes formed an elaborate decorative crown to the entire work. The bell had been hanging there since 1786; eight feet in diameter and almost twenty-five feet in circumference, it was the ninth-largest bell in the world. It had been commissioned by Pope Pius VI after the previous *campanone*, with only thirty-three years of service, cracked one day as it rang at full peal. Like many things at the Vatican, the new *campanone* had a checkered history. The pope had awarded the job of designing and casting the bell to Luigi Valadier, a well-known Roman silversmith who had executed numerous commissions for church decorations and altar figures around the world. As it turned out, though, Valadier was not really a bell maker. The tone of a bell depends on many things, including the dimensions, the quality of the bronze and the finishing work. It requires not only specialized knowledge but also experience. Rumors began circulating around Rome's artisan workshops that Valadier wasn't up to the task, that he was having problems, that the design was flawed, that the tone would be off, that cracks were likely. On September 1, 1785, Luigi Valadier walked from his workshop to the city's docks and threw himself into the Tiber River. Boat workers tried to save him, but Valadier had drowned by the time they pulled him out. His suicide shocked Rome, but he was given a fine funeral and buried in the Church of San Luigi dei Francesi, a few steps from the Pantheon. Ten months later, his bell was hung, and everyone pronounced it magnificent.

From the front chamber of the bell tower, it was impossible to see into Saint Peter's Square below, but Fiorucci knew it would be filling up with a lot of foreigners; the Romans were always the late arrivals, and would come rushing down only at the last minute, or when the words *fumata bianca* spread like lightning through the city. The foreigners cheered everything, even when a mere monsignor in red piping would walk through the square. "Look, it's one of the cardinals!" The night before some had cheered when the bells rang the eight o'clock hours. They thought a pope had been elected. Of course, that was silly—the slow *tocco* of the hours and the free swinging of the bells *a distesa* were completely different.

But how could they know that? They didn't speak the bells' language. Fiorucci heard a little click and instinctively plugged his ears, stepping away from the big bell. It was ten a.m., and a small hammer on the side of the *campanone* went into its mechanical routine, pounding out the hour. Although that used to be done by hand, now it was automated.

Fiorucci walked over to a small cabin in the corner and kicked away some of the pigeon feathers. He pulled out a plastic chair and sat down in front of a console where a series of black switches controlled the bells. The first one on the left, No. 1, turned on the *campanone*. Before turning it, of course, Fiorucci would have to be sure that a pope had really been elected. That didn't worry him particularly, but he didn't take the task lightly. "If I turn that switch and it turns out to be black smoke, it's my neck," he acknowledged. Fortunately, Fiorucci would not be required to read smoke signals—he couldn't even see the smoke from the bell tower, as the Sistine chimney was on the other side of the basilica. Instead, he would be duly informed, or so he was told. The details had never been fine-tuned. He was supposed to be in the tower for the midday smoke; in the evening, since the basilica was closed, he would wait in front of an identical console in a small ground-floor room just off the sacristy. Up here, he had a cell phone and a walkie-talkie. But the electronic jamming for the conclave and the thick walls of the basilica made both unreliable. Fiorucci reached over and pulled a heavy brown telephone closer to his chair. It was an old model, a rotary dialer that had probably been up there for decades. He picked up the receiver and heard a dial tone. That was the important thing.

It was starting to get warm. He took off his jacket, sat back down and closed his eyes for a moment. All he could hear were pigeons cooing and a distant hum from the piazza.

At eleven fifty-two a.m., the phone rang. "Black smoke. At least it *looks* black," one of his usher friends announced. But before he could leave his post, Fiorucci had to wait for the official all clear from Bishop Lanzani, which came a few minutes later. As he pulled on his jacket and started down the stairs, he heard the *campanone* start to ring out the deep tones of twelve o'clock. Down in the square, the innocents began cheering.

"I want it to be over. The pressure, it's too much," said Sophie de Ravinel, a young reporter for *Le Figaro*, as she stuck her head in our Catholic News Service booth and heaved a great sigh.

It was three p.m. on Tuesday, the second day of the conclave, and the atmosphere in the Vatican press office was charged with an unhealthy nervousness. The evening before and that morning, the Sistine Chapel smokestack had belched out two batches of black smoke. But despite the Vatican's pre-conclave assurances and the use of chemical color packs, the smoke had looked gray. Then white. Then black. Then gray again.

In the corner of our cubicle, a television showed a live feed of the Sistine chimney. The cardinals, unseen, were on their way back inside for the fourth ballot of the conclave.

Over the previous forty-eight hours, many of my journalistic colleagues, sleep deprived and overworked by the events of the last two weeks, had begun to fray at the edges now that the cardinals were locked in and we were locked out. The strange thing was, I was enjoying it. I was probably no more prepared than anyone for white smoke, but, as I told Sophie, I couldn't help loving every minute. "For all we know, we could be here another hour or another week," I said. "We have no idea, and no idea how right or wrong we'll turn out to be. It's exciting. It's great."

I believed that, too. History was being made behind closed doors. It was undemocratic, it was nontransparent and it was wonderful. The uncertainty and apprehension in the crowded press room added to my delight. The crowning touch was the chimney. There was something marvelously surreal about an institution that announced the pope's death via an e-mail to news agencies, and two weeks later announced the election of his successor with a smoke signal.

But like Sophie's editors, my own desk people in Washington would be watching the smoke pour out of the chimney. That much they could see for themselves on TV. What they expected me to know was what it meant. Somehow, twenty-five years of covering the Vatican were supposed to give me greater insight into distinguishing the different shades of gray smoke.

In fact, I had been in Rome for the two conclaves in 1978 that elected the two John Pauls, and the smoke then had caused no end of problems. More than once the crowd in the square had been convinced it was white and, after waiting in vain for a new pope to appear, went home grumbling. When John Paul II was finally elected, the smoke looked dark—but when people started to leave, they were startled to hear the Vatican's loudspeakers crackle to life, telling them to stick around, it was white smoke. On that occasion my editor at the *Rome Daily American* wanted to run a page-one photo of the smoke pouring out of the Sistine. "It's gray," she complained when she saw the photo, and grabbed a bottle of Wite-Out to fix it.

This time, of course, things would be different. Or so we were assured. Two days earlier I had been among a small pool of reporters escorted into the Sistine Chapel to see the conclave layout. In the chapel's main section were arranged twelve long tables draped in beige and maroon felt, complete with name cards. The chairs were crammed close together—so close that I had a mental picture of cardinals having to shield their ballots as they scribbled their choice. The beautiful marble pavement had been covered with a carpeted false floor. Except for Michelangelo's fresco of the Last Judgment, which loomed menacingly at the end of the room, it looked a little like a business convention at a Holiday Inn.

But the real reason journalists had been brought to the Sistine Chapel was to admire the stove that sat at the far end of the room. On the right was the black cast-iron cylinder that had been used to burn the ballots in every conclave since 1939. But connected to it, on the left, was a new, smaller electrical unit with a control panel and a red "start" button. Its purpose, a Swiss Guard proudly explained to me, was to burn chemical canisters to enhance the color of the smoke and to preheat the copper smokestack to improve the draw. I went over to take a closer look and found Phil Pullella, the Reuters Vatican correspondent and a chronic snoop, already poking around a metal box next to the stove. He lifted the cover up, revealing rows of strange electrical gizmos. Immediately the guards pounced, shooing us away and closing the box. Clearly, they weren't telling us everything.

Pullella sidled up to another guard to ask why the floor had been raised almost a meter. Was it to allow disabled cardinals to have easier access? The guard should have said nothing, but had a juicy bit of information that was too hard to hold back. "Where do you think we put the jamming devices?" he said proudly, apparently not realizing that he had just given us the lead to that day's story. In their mania for secrecy, the Vatican had hired specialists to install electronic equipment capable of disturbing cell phone or radio signals and preventing wireless eavesdropping. No one would be text messaging from inside *this* conclave.

Walking out of the Sistine, back down the long Sala Regia stairway toward the Bronze Doors, I wondered whether the techno-stove would increase or decrease the margin for error. It all seemed slightly redundant anyway, since the Vatican had recently put a fail-safe backup signal into place: the bells. When a pope was elected, the bells of Saint Peter's would begin to toll. Not all the bells, actually, but the giant *campanone*, the "great bell," the ten-ton workhorse that rolled into action only at the most important ecclesial moments of the year. When Archbishop Piero Marini, the papal master of liturgical ceremonies, announced that the election of the new pope would be confirmed by the ringing of the *campanone*, a lot of conclave veterans were disappointed. It seemed to kill the fun of watching the chimney. In fact, why bother with the smoke at all?

But once the voting had begun, journalists were happy to have the *campanone* as the great arbiter. That's why it paid to be in Saint Peter's Square instead of watching the smokestack on the video feed. As soon as smoke began chugging out of the chimney, the smart move was to keep an eye on the bell, which stood motionless at the top of the tower on the left side of the facade. It would begin to rock silently back and forth before the first deep notes resounded across the city. No bells, no pope. It was the media's safety net.

Outside the locked doors of the Sistine Chapel, a Swiss Guard stood at attention and let his eyes wander across the marble inlay patterns of the floor of the Sala Regia. The grand hall was empty, and his presence there might have appeared pointless. But the guards and the conclave masters knew that, despite its reputation for being hermetically sealed, the Vatican was actually quite permeable—sometimes embarrassingly so. Although it seemed preposterous, you couldn't rule out the possibility that someone might try to crash the conclave, or simply wander through inadvertently. Not the regular pilgrims and tourists, who would be stopped at the Bronze Doors in Saint Peter's Square three floors below or at one of the three main gates to Vatican City. No, the risk came from people with connections to a Vatican employee or a resident monsignor, who would proudly escort them through the premises as if he owned the place. Over the years the guards had found individuals and groups meandering ingenuously through the hallways of the Secretariat of State, their eyes fixed on the frescoed ceilings, or straying into the courtyard that lay just below the pope's apartment, or simply lost in the warren of more than two hundred offices that make up the Apostolic Palace. There were the nutcases, too. Once—it mortified the guards to even remember this—a crazed Italian claiming to be the personal physician of John Paul I had been waved past the normal checkpoints all the way up to the papal apartment. He fell at the feet of the pope, the easily flustered Albino Luciani, who sputtered, "Get him out of here!" That incident was hushed up, because so few people were aware of it. But a conclave was different. If an outsider reached the door of the Sistine Chapel, everyone would know, and the guards would be ridiculed.

The door to the Sistine was locked, of course. But an incident outside would be noticed on the inside. Of that the Swiss Guard was certain, because he himself could hear the cardinals, and at times could even hear what they were saying. Incredibly, their voices occasionally carried through the door, especially when the vote counts were being announced on the internal PA system. It was distracting, and a little bit discomfiting, to be the involuntary recipient of secrets he could never tell. For he, too, had taken an oath never to breach the conclave's inner proceedings, under pain of excommunication.

The guard couldn't hear everything, but it sounded as if Cardinal Ratzinger was ahead in the count, which was not surprising. For months, the buzz inside the Vatican had been about Cardinal Ratzinger. The Swiss Guards liked him. The Roman Curia liked him. The papal household liked him. The people in the Secretariat of State were wary—Ratzinger had a reputation for favoring doctrine over diplomacy—but that only enhanced Ratzinger's standing with the others. Most of the Vatican's top people knew he was the most qualified to be the next pope, and had known it for years. They had wisely refrained from saying so until recently; this could not be seen as a curial campaign, or it would be doomed. What it would come down to was the number of votes, and Cardinal Ratzinger would need seventy-seven to cross the two-thirds mark needed for election. Last night he had begun well, and had gained more support this morning. But this evening's balloting was the moment of truth: If Ratzinger pulled up short now, the cardinals would turn to other candidates rather than engage in a prolonged electoral battle.

When the cardinals filed back into the Sistine for the two evening ballots, the guard looked closely at their faces. They seemed relaxed. Some were smiling. Smiles, he had decided, meant a quick conclave. The cardinals were human, and they knew that the world was waiting impatiently outside. A conclave that lasted even four or five days would be described as an impasse, a hopeless deadlock, a sign of a divided church. No one wanted that.

At four p.m. the doors to the Sistine Chapel closed. At the end of the two votes—or after the first vote, if a pope was elected—the ballots, along with the cardinals' notes and tally sheets, would be burned in the stove. Already, there had been problems. Smoke had begun to leak out into the Sala Regia at the end of the first two voting sessions. That had made the guards nervous—it meant there was considerable smoke inside the chapel.

Not as bad as 1978, when a downdraft sent dark fumes back into the Sistine and the cardinals came out hacking and wheezing. But it was enough this time to bother some of the prelates and to arouse the alarm of Vatican museum officials, who had spent ten years daubing away the black residue of candle smoke from Michelangelo's frescoes on the ceiling.

"It's a good thing there were no art historians inside," Austrian Cardinal Christoph Schönborn had commented. He was joking, but not everyone was amused.

Now the Swiss Guard could again hear the voices from inside, no doubt announcing another vote count. He resisted the temptation to move closer to the door and glanced at his watch. It was just after five thirty. It took so long to vote because of the special rite of collecting the ballots. Folding, unfolding. And to gather the ballots, they were using new oddly shaped urns that the traditionalists hated—flying saucers, the press had called them. Suddenly, the guard heard a sound like falling rain. It was a second or two before he recognized it as applause coming from the other side of the door. It began slowly, then grew to a sustained ovation. His pulse quickened, and he knew. It was Ratzinger.

The press office had become so crowded by five p.m. that reporters were bumping into one another. I had just finished prewriting two stories: one saying Cardinal Ratzinger was the new pope and the other, much shorter, saying Italian Cardinal Dionigi Tettamanzi had been elected. I considered Tettamanzi a long shot (I had little idea how long), but I thought the cardinals might turn to him early in the conclave as a compromise choice. In my heart, though, I knew that if white smoke came tonight, it could only be Ratzinger. On day two of the conclave, there hadn't been enough time for any other cardinal to gain traction. All of us had profiled third-world *papabili*, but none of them would be elected this quickly, on a fourth or fifth ballot.

My colleagues in the Sala Stampa had been divided about Cardinal Ratzinger's chances. The argument against the German cardinal was that he was too doctrinaire, too old and too unpastoral to be elected. Only a few months earlier, the idea of short-listing Ratzinger as a potential successor to John Paul II was dismissed by reporters—with one exception. In January Jeff Israely, the *Time* magazine correspondent in Rome, had penned a short but intriguing article that quoted a Roman Curia official: "The Ratzinger solution is definitely on." Three months before Pope John Paul died, the gears were already in motion. Over the past two weeks, as dean of the College of Cardinals, Ratzinger had presided ably over John Paul's funeral and various assemblies of the cardinals, and it became easier to imagine him as pope. Given the scarcity of other *papabili*, his candidacy had suddenly taken on an air of inevitability among the voting cardinals, and journalists were picking up the vibe.

I left CNS correspondent Cindy Wooden in our booth and walked out the Sala Stampa door, past the guards who checked credentials and past small knots of journalists interviewing journalists. Saint Peter's Square in front of me was teeming with life. The place was filling up quickly, and reporters stood like sentries on the perimeter. I watched Alessio Vinci, halfway up a small ladder, do a quick live report for CNN. *It wasn't like this in 1978*, I thought. That year, when the "white smoke" announcement came over the wires for John Paul II, I had ridden my bicycle from our newspaper office near the Trevi Fountain to Saint Peter's and walked to a spot right under the central loggia, all in time for the *habemus papam* announcement. Now the square was so packed you couldn't get close to the basilica.

I spotted Monsignor Michael Magee, a fortyish Philadelphia native who worked at the Congregation for Divine Worship and the Discipline of the Sacraments. He was talking with a fellow Vatican official at the edge of the square. Theoretically, they were both supposed to be working this afternoon, but who would stay in his office at a moment like this? I stopped to chat with Magee, and we agreed that if smoke came early, it probably meant election, since there was no way they could do two ballots in less than two hours. It was five forty p.m., according to the clock above the bell tower. We both saw the first puff of smoke at the same time. Then another, and the first of many loud cheers went up from the square. "Oh, my God— we have a pope!" Magee yelled, and he and I took off running in opposite directions.

Magee hadn't even stopped to double-check the color of the smoke, and neither had I. We figured it had to be white. I tore back to the press room, where reporters stood in tense confusion below the TV monitors. I quickly realized that opinions were again divided.

"Too dark," a Spanish colleague argued, and screamed something into his cell phone.

"It's white! Of course it's going to look gray, especially close up on TV, because there's no such thing as 'white' smoke. But it's not black," Pullella said. Just then the smoke turned darker—or was it just the camera angle against the late afternoon sky? Everyone filed "smoke poured out of the chimney" stories. The stories said it looked white or gray and people were cheering. No one dared to state that a pope had been elected.

Father Ciro Benedettini, the vice director of the Vatican press office, scurried through the press room, igniting a small explosion of questions. "Don't ask me," he said. "I know as much as you do."

I called Benedicta Cipolla, one of our reporters in the square. People were excited, she said. They were positioning themselves under the balcony for the announcement, making cell phone calls back home, waving flags—and asking one another whether the smoke was really white. The scene was a mix of elation and confusion. Ten minutes had now passed since smoke had first appeared, and it was still coming out. And the bells?

"They're not ringing."

In the corner of the Sistine Chapel, there was a problem. Every time the stove was opened to add new ballots and papers, it belched dark smoke back into the room. And the chemical cartridges fired in the auxiliary burner were taking too long to ignite, so the smoke that did make it out the chimney was darker than it was supposed to be.

"I don't think they practiced this. They should have practiced this," Cardinal Roger Mahony of Los Angeles remarked.

All the cardinals who described the scene afterward had advice—on the timing of the chemical ignition, on the amount of air being let into the cast-iron burner, on how many ballots to put in at one time. Some wondered about the wisdom of running two copper vent pipes—one for each stove—and then joining them halfway up toward the roof. Wasn't that playing havoc with the draw? As my colleague Cindy Wooden remarked, it sounded a lot like men gathered around a barbecue, debating the finer points of cooking with charcoal.

The smoke was only one of the problems facing Archbishop Piero Marini. As master of liturgical ceremonies, he had been summoned as soon as the final ballots were counted and announced. He arrived in the Sistine Chapel in time to hear Cardinal Ratzinger being asked: *"Quo nomine vis vicari?"*

The choice of a name was a mini-drama in itself, a new pontiff's first act and a signpost of his papal agenda. Ideally, the name would establish continuity or at least a connection with an earlier pope—but who? "John Paul III" would leave Ratzinger forever in the shadow of his predecessor; "Pius XIII" would appear to signal a retrograde, pre–Vatican II pontificate; "John XXIV" was out of the question.

"Vocabor Benedictus," the new pope replied. And again the place erupted in applause.

Benedict XVI. For Archbishop Marini, the choice was not surprising: Benedict, one of Europe's patron saints. As far as the universal church went, Europe was back in the center. Ratzinger would see to that. There would be fewer trips to Africa and Asia.

The scrutineers gathered the 115 ballots and all the notes the cardinals had made during the voting, which wouldn't make for much of a fire, and that was part of the problem. They'd have to burn some extra paper again. And soon the smoke began to back up into the chapel.

Archbishop Marini stood and surveyed the scene. Not one to fluster easily, the sixty-two-year-old, silver-haired prelate had spent the better part of the last ten years guiding an increasingly frail John Paul II through his public paces. The pope would nearly stumble on the altar, and Marini's arm would be there to grab him. The pope would lose his place in a reading, and Marini's finger would guide him back to the text. It was Marini who had modified the papal liturgies to accommodate a disabled celebrant, and who had helped design a mobile chair that could be raised and lowered pneumatically, enabling the pope to preside at the altar while sitting down. Marini knew that the world watching on TV would barely notice, and that flowing vestments would cover the strap used to keep the pontiff in his chair. And while the past years had brought many near disasters on the altars of the world, Marini had never once panicked. At the end of 1999, people thought he was crazy to let the pope open the Holy Door by himself; John Paul had teetered on the top step in his long Technicolor chasuble, barely able to stay on his feet, but had pulled it off through sheer willpower. As Marini explained afterward, that was the pope's moment; he could not have his master of liturgical ceremonies propping him up. On this and countless other occasions, Marini had worried along with the rest about ceremonial debacle, but he never showed it on his face. He was unflappable, and it was this sense of composure that at times seemed to hold everything together. When the pope died, Marini unlocked a desk drawer and drew out two volumes of liturgical prayers and ceremonies that he had worked on painstakingly for more than a decade. The books covered virtually every moment from papal death to papal election, and they became the script for what many consider the smoothest papal transition in modern history. The funeral Mass for John Paul was so well staged that when the wind gently blew the pages on the open Gospel atop the pope's casket, one Vatican official remarked that it was Marini's finest touch.

Marini handled the pope's infirmity and his funeral so deftly that even his enemies grudgingly gave him credit. And make no mistake, he had enemies. The Roman Curia was split down the middle on his liturgies. The traditionalists despised what they considered the increasingly showbiz aspects of papal Masses over the years—the native dancers from third-world countries, the exotic music, the showcasing of multicultural gifts and intentions and vestments. They hated the flowers, which flowed over and under and around the altar, *in clear violation of the Vatican's own rules!* They blamed Marini, and were convinced he was a marked man. Especially if Cardinal Ratzinger, a vocal opponent of liturgical innovation, was elected pope.

At that moment, however, Archbishop Marini had no time to reflect on what the cardinals' choice might mean for his ecclesial career. As he and his assistants were adjusting the stove, someone thrust a piece of parchment into his hands. It was the certificate of acceptance of papal ministry, and part of his job was to fill it out and notarize it. He worked quickly, because soon he would have to attend to the new pope and help him choose the proper-sized vestment from the three sets hanging in a small dressing room nearby. Ratzinger, he figured, would be a medium.

By now the cardinals were going up one by one to kiss the hand of the pope, who stood looking very happy and somewhat overwhelmed. It was only then that someone remembered about the bells. Archbishop Marini or one of his top *ceremonieri* was supposed to call the Fabbrica, where Bishop Lanzani would give the order to the bell ringer. But no one had called the Fabbrica yet. Cell phones were jammed, so that meant sending someone to a landline. On his way to vest the new pontiff, Marini whispered to one of his assistants, who ran to a door, opened it and saw the single Swiss Guard standing at attention outside.

"Find a telephone!" he ordered the guard. "Tell them to ring the *campanone*! *Habemus papam!*"

Few people noticed Bishop Vittorio Lanzani as he hurried out of Saint Peter's Square and past the Arch of the Bells. Although he was the number two official at the Fabbrica, he was not someone any tourist would recognize. Lanzani was part of the Vatican's invisible hierarchy, and he liked it that way. A slight and unassuming man with thick glasses, he had no appetite for celebrity. At age fifty-three he was already on a track that would no doubt lead to the cardinal's hat one day. But for now, he seemed happy to work behind the scenes. The important thing was to do his job well and, especially at this critical juncture—with the world watching—to avoid a misstep.

The last two and a half weeks had turned Lanzani's world upside down. The simple tasks of opening and closing Saint Peter's Basilica, and keeping it clean and maintained, had suddenly been thrown into chaos by the arrival of more than three million pilgrims. To his workers, he called the interregnum a "beautiful emergency," but privately he had serious doubts about whether the basilica and the Fabbrica staff could withstand the round-the-clock schedule that had been imposed. Saint Peter's was designed to hold up to eight thousand people at a time, but these days there were twenty-one thousand people entering the basilica every hour.

The bells were another problem. Most people figured ringing the bells was a simple task, easily executed by anyone who could grab a rope. Lanzani recognized it was more complicated than that. The bell ringer at Saint Peter's needed to know his way around the electrical console. That was Giuseppe Fiorucci's domain, and Fiorucci was as good as they came. But Fiorucci was a layman who went home every night after work. On the night John Paul II died, that had almost led to disaster. Lanzani had been in Saint Peter's Square beneath the dying pope's apartment, helping to lead the rosary for tens of thousands of pilgrims, when a superior whispered to him that the pope had passed away. Lanzani suddenly realized they had no one to ring the bell. "Call Fiorucci!" he told an aide, hoping the bell ringer was not already in bed. Reached at home, Fiorucci sped to the Vatican, while church officials in the square kept praying the rosary. When John Paul's death was finally announced to the crowd, Fiorucci was at the console, and the slow, steady tolling of the bells began on cue. Traditionally, the death knell marked the moment of passing, but in this case, as Lanzani later recalled, "I think the pope had been dead for some time."

And now, once again, the world's attention would be focused on the bells. Fortunately, Fiorucci was in place this time. Lanzani had just reached his ground-floor office in the Fabbrica when the call came to the switchboard. Fiorucci picked up. But the caller was not Archbishop Marini. It was someone speaking excitedly in heavily accented Italian.

"You must ring the *campanone*! The pope has been elected!"

Fiorucci put him on hold and called Lanzani. "There's a Swiss Guard telling me to ring the bell."

Lanzani frowned. The order was supposed to come from Archbishop Marini's office. "Who is this Swiss Guard?" he asked. Fiorucci had no clue. "He's very insistent. He says he's outside the Sistine Chapel."

On the other end of the line, the Swiss Guard was beginning to panic. He pleaded with Fiorucci to ring the bell.

Lanzani had already decided, though: This was not the way things were done. How did he know it was really a Swiss Guard at all, or that he was standing outside the Sistine Chapel?

"We can't start ringing the bell just because some anonymous Swiss Guard calls up and says so. Tell him we need to hear this from someone in authority. A *ceremoniere*," he told Fiorucci.

CNN had interrupted its regular programming as soon as smoke began pouring out of the Sistine chimney. Now, in a live report from a terraced hillside above Saint Peter's, veteran correspondent Jim Bittermann along with John Allen, the Vatican correspondent of the *National Catholic Reporter*, were trying to figure it out.

For Bittermann, it evoked the fiasco of 1978, when he was a Rome correspondent for NBC and his network made the wrong call. After proclaiming white smoke, NBC waited a half hour in vain. No one appeared at the balcony to announce a new pope. The square was emptying out by the time the network acknowledged the false alarm. It was a story Bittermann loved to tell, but he was not about to make that mistake again. And in his mind, he wouldn't have to—the bells would end all doubt.

Someone handed him a sheet of paper. The Italian news agency ANSA had just pronounced the smoke white. That didn't impress Bittermann. The agency had called yesterday's smoke white, too. Italian journalists looked upon such moments more as theater than as history in the making, and if the color went from white to black it only added to the drama and detracted nothing from their own credibility.

Bittermann watched the crowd grow more excited by the minute. If that smoke turned out to be black, this would be the mother of all false alarms. "The crowd seems to think this is white smoke, that's for sure," he announced to his audience.

The hourly toll of bells suddenly rang across the square.

"There go those bells, Jim," John Allen said.

"Right. There go the bells, but it is also six o'clock."

"Quite right," Allen acknowledged.

Bittermann watched the CNN camera feed from the *campanone*. It still wasn't moving. Twelve minutes had passed, and the smoke was still puffing out the chimney. What the hell was going on?

Inside the Fabbrica two men waited for the phone to ring.

Giuseppe Fiorucci sat before his console and listened to the excited voices in the sacristy down the hall. "White smoke!" "Black smoke!" "We should be ringing the bell!" Everyone had an opinion. But back there, deep inside the basilica annex, you couldn't see the smoke or the square or anything else.

People spoke about the "honor" of ringing the bell, but Fiorucci knew better. He sat at these controls because he'd worked at the basilica forty years, not because he'd shown initiative or good judgment in times of crisis or an ability to push the buttons better than anyone else. If people thought he might be nervous or excited to ring the bells for a new pope, they were mistaken. No more than when he had rung the death knell for the old pope. It was what he did, and it wasn't that special. The important thing was to not screw up, not jump the gun. After all, you can't start ringing the *campanone* and then change your mind. You have to be sure. And with those thoughts, he soothed his mind.

A few doors down the hall, Bishop Lanzani was less philosophical. He stared at the phone. Why didn't it ring?

Someone stuck his head in the door. "They say it's white."

A nightmarish thought crossed his mind: What if no one called over in time? What if the new pope appeared on the balcony before the *campanone* had begun to ring? Lanzani knew that something like that would not be forgotten.

A new pope. *It has to be Ratzinger*, he thought. No one else could have pulled it off in four ballots. And that was fine. In Lanzani's view, the church was like a massive ocean liner, and Ratzinger was the only one capable of taking the helm. Unlike most of the cardinals, Ratzinger was a familiar figure to the people who worked at the basilica. He crossed the square daily in his black beret, holding his briefcase, looking very much like a university professor. He often celebrated Mass in the basilica's Holy Sacrament chapel—in Latin. He would protect the church's tradition, and that could only be good. True, Ratzinger was German, and German popes through history had not distinguished themselves. But the Italians at the Vatican considered him almost one of their own; he'd worked there twenty-four years. And besides, there really wasn't an Italian *papabile*.

In the past, when the Italian cardinals were split between two of their own candidates, they still had the influence—and the votes—to impose a third Italian, a compromise choice, on the rest of the College of Cardinals. But by now Italian votes had shrunk to 20 out of 115, not nearly enough to set the agenda, and the Italian cardinals themselves were hopelessly divided between Cardinal Tettamanzi of Milan and Cardinal Camillo Ruini, the papal vicar of Rome. Liberals still dreamed of Cardinal Carlo Martini, but he was likely to receive only symbolic votes from the "stop Ratzinger" crowd.

Faced with an impasse, the conclave might turn to the third world. But who? Everyone talked about Latin America, but the U.S. cardinals, and to tell the truth many Europeans, were wary of the Latin Americans. The way Lanzani saw it, they were just too unfamiliar with the ways of Rome and would never be able to manage the Roman Curia. Others whispered the code word "maturity"—the Latinos and the Africans represented local churches that were not quite mature enough to produce a pope. Maybe next time. Then there was Asia, but the only cardinal who had much of a chance was India's Ivan Dias, a man who had spent most of his career in the Vatican's diplomatic service. Once he arrived in Rome, Dias was given a lesson in how quickly a candidacy can be killed. The *voci* that were planted in the Italian press said Dias was sick, diabetic and needed a personal nurse to help him to and from the cardinals' secret meetings every day. His own denials couldn't seem to get into print.

From inside the Vatican, then, all this talk about a third-world pope appeared as fantasy. Roman Curia officials sensed the wind was blowing the other way. After twenty-six years of church expansion under John Paul II—the boom in third-world conversions and vocations, the trips that spotlighted every African village with a Catholic church, the endless dialogues and meetings with leaders of other faiths, the historic gestures of visiting a synagogue or a mosque—it was time to reconsolidate, to take stock, to look inward again. The Catholic Church needed some internal attention, some housecleaning. The odds favored an insider, and Ratzinger was the ultimate insider.

Lanzani looked at the clock. Another five minutes had passed. Then he saw the switchboard light up with an incoming call. He raced out of his office and found Fiorucci's cubicle already crowded. Fiorucci put his hand over the phone.

"He says to ring the bell."

"Who is it?"

Fiorucci pronounced the name of a monsignor who worked under Archbishop Marini.

Lanzani nodded, satisfied. A *ceremoniere*. "Now we know," he said slowly, as if offering a lesson to everyone in the room. "*Now* we know."

He let the message sink in.

"Ring the *campanone*."

Fiorucci flicked a set of switches. In the tower above, a small electric engine hummed and the giant gears turned slowly. A few seconds later, the big bell would begin to move. *Habemus papam*.

CHAPTER TWO

UP IN THE AIR

EVEN AT THIRTY-THREE THOUSAND FEET Pope Benedict XVI had an understated way of making an entrance. Dressed in his best white cassock, his hair recently trimmed for the trip, the pontiff glided quietly into the coach section of his plane and stood in front of the bulkhead, smiling wanly at the sixty-five journalists who accompanied him on the *Volo Papale* from Rome to São Paolo, Brazil. To his side, nervous technicians from Vatican Radio held a microphone, hoping they had made the right connections after forty-five minutes of fiddling with speakers, jacks and wires. Benedict, not one for standing around idly, launched into an impromptu riff about the purpose of his journey and the future of Christianity in Latin America. The microphone finally worked, to the relief of the technicians, and the pope's first airborne press conference was rolling.

I had what should have been a pretty good seat, about ten feet from the pope on the right side of the plane. But I now noticed that the PA system was set up on the plane's left aisle, which meant the microphone would never make it over to my side for questions. Moreover, the Vatican had reserved the first three rows of seating for photographers—it was pretty much standard procedure to favor TV and photo people over print journalists on these trips. So even from my prime perch, a jungle of cameras obscured my view and a fuzzy boom mic was in my face. I felt a fleshy pressure from behind: A newspaper correspondent from Brazil had climbed halfway up my back for a better view. Looking down at my seat, I saw that one of her stack heels was planted firmly on the cover of my laptop.

I tugged on her sleeve. "That's my computer." She moved her foot to the seat cushion, simultaneously digging an elbow deeper into my shoulder.

It was a Wednesday morning in May 2007, and for those of us on the *Volo Papale*, the working day was already four hours old. It had begun with an early check-in, complimentary orange juice in the VIP lounge and—the most characteristic ingredient of papal trips—long periods of waiting. The *Volo Papale* generally carries sixty or seventy international reporters, including seven or eight American regulars. We're supposed to feel privileged, since requests for seats usually outnumber available places, and because we are, after all, considered part of the papal party. In theory, that should mean closer access to the pope throughout the duration of the trip. We receive advance copies of papal speeches in several languages, travel with police escorts to and from papal events and often enjoy our own special "Papal Flight" section in the host press centers. Outsiders would say we are coddled. But we are also closely controlled, in ways that actually make it harder to cover the pope.

As we waited at the gate to board the pope's Alitalia charter jet, a bearded figure loomed into view and looked us over with a jaundiced eye. In his right hand he held a small red plastic case.

"Hi, Vik. Bring your harmonica?" I asked, nodding at the container.

In silence, he opened it to reveal a cache of metal chains. Then he resumed his prowl.

Vik van Brantegem is our Vatican warden on these trips, a Belgian layman whose by-the-book mind-set is legendary among Vatican reporters. He had a smile on his face, but it was not a cheerful start-of-the-trip smile. It was a sardonic smile that said, *How did you think you could get away with that?*

He focused his attention on Greg Burke, the Fox News correspondent. "The blue cord. Off."

Burke was puzzled.

Van Brantegem flicked the blue ribbon that held Burke's press badge around his neck. From his red case, he pulled out a chain and dropped it in Burke's hand. Then he walked away, shaking his head at our ignorance. The blue ribbon bore the words "Holy See" and had been handed out by the Vatican. But—and Vik was amazed at how often he had to explain this to *Volo Papale* reporters—on papal trips the ribbon was no good, because the local press badges were designed to slide onto chains, not ribbons. Even the chains, as van Brantegem knew well, could be problematic in the hands of a dim-witted journalist. How many times had he watched reporters put their badges on backward, or let them accumulate in a floppy plastic necklace, or attach them through one hole instead of two? On this last point, van Brantegem finally had to spell it out in writing: "Journalists are requested to take the metal chain consigned by the Holy See press office and pass it through the two holes of the local press pass. In order not to create confusion at security controls and not to deform the plastic sleeve, journalists are requested not to stick things into the sleeve that don't belong there."

That warning was included in the play-by-play booklet van Brantegem prepares for reporters before each papal trip. The booklet first appeared as a two-page addendum to the pope's own schedule, but over the years it has grown to an epic of logistical detail, thirty or forty pages of minute-by-minute instructions on when to get up, when to eat breakfast, when and where to collect speeches, what kind of weather to expect, when to line up for the bus, when to get on the bus, where to stand when the pope arrives and even when to gather for the daily Mass for journalists, which is celebrated in van Brantegem's hotel room (and typically draws only one or two reporters—the flying press corps is not an overtly religious bunch). The booklet, dubbed "Vikipedia" by the press corps, features color-coded directives: The pope's schedule is in blue, general information is in black and journalists' movements are in bright red. One full page, in tiny type, lays out exhaustive instructions on how to behave and how not to behave at papal events.

A cruel sport among the *Volo Papale* veterans is to encourage a first-timer with a doubt or complaint about our schedule to go over and ask van Brantegem for an explanation. "Just ask Vik," someone will say, and we stand back to watch the fun begin. You can almost see the Flemish bile rising in van Brantegem's throat. A tongue-lashing of the reporter inevitably follows; Vik's answer always begins with the words "It's in the book." And it always is.

Bogged down in this realm of minutiae, most reporters experience papal trips as an endless logistical ritual in which the pope himself is rarely, if ever, physically present. The reporting pools for many of the pope's appearances are tiny, only five or ten journalists, and they are typically offered no more than a brief glimpse of the pontiff as he enters a church or a stadium or a presidential palace. As a result, almost all the journalists on the *Volo*

Papale cover papal events from press centers, where they can watch them on TV. Lest we Americans grow too comfortable in the press rooms, we have for years held ourselves to an unofficial rule: We have to eyeball the pope at least once during every trip.

So when Pope Benedict strolled back for his flying press conference above the Sahara Desert, the coach class buzzed with excitement. This is what our companies were paying the big bucks for—access to the man in white. This is where our expertise as *vaticanisti* would pay off, in prodding the pontiff on tough issues and interpreting his unrehearsed answers. This is where we watched the pope up close and took his measure. This is where the *Volo Papale* meant something.

And this press conference, we had been told, would be the real deal: a wide-ranging, give-me-your-best-shot encounter with reporters. On earlier trips, Pope Benedict had answered a few token questions before takeoff and quickly returned to the front of the plane, leaving many of us nostalgic for the days when John Paul II would field our questions at length during his flights, roaming up and down the aisles, even during turbulence. Benedict, it seemed, was the type who liked to keep his seat belt fastened.

But now here Benedict was, smiling and talking a mile a minute in an Italian that was perfectly fluent, though starched with a German accent. A first question about violence in Brazil was followed by one that got everybody's attention: What did the pope think about Mexico's recent decriminalization of abortion? Did he support the Mexican bishops on excommunicating Catholic legislators who approved this law?

The pope answered the first part of the question, talking about the value and beauty of human life, and ignored the second part. But a few minutes later Marco Politi, a veteran reporter for the Rome daily *La Repubblica*, pressed the issue again: Do you agree with the excommunication of Mexican legislators on the question of abortion?

This time the pope waded straight into the swamp. "Yes, this excommunication was not something arbitrary but is foreseen by the Code of Canon Law. It is simply part of church law that the killing of an innocent baby is incompatible with being in communion with the Body of Christ. Thus, the bishops didn't do anything new, anything surprising or arbitrary."

Benedict went on to speak for another twenty minutes, but already some of the major agency reporters were pounding furiously on their lap-tops. They had heard two magic words: "abortion" and "excommunication." The story line was simple: "Pope supports excommunication for pro-choice politicians," and it was soon on the wires.

The pope had barely retreated to his first-class seat when Jesuit Father Federico Lombardi, the Vatican spokesman, came back and tried to spin the story in an entirely different direction. The reporter's question, he told us, had been based on a false premise, because the Mexican legislators had not, in fact, been excommunicated by their bishops.

"And if the bishops haven't excommunicated anyone, it's not that the pope wants to do so," Lombardi said.

But Lombardi, a gentle soul with a sharp mind, was selling some-thing reporters weren't interested in buying. In years past, backpedaling on a pope's verbal miscues was easy because, quite simply, journalists couldn't file their stories until the plane landed several hours later. But the Alitalia 777 was equipped with phones, and the genie was already out of the bottle.

"I'm not going to use that. It ruins the story," said one American jour-nalist after hearing Lombardi's spin.

As the Alitalia flight attendants began rolling out lunch (lasagna with artichoke and mint, grilled turbot with almonds and *taggiasca* olives), heated debates began erupting among reporters. Several of us knew that canon law, the church's internal legal code, stipulates excommunication for those directly involved in an abortion, not for legislators who may have helped make it possible. Surely Pope Benedict, who had been the Vatican's top doctrinal official for twenty-four years, was aware of that. He must have known that the Vatican's own legal experts would consider automatic ex-communication of pro-choice politicians a misapplication—an abuse—of canon law.

While dessert was being served (miniature raspberry *crostata* and white chocolate Bavarian cream), Father Lombardi returned with more ammuni-tion: The pope was not saying pro-choice politicians were excommunicated, but that by their actions they had excluded themselves from the Eucharist. In other words, they shouldn't go to Communion. This, of course, was quite different from being excommunicated. Perhaps sensing the journalistic skepticism, Lombardi added that he had been "authorized" to make this clarification—in other words, it came from the pope. The wire service reporters reluctantly pushed aside their Bavarian cream and pulled out their laptops. The story was now officially muddled.

Meanwhile, someone in the Secretariat of State was already taking the eraser to the pope's remarks. When the official transcript of his press conference was published, we saw that it had been neutered: The pope's first word, "yes," the direct answer to the question about excommunication, was gone, as were all specific references to the Mexican bishops. The pope's statement about pro-choice politicians not being in communion with the church was changed to refer to "going to Communion, in which one receives the Body of Christ."

Editing Pope Benedict's extemporaneous comments had been a common practice from the very first day of his pontificate. Vatican officials justified it on the grounds that the pope's Italian might need cleaning up, and an imprecise or inelegant phrase should be quickly amended. The idea of a midlevel bureaucrat fine-tuning Pope Benedict's language may sound strange, but it reflects a deeply entrenched conviction that the actual words a pope pronounces are not definitive until the "official version" is published. Usually the editing was merely annoying, but in this case it was an attempt to rewrite reality.

By the time we landed in São Paolo, more than twelve hours after boarding the plane, reporters were asking themselves how this pope, reputedly the sharpest mind in the Vatican, could fumble so badly on an issue he had followed so closely. Perhaps he had simply misspoken, or perhaps he was allowing his aides to tone down his warning to Catholic politicians. Either way, it seemed strange. And it didn't make the Vatican press corps look so great, either. To our editors, it must have seemed as if we were guessing—perhaps wrongly—at what the pope meant.

As we lined up to disembark, Victor Simpson, an Associated Press reporter who had been flying with popes for more than thirty years, turned to me and remarked with an ironic laugh: "I think this may be the last time Pope Benedict meets the press."

A few minutes later van Brantegem, arms flailing, herded us into a dim hangar for a welcoming ceremony. From where we were positioned, the

pope was a distant figure on a platform, standing next to the bearded Brazilian president, Luiz Inácio Lula da Silva. Soon the pope disappeared into
a popemobile and a motorcade. We were moved onto a bus.

"Hurry up," van Brantegem, checking his watch, said to a few stragglers.

Someone asked whether the bus stopped first at the hotel or the press
center. Van Brantegem didn't even look up.

"It's in the book."

When I tell friends and relatives back in my native Minnesota that I travel
on the pope's plane, their faces inevitably express a "How cool is that!" kind
of respect at my supposed familiarity with the leader of the Catholic
Church. The assumption, no doubt shared by my editors who pay outrageous fares for my seat on the *Volo Papale*, is that we constitute a journalistic inner sanctum that sticks like glue to the pontiff in all his peregrinations.
In their minds we're the ones who can read his body language as he meets a
prime minister in his office. We're the ones who catch papal ad-libs as he
makes his way out of a mosque. And we're the ones who hear him chatting
with aides as he hops into the popemobile. Anyone can watch the pope on
TV or on Internet streaming video, but we're the people who know what's
really going on, because we're there—right there, just off camera, like the
pope's own shadow.

One of the great ironies of traveling with the pope is that, because of the
practical difficulties of moving us to and from his venues, we're often the
only people who *can't* see him.

In September of 2007 we found ourselves inside yet another dimly lit
airport hangar watching Pope Benedict give a speech, this time in Vienna.
He stood on a dais at the end of a long red carpet lined with Austrian soldiers. It was cold and raining hard outside. From the airport the pope
would go directly to Vienna's crowded main square, where he would pray
before a statue of Mary and then visit a Holocaust memorial. These were
the newsy events of the day, and already our schedule was tight. Van Brantegem's book instructed reporters to get on a bus before the pope left the
airport, but as I watched the pontiff disappear out the hangar door, I realized that was not going to happen. Our bus, it seemed, was nowhere to be
found.

We huddled near the door and began to worry. Unless we left soon, we would miss seeing both papal appearances that day. I looked around. There was not even a TV in the hangar. We were totally cut off. I smelled disaster.

A young Austrian was waving his hands.

"Attention! Welcome in Austria! We are trying to find your bus to take you to the press center, so we ask for your patience."

This was met by a few groans and much indifference.

You would think that moving journalists from an airport to a papal event would be a pretty straightforward matter. But the history of papal trips is full of false starts, misplaced vehicles and hours wasted. Often it's a case of the host country trying too hard. In Zambia, where the government gave the airport a security makeover before the pope arrived, our press minibus got hung up on an extra-large speed bump and swung there like a teeter-totter as the pope's motorcade sped away. In Azerbaijan, the government put us in a newly purchased, oversized motor coach that promptly had its roof ripped off at the first underpass outside the airport; the driver kept going at full throttle, thinking it was a terrorist attack.

In Austria, happily, our buses did finally show up. One vehicle took a small reporting pool, mostly TV people, to the square so they could see the pope live. The rest of us were supposed to be whisked to the press center to watch the event on monitors. With any luck we would make it in time, and we had a police escort to ensure a fast trip. But as soon as we hit the highway, the police car peeled off and disappeared for good.

A half hour later our bus was stuck in gridlocked traffic in the center of Vienna. Five minutes passed. Ten minutes. We weren't moving. The pope, meanwhile, was arriving downtown. At this point some of us turned to what I call the "Telepace solution." Telepace is a small Catholic TV station in Italy that runs live coverage of papal trips, with syrupy voice-over by a priest named Don Guido. From the bus I phoned our Rome office and asked my CNS colleague Carol Glatz to turn on Telepace and tell me what was happening. Carol described the scene in detail, right down to the yellow slickers the young people were wearing as they jumped up and down and cheered the pope in Am Hof Square.

"They're soaked. Those poor kids. It's pouring down rain," Carol said.

I jotted it all down in my notebook.

"Hey, the pope stopped talking all of a sudden," Carol continued. "He's just standing there. Something's going on, but I can't tell what."

I gritted my teeth and silently cursed the bus, the traffic and especially the trip organizers. I asked Carol whether someone had interrupted the pope. Did they take him off the stage? Was it the rain?

"No, they're all just standing there. Cardinal Schönborn's smiling, so it can't be too bad."

Someone phoned our journalistic pool at the event. They should have been with Pope Benedict by now and could tell us what the problem was. But they had been moved out of the square and, nowhere near the pope, were standing pointlessly in the rain. Somehow, that didn't surprise us.

My colleagues on the bus began making calls to their Rome offices, or to their spouses or children at home. "Turn on Telepace," they said.

It turned out the pope's mic had gone dead, which left him trying to communicate with the young crowd through gestures—not his strong suit. He soon gave up.

Our bus, meanwhile, remained immobile. I asked our Austrian minder what could be done. "Nothing. Normally it isn't this bad, but today the pope is here," she explained helpfully. "Can we walk?" I asked. She pondered that a few seconds and then sprang into action, announcing on the intercom that we would now disembark and take the subway. The subway? This would be a first for the *Volo Papale* crowd. We all got off the bus and hustled through the rain to the nearest subway stop. Our minder, holding her yellow umbrella high above her head, steered us through foot traffic as one might guide grade school students on an urban field trip.

The subway came after a few minutes, and fifty-five Vatican journalists, their *Volo Papale* press badges dangling from their necks, boarded the car. Ten minutes later we reached the press center in a wing of the Hofburg Palace. By the time we got through the metal detectors and entered the work area, the pope was winding up his outdoor events. We watched him step back into the popemobile and drive away. Then we sat down to write our firsthand account of Benedict's first day in Austria.

Not being there is actually a big part of papal trips.

Under van Brantegem's scheduling, the reporting pools often include only a TV crew, a couple of photographers and two or three print journal-ists. The explanation is that space is tight; the real reason is that it's simpler to deal with ten reporters than twenty or thirty. Typically, the same pool must cover a succession of papal events, so we leapfrog from one venue to another. As the pope arrives in one place, we're often getting on a minibus to the next site. There are usually no pool reports because, of course, we have witnessed virtually nothing, while the rest of our colleagues have watched it all on TV back in the press center.

Some events, like outdoor papal Masses, are open to all but there's little advantage to being physically present. Reporters are typically guided to a press section somewhere off to the side of the altar and told not to move; there's not much chance for interviews, unless you want to interview people working at the Mass, or first-aid volunteers or other reporters. I always try to slip away for a few minutes to mingle in the crowd and talk to people, and always pay a price when the eagle-eyed van Brantegem sees me return-ing to our corral, clutching my notebook full of illicitly gained quotes.

On Pope Benedict's first trip to Germany in 2005, I had managed to escape the press pen and actually speak to young people at a World Youth Day gathering. As I sidled back, van Brantegem was waiting for me. I braced myself.

"Who said you could wander off?" Van Brantegem glared.

I shrugged and looked repentant. But Vik was just warming up.

"You people are like children. You think there are no reasons for these rules. Here you have a place near the altar. But it's not good enough? I don't care. Do you think it was easy to find a place for journalists near the altar? But no, you have to go somewhere else. It's unprofessional. Do you think these security people want you strolling around? You act like children at a picnic. Fine—then you'll be treated that way."

It was a relatively mild rebuke, say, 3.2 on the Viktor scale. His face had flushed, but the veins on his forehead were not even throbbing. And at the corner of his mouth was just the hint of a smile. That's why we all love Vik.

Given the limitations placed on us, it's no surprise that many reporters on the *Volo Papale* simply stay away from papal venues and never leave the press center. But sometimes history is being made, and you have to be there. Or at least try.

In 2001, on a trip to Syria, Pope John Paul was scheduled to visit the ancient Umayyad mosque in the center of Damascus. It was the first papal stop ever at an Islamic place of worship, and I was one of the few lucky reporters to have a spot on the pool. I would personally witness another interfaith milestone.

It was a Sunday afternoon, and van Brantegem's playbook called for us to line up for press passes in the lobby of the Sheraton Damascus at three forty-five p.m. As Vik called out our names, we came forward one by one to receive the plastic badge for an event he had mysteriously designated CE/SI-08. (We could never decipher his coding system.) Then, like a general about to send his troops into battle, Vik walked slowly among us, hands behind his back, inspecting the way the press passes had been strung on our chains. Apparently satisfied, he gave the order to board the bus.

We arrived at the mosque two hours before the pope, and the first sign of trouble came when local authorities insisted we take positions in a square outside the building. Van Brantegem disappeared in a huff, presumably to negotiate our way inside. Shortly afterward we were allowed to assemble at the door of the mosque. For a moment, it looked as if even the Umayyad authorities had been impressed by our *Volo Papale* status. Then we saw Vik coming toward us from inside the mosque. His face was dark with anger and his lip was bleeding. No, on closer examination, his nose was bleeding and he had a big bump on his forehead. He waved us all back to our places in the square. Clearly some disaster had occurred.

Although the details would emerge only later, van Brantegem had had a dustup with the Umayyad security people. The idea of Vik's fighting for our journalistic rights was heartening, but in fact the incident had centered on another matter. Van Brantegem had seen the mosque guards refusing entry to Cardinal Walter Kasper, the Vatican's chief ecumenist. Concerned that the Vatican's honor was being besmirched, van Brantegem hurried after them to insist that the cardinal be allowed inside. Inadvertently or not, one of the guards slammed a door in Vik's face—literally—and he was now bleeding all over this moment of interreligious harmony.

The Vatican press corps buzzed excitedly about van Brantegem's bloody nose, which looked as if it might be broken. But none of this helped our cause. I stood next to CNN correspondent Jim Bittermann, who shook his head. "This doesn't look good," he said. We looked around the square for a TV monitor, but found none. Not only that, our cell phones weren't picking up a signal.

"Let's take a walk," Bittermann suggested.

We stole quietly away from the mosque and turned down a dusty side street in the ancient city. There, tucked into the ground floor of an apartment building, was a household goods shop. We glanced inside and saw the owner, a young man, sipping tea at the cash register in the middle of the store. Above him was a black-and-white television, tuned to what looked like a Syrian soap opera.

Jim looked at me hopefully. "Worth a try," I said.

The store owner, Muhammad, spoke just enough English to make us feel most welcome in his shop. Once he understood that we were journalists following the pope, he turned to the state channel that would carry the mosque visit live and invited us to make ourselves comfortable. I sat down and pulled out my notebook. Jim bought an ice-cream sandwich from the store freezer. Then he saw a telephone next to the cash register. Would it be possible, he wondered, to briefly phone his desk in London and have them call back? He would pay for the call, of course. No problem, Muhammad replied. An old man and one of his young children had now joined us. Jim finished his ice cream in a decidedly better mood. What more could we ask for?

Fifteen minutes later we watched on the small TV screen as Pope John Paul, hobbled and bent, removed his shoes, donned a pair of white slippers and shuffled into the prayer hall of the eighth-century mosque, listening to a Muslim guide. Bittermann, his eyes glued to the TV set, was doing commentary into the phone for CNN's broadcast, fielding questions with skill and adding insightful asides about the pontiff's demeanor as he moved through an Islamic place of worship. In the broadest sense of the phrase, Bittermann was indeed "with the pope in Damascus." Muhammad, his shop now filling up with friends, beamed with pride.

It was over in twenty minutes, and we walked back to our assembly point outside the Umayyad mosque. Our fellow pool reporters, who had remained outside for the duration, shut out of the story, were being herded by van Brantegem onto a bus. His nose had stopped bleeding, but it would be some time before the swelling went down.

+ + +

Shortly after his election, Pope Benedict announced he wouldn't be traveling as much as his predecessor. Yet Benedict made eighteen trips during his first six years in office, perhaps realizing that a twenty-first-century pope cannot just remain ensconced in the Vatican. But while John Paul took obvious enjoyment in his far-flung journeys, Benedict seemed merely to endure them, keeping strictly to his schedule and avoiding both detours and crowd-immersion events. At times he seemed like a meticulous tourist, crossing things off his checklist.

Perhaps the biggest difference between the two pontiffs is that John Paul had a constant awareness of being on the world's stage during his global travels. When he landed in a country and kissed the airport tarmac, it was like the opening curtain of a religious drama. In contrast, Benedict eschewed the ground-kissing ritual as too theatrical. In fact, as the *Volo Papale* photographers quickly discovered, Benedict would often hustle out the front of his plane before the photogs had exited the rear, which meant they missed the arrival picture completely. The German pope was not interested in putting on a media show, but in getting down to business. And the business of such trips is the program of ceremonial meet and greets, speeches and liturgies—not much for the press to chew on.

One reason Pope John Paul's trips were more interesting to reporters was that he ventured farther from Rome, out of the European safe haven and into missionary territory. When he barnstormed into an African country, John Paul was welcomed by tribal dancers in feathered headdresses, rag-clad children reading poems and teenaged bands playing rock music along the papal motorcade route. Benedict, on the other hand, was more likely to find himself in a concert hall filled with dignitaries like himself, listening to Mozart.

I boarded my first papal flight in 1984, when the pope traveled to the Dominican Republic and Puerto Rico. These were pre–Vik van Brantegem days, and no one seemed to be in charge. From the moment we boarded the Alitalia 747, a genial chaos reigned. Rudi Frey, a photographer for *Time* magazine, prowled the aisles and made sure everyone had a glass of champagne or a Bloody Mary. Rudi had close-cropped white hair, a wild look in his eye and an intimidating way of offering a drink.

"No, thanks," I said as Rudi instructed a lithe flight attendant to pour me some Krug Grande Cuvée. It was seven a.m.

But Rudi took the flute of champagne, handed it to me and stuck around to make sure I drank it. Then he ordered another Bloody Mary for himself. Well before takeoff, half the plane was mildly lit.

The flight attendants were soon busy handing out gift after gift—designer tote bags, perfume and cartons of cigarettes. The plane was huge, and we each had a row of seats to ourselves. Unfortunately, I had developed an intense fear of flying, and even with Rudi's tonic refreshments this day would be eleven hours of private terror. I settled in and popped a beta-blocker, hoping it would help calm my nerves, along with Roy Orbison on my Walkman. As we began crossing the Atlantic, we were handed two texts the pope would deliver in Santo Domingo later in the day, his arrival speech and a Mass sermon. We scanned them rapidly, circling a paragraph that spoke of injustice and oppression and another that seemed to be a dig against liberation theology. We all pulled out portable typewriters and pounded away, prewriting big chunks of our stories. Then we stashed the typewriters and took more drinks from Rudi.

As we approached Santo Domingo my knuckles eased their grip on the hand rests, and relief began to trickle through my bloodstream. When we descended to treetop level, I looked out the window and saw a cheering multitude gathered on the ground below, swarming near the terminal. As the plane eased down clumsily, wings tipping from side to side, the engines suddenly accelerated. Then we were lifting up with a roar, straining against gravity, climbing back into the sky. Stunned, I looked around the aircraft and saw some of my colleagues laughing. Latin Americans, it seemed, just loved it when the pope's plane made one low pass over the crowd, buzzing them before landing. I took a deep breath. By now we were circling again for the real landing, which came with an anticlimactic thud. I pulled out my notebook and wrote: "Pope knows how to put on a show."

Several months later I found myself on the *Volo Papale* en route to India. By now I had increased my dose of beta-blockers and added Don Williams, the "Gentle Giant" of country-western, to my in-flight song list. We landed in New Delhi without a low-altitude flyover and without a cheering crowd; few people here, in fact, seemed interested in the pope's visit.

For the press corps, India was a week of predawn wake-up calls and bureaucratic punishment. The Indians were in love with duplicate forms and rubber stamps and waiting in line, and they gave that funny head roll when you asked them a yes-or-no question. If you complained, they promised "VIP treatment" and disappeared. Filing stories was a nightmare; the Indian telex operators were supposed to input our typed copy, but they kept losing pages and mixing them up. The telex room looked like a scene out of a Marx Brothers movie. After forty-eight hours we were exhausted, and I could feel my vague but deep-seated sympathy for the third world being replaced by pure irritation.

On day three, we flew to Calcutta and had to hurry from the airport to a waiting bus. As we ran out of the terminal, I nearly tripped over what turned out to be a human being lying next to the curb begging. He had no forearms, and his legs were cut off at the knees, but he managed to quickly drag his torso across the street and out of the way of the stampeding press corps. From there we went directly to Mother Teresa's home for the dying in the crowded Kalighat quarter of the city. The stench from open sewers wafted along our bus route. On the side of the road, people were making little dung pies to dry for fuel. Others waded into the wide Hugli River to beat their clothes clean. Our bus honked its way furiously through heavy traffic, past billboards that paid tribute to the city's very important guest: "Breezy Welcome to H. H. John Paul—Polar Fan Co."

When we arrived at the two-room center, I watched in the dim light as Mother Teresa took the pope to greet the men and women residents. Most of them were unable to rise from their mattresses on the floor. Mother Teresa gave the pope plates of sweet curd to hand to each of them, and curtly directed his movements. One woman began screaming in Bengali, and the pope wanted to know what she was saying. "She says, 'I am alone, I am alone, come back again,'" Mother Teresa told him, and moved him briskly along to the next bed. Near the entry a blackboard on the wall held the day's report: "Feb. 3, 1986: Entered 2, Discharged 0, Died 4. This we do for Jesus." A few minutes later the pope emerged into the packed street and stood on a platform as the crowd quickly pushed in from all sides. He brought Mother Teresa up to take a bow. "This is the happiest day of my life," she said, beaming like a schoolgirl.

The next day a hotel bellhop began pounding on my door at three a.m. It was time to go to Calcutta's Dum Dum Airport for a flight to Shillong in the northeast corner of India. We flew in a Fokker prop plane, and I was too exhausted to feel even the slightest distress. The aircraft was tiny, and only a few of my colleagues were making the trip; the rest were still asleep at the hotel. We landed, and as the sun rose our bus wound through the hills near Shillong, where people with Chinese features were stirring around their huts. Incongruous as it seemed, the pope's Mass would take place at "Golf Links," a course built by the British during the colonial period. We arrived early and I surveyed the crowd that had gathered on a grassy fairway. Since I did not speak Khasi, the indigenous language, I found a local who was delighted to accompany me and act as interpreter.

In front of the papal altar was a group of tattooed men wearing tribal dress and carrying long, sharp swords. This looked like a reporter's jackpot. Indeed, as my translator soon discovered, these were Naga headhunters, or rather former headhunters, since they had converted to Christianity more than a decade earlier. I spoke with the leader of the contingent, a strong man who wore wild boar tusks on his forehead and five tiny brass heads across his chest. He unsheathed his machete and showed me the keen edge.

"I only use it to scalp monkeys now," he said with a bit of nostalgia in his voice. The little brass heads, it turned out, were symbolic reminders of his last big hunting foray, when he killed five rival tribesmen and brought their heads back to his village.

Why had he converted to Christianity? I asked. He shrugged.

"Everybody else in Nagaland was going Christian."

During the liturgy a bemused pope watched as the ex-headhunters performed traditional dances. There was nothing to suggest violence or swordsmanship; instead, they did a couple of tamer numbers, like the flight of the legendary woodpecker.

The pope's Indian sojourn lasted an incredible ten days. To sleep-deprived reporters, it seemed as if it would never end. We crisscrossed the subcontinent, down to Madras on the east coast, over to Goa on the west and ended up in Bombay. After one last day of interminable papal events, we arrived at the airport for our night flight home and discovered there was a problem: Strong headwinds were forecast across the Middle East, which meant that the pope's Air India Boeing 707 would have to be fueled to the max. As a result, we were informed, the pope's gifts and the reporters' luggage were being left behind. When we boarded, we found that the coach section was quite small and every seat would be filled—hardly the "VIP treatment" to which *Volo Papale* reporters were accustomed. It would be a long and cramped nine hours. A reporter for the Italian state television RAI was crestfallen to learn he would not be able to board a souvenir he had been hand carrying since the second day of the trip, a four-foot-long sitar. Meanwhile, we were told the weather had turned nasty in Italy, and a rare snowstorm was hitting Rome. I sat back in my seat and, despite my fatigue, felt the adrenaline begin to pump. I suspected it would take more than beta-blockers and Don Williams to get me through this flight.

The pope came back soon after takeoff, looking every bit as irritated as the rest of us. He tried to walk down the single middle aisle of coach but didn't make it very far in the crowded quarters. I saw the pontiff's face cloud over when he was asked about population growth in India and the church's teaching on contraception. The pope didn't like the question, and he began raising his finger to punctuate his remarks. He soon returned to his first-class seat as the drinks were rolled out.

Many hours later I awoke in the darkened plane. Everyone was asleep, but I recognized a Vatican official slowly making his way up the aisle. He leaned over and told me, sotto voce, "We're landing in Naples," and then disappeared without explanation. I looked out the window and saw below us the curved rim of a mountain, and then a deep dark hole. We were flying directly over Mount Vesuvius, at very low altitude. I was pretty sure you're not supposed to fly over an active volcano, and mentally chalked up a safety demerit for our Air India pilot. But I later learned that the pilot had, perhaps, saved us all from disaster. As we slept, the plane had circled Rome pointlessly before Italian air traffic controllers finally announced that all runways were snowed in and instructed the pilot to proceed to Pisa. The pilot wisely looked at his fuel gauge, however, and realized the plane would never make it there. We were flying on empty. He turned south instead and took the most direct route to Naples, where we then landed. It was snowing there, too. But we were on the ground.

And then, in one of the most bizarre endings to a papal trip, we were whisked by bus to the Naples train station. It was three in the morning, and the Vatican had decided to put the pope and the rest of us on a two-car *Treno Papale* to Rome. The Naples train depot was nearly deserted at that hour, but several bleary-eyed bums stirred on benches and watched, incredulous, as the white-robed John Paul strolled by, followed by his retinue and a haggard pack of journalists.

Out of the corner of my eye, I saw Phil Pullella slip into the single phone booth on the platform. This was the pre–cell phone era, and Pullella routinely carried in his briefcase a roll of *gettoni*, the slotted Italian telephone tokens. Now he was feeding them furiously into the pay phone as he tried to quickly dictate a story to the Reuters desk in Rome or London. What surprised me was that none of the Italian agency reporters were rushing to find telephones. Then I heard one of them, ANSA's Federico Mandillo, scream in Pullella's direction, "We had a deal!" Apparently, the exhausted Italians had agreed that none of the agencies would file a story on the pope's dramatic detour before they reached Rome. Pullella wanted no part of such an arrangement, of course, and was now getting a scoop. He appeared to be hyperventilating a bit as he read from his notebook into the mouthpiece, still feeding *gettoni*, and all the while bracing the doors of the booth against Mandillo, who was trying to punch him in the face.

The train was a romantic image, gliding through the snow-covered hills at dawn, but it had no heat. The pope passed the journey covered in a blanket, asleep in a front compartment. Many of us were in the lightweight shirts we had been wearing in balmy Bombay, and we jumped up and down to stay warm. When we arrived at Rome's small Trastevere train station, the pope stood on the platform and said he'd never imagined coming back from India like this. "That's the way things go sometimes," he added. And that was really all there was to say.

The Roman streets were still clogged with eight inches of snow, and I ended up walking the two miles home, still in my short-sleeved shirt, lugging a briefcase and a portable typewriter. When I rang the bell, my wife answered the door. I heard her cheerful voice: "How was the trip?"

John Paul traveled to Africa fourteen times, and it was there that the *Volo Papale* often came unglued.

In 1988 the pope set off on a five-country southern African tour that pointedly excluded South Africa and its Apartheid regime. On the third leg of the trip, the Vatican press corps was waiting outside a Botswana airport for a flight to Lesotho, a tiny country bordered on all sides by South Africa. We had heard forecasts of storms around Maseru, the Lesotho capital, our destination that day. I saw our Air Zimbabwe pilot and walked over to ask him about it. Sure enough, he said, they were reporting bad weather ahead. He seemed friendly and chatty. The problem with Maseru, he explained, was that the airport was located not far from the sheer face of a mountain, and it was a very tricky approach in a storm. I ventured that he must have flown there many times. He smiled. "Never been there, actually. This is my first."

I looked out on the tarmac at our Boeing 707, an old plane that had obviously been mothballed by a first-world airline before ending up in the Air Zimbabwe fleet. At each of our previous stops in Zimbabwe and Botswana, a mechanic had worked on one of the engines—right up until the moment the pope boarded the plane, when the cowling would quickly be screwed back on for takeoff. Even now, I noticed, two mechanics were up on the wing examining engine parts. Before long, sirens could be heard in the distance: The pope was arriving. We boarded the plane and, sure enough, by the time we reached our seats the cover was being bolted back onto the problem engine.

On previous trips all this would have frozen me with anxiety. But whether it was the beta-blockers or a metaphysical attitude adjustment, I felt no fear—none whatsoever. And as this particular flight turned nasty—the weather had indeed become bad, and the faulty engine was causing problems—I found myself immune from the sickness that soon overtook most people on the plane. In fact, I was eating my meal with gusto even as others were tossing it back up into paper bags. We circled Maseru, waiting for what we presumed was a break in the storm. Although we didn't know it at the time, the real reason for our predicament was a combination of weather, mechanics and protocol. Lesotho's King Moshoeshoe II, who was to greet the pope at the airport, was himself on a flight to Maseru, running late and racing to arrive before the pontiff. Air traffic control held up our plane until the king had landed, but at that point the storm worsened and the airport's navigation beacons and radar signals went out. The *Volo Pa-*

pale, stuck in the air with a bad engine and above a mountain hidden somewhere behind the clouds, lurched through the storm in an endless loop. Federico Mandillo, the ANSA reporter, suffered what turned out to be a stroke. Then the plane suddenly leveled off.

Moments later a beaming stewardess walked back to our press section and said loudly, "Jo-burg." The plane erupted in a cheer, and a half hour later the pilot put us down at Johannesburg's Jan Smuts Airport. Frantic to find telephones and file our stories, we rushed out of the plane. Barry Moody, the Reuters correspondent, watched in horror as the semiconscious Mandillo, now slumped in the aisle, was trampled by his colleagues. South African officials were eager to play host to their unexpected guests. They quickly assembled a bus caravan to take us overland to Lesotho, the pope riding in a bulletproof BMW in front. At one point, when his car pulled into a gas station and the pontiff stepped out of the backseat, the astounded attendants fell to their knees and began to pray. The pope handed them each a rosary.

It was a five-hour trip, and along the way we learned that a dramatic hijacking story was unfolding in Lesotho. Gunmen had seized a bus full of Catholic pilgrims on their way to the papal Mass and were demanding to see the pope. A South African SWAT team was being sent in to surround the vehicle. As our own bus sped past bean fields and cattle ranches, we followed the story on my portable radio. Up in his armored BMW, the pope had been informed that a pilgrim bus had been seized, but not about the hijackers' demand to meet with him. Witnesses later said the young men who had commandeered the bus were a strange bunch, wielding AK-47s and singing religious songs with the pilgrims throughout the ordeal.

In the evening we finally crossed the Lesotho border and arrived in Maseru. John Paul got out of his car and walked along a muddy roadside to shake hands with pilgrims who had camped out to see him. The pope's motorcade continued and passed close to where the gunmen were holding the bus, but it did not stop. The pope had still not been told the hijackers wanted to meet him, and Vatican officials, concerned about the pontiff's safety, did not for a moment consider bringing him to the site. A minute after the pope passed by, the gunmen ordered the bus driver to ram the gates of a nearby British embassy building. Before he had a chance, the

South African SWAT team stormed the vehicle, killing the three hijackers and a sixteen-year-old schoolgirl. As we arrived at our hotel a few blocks away, we heard the sirens of ambulances taking the injured to hospitals.

The deaths cast a pall over the Mass the pope celebrated the next morning. For reporters, the hunt was on to find the pilgrim survivors from the bus, who were here at the Mass, but no one would tell us where. The last thing organizers wanted was to make these traumatized people face the media. I broke from the press pack and scanned the crowded field. If the survivors were here, I reasoned, they would be brought to the front, where they could receive Communion from the pope. As the liturgy began, I crept through the grass toward the altar, moving furtively among the worshipers. To those who eyed me with suspicion, I held up my press badge and said simply, "Vatican." I explained that I needed to find the people from the hijacked bus. Someone helpfully pointed to a kerchiefed woman seated on a blanket. "She was on the bus."

I approached the woman, who was flanked by two friends. Could I ask some questions? The friends looked doubtful. I held up my press pass, and the woman nodded reluctantly. This was like striking gold, and I wanted it all to myself. I looked around and pulled a rain hood over my head, lest my colleagues see me. The woman was a forty-nine-year-old schoolteacher who had been accompanying the younger people on the bus. I whispered questions into her ear as the people trying to follow the Mass shushed me. She didn't answer at first. Perhaps she didn't speak English, after all. Then I realized she couldn't speak because she was crying. Eventually she dried her tears and described the scene on the bus: how they had prayed the rosary with the hijackers, how the gunmen thought the pope could help them change the Lesotho government, how they all hid under the seats when the shooting started. She knew the sixteen-year-old girl who died in the shooting.

"She was so excited about the pope's visit. She was just a schoolgirl," the woman said before breaking into sobs again. Even the most callous reporter will at times feel that he is trespassing on someone's raw emotions, and this teacher's grief led me to close my notebook. I said good-bye and slinked back through the grass to the press pen. I had my story. When I looked back, the woman was once again indistinguishable in the field of worshipers.

+ + +

We were all happy to leave Lesotho and roll into Swaziland, where the pope was to say Mass in a soccer stadium. It was a splendid sunlit day, and at the stadium I strolled through a crowd that seemed more curious than devout. Over near the papal altar, I spied Father Roberto Tucci, frowning.

Tucci, a gregarious prelate in charge of organizing these trips, was a favorite of Vatican journalists. A big man with an oversized head, he looked like a country farmer. His droopy face was deeply furrowed and sprouted eyebrows that had grown out of control. No one would have guessed he was a Jesuit. He had a down-to-earth style of talking and a bluntness that had occasionally gotten him in trouble with the Vatican's diplomats. He seemed to lack the discretion that made most Vatican officials such bad interviews. When Tucci met the press (often on a smoke break during papal ceremonies), he actually told them what was on his mind—a dangerous practice. As the Vatican's advance man, he had negotiated with governments all over the world and knew the dubious things they wanted the pope to do: parades, private blessings, public approbation, visits to state factories, prayers at their relatives' graves, triumphal tours of housing projects. Many government leaders, especially the dictators, saw the pope's presence as a giant PR opportunity. Tucci was the man who told them, quietly but firmly, to forget it.

Once the papal program had been whittled down to the reasonable, Tucci's job was to make sure it went off without a hitch. He lined up transportation, counted the steps the pope would have to climb, measured the angle of the sun on papal altars. He was the show's producer.

Few people know it, but Tucci and John Paul went back decades. They had met during the Second Vatican Council, when the pope was a young archbishop and Tucci was a theological adviser on several council documents. Though to listen to him he might seem like the guy sitting on the next bar stool, Tucci was, in fact, an intellectual, and for many years directed the team of Jesuits who wrote for the prestigious journal *La Civiltà Cattolica*.

I walked over and chatted with him in the Swazi sunshine, and soon learned the cause of his consternation. The Mass was ready to begin, but the Vatican was waiting for Swaziland's twenty-year-old king, Mswati III, who had a habit of arriving late. As Tucci glanced at his watch, a government official in a dark blue suit approached us.

"Coming a little bit late is considered a sign of respect in our country," he explained. Tucci said nothing. His eyebrows heaved in exasperation; he badly needed a cigarette.

Already the Swazis had flubbed John Paul's arrival. When the pope drove into the stadium, a squad of staff-wielding Swazi men closed in around his open truck and raised their shields high in salute. But then the truck took a wrong turn at the end of the track and had to slowly back up, as the pope sat wondering what was going on. For reasons Tucci couldn't understand, this miscue triggered wild cheering by the crowd.

By now the king was fifteen minutes late, and the pope was at the altar, waiting. Tucci surveyed the scene, saw something he didn't like and spoke abruptly into a walkie-talkie. The heavily armed soldiers, he said, were too close to the altar, and a machine-gun nest was visible behind the pope. They had to be moved, or the Mass would look like a military exercise.

The pope began celebrating the liturgy, and a few minutes later a cheer went up. King Mswati had finally arrived, riding along the stadium track in a vintage Cadillac toward his seat of honor. I watched Tucci grumble into his walkie-talkie and shake his head.

"Get a load of this," he muttered. I looked up and saw the young king was accompanied by two of his four wives.

Polygamy is widespread in Swaziland, and King Mswati always made sure he got first connubial dibs among the country's female population. Three weeks before the pope arrived, Swaziland had held its annual "Reed Dance," in which tens of thousands of young virgins gather to dance bare-breasted, twirl reeds and sing in an effort to be noticed by the king, who chooses a new bride from among them. For the girls, selection as the king's latest wife is a unique chance to escape poverty—or at least, that was the line I got from Swazi officials at the Mass. They also explained that it wasn't as easy as it looks to pick a bride from twenty thousand girls dancing in a field. This year the king, not wanting to rely on first impressions, had video-taped the dance and made his decision afterward.

In a bit of irony that probably went right past everyone in attendance, the pope's sermon at the stadium Mass defended Christian marriage and sharply criticized polygamy, saying it was disrespectful to women. If the king and his wives were offended, they didn't show it. Mswati greeted the pope warmly at his palace later in the day, a ceremony overseen by an imposing, no-nonsense female who stood off to one side.

"Who is that?" I asked a black-suited Swazi bureaucrat.

"That is the king's mother, the Indlovukazi." He consulted briefly with his colleague. "In your language, 'the Great She-Elephant,'" he said, as if that would ring a bell. My face must have told him it didn't.

"She is a very important person in Swaziland," he said slowly. Indeed, I later discovered that this turbaned figure with the baleful stare ruled jointly with her son, by constitutional decree. She also helped screen the king's new brides.

The pope's eight hours in Swaziland and his strong defense of monogamy blew over like a summer cloud. Polygamy continued to flourish in the country, and the Reed Dance drew increasing numbers of maidens. Years later, I opened the newspaper and read that King Mswati, now thirty-seven, was in trouble after choosing a seventeen-year-old virgin—Miss Teen Swaziland, no less—as his thirteenth wife. In doing so, it seems, he had violated his own chastity decree for girls under age eighteen, which he had established as an anti-AIDS measure. After breaking the ban, the king showed that he was not above the law: He fined himself a cow.

In late September of 2001 Pope John Paul spent three days in Armenia after a four-day visit to Kazakhstan. The trip was too long for the ailing pope, now eighty-one and suffering from Parkinson's disease. He needed to be constantly steadied by aides when he walked, had trouble getting to his feet during liturgies and at times slumped in his chair in apparent exhaustion. His hands trembled, and Vatican planners had devised a laptop podium to help him keep his text together. That idea backfired when the podium slid off the seated pontiff, scattering the pages of his speech. To those of us who had accompanied him through the years, the slow transformation was painful to witness. It was clear he'd soon be in a wheelchair.

For *Volo Papale* reporters, the trip also raised the delicate question of whether the pope was really running the Vatican these days—an issue that came to a head in Kazakhstan. It was only two weeks after the September

11 attacks, the Afghanistan border was a few hundred miles to the south and journalists were pressing to know the Vatican's position on the imminent U.S. attack against the Taliban forces. Neither the pope nor his top foreign policy aides had said much about the buildup to Operation Enduring Freedom. But in the Kazakh capital of Astana, the Vatican spokesman, Joaquín Navarro-Valls, suddenly filled the void. During a lull in the papal program, he declared that the Vatican would understand if the United States went after terrorists around the world as an extension of the principle of self-defense. The surprisingly hawkish comments totally upstaged whatever the pope was doing in Kazakhstan. Watching John Paul struggle just to say Mass, we wondered whether he was even aware of what his spokesman had just told the world.

By the time we reached Armenia, Navarro-Valls was spinning in a different direction, emphasizing how alert the pope was despite his physical infirmity. If only you could see him up close, he said, you'd realize that his mind remains sharp. It seemed to me that Vatican higher-ups were behind this new insistence on papal competence. No doubt they had noticed the problem with Navarro-Valls enunciating John Paul's views on the "war on terrorism": It looked as if the pope could no longer speak for himself.

Andreas Englisch, an astute reporter for the bestselling German newspaper *Bild*, picked up on all this and wondered aloud who was calling the shots.

"Do you think Navarro did this on his own? Never! Of course it was orchestrated, but who is directing the orchestra? And now they have to convince us that the pope is 'mentally alert'! That the pope is really in charge!" he said with a big laugh.

Englisch and I had discovered strangely marked orange canisters stowed on the papal plane, produced by a German manufacturer. We Googled them and discovered they were oxygen tanks, obviously carried for papal emergencies. All this added to the impression that a moribund pope was being carted around the world for show, while the Vatican chain of command was falling apart.

On the trip's final day, reporters lined up to get on a bus in Yerevan. A weary Vik van Brantegem stood sentry at the door, checking us off a list to make sure no one was left behind. Missing the bus to the airport can be disastrous, and it's only happened to me once, in Mozambique. On that occasion, I ran out to the main road and hitchhiked, waving a fifty-dollar bill. The first driver stopped and sped me to the terminal, refusing any payment.

In Armenia, the bus drove us to the airport, and we trooped onto an Airbus as the pope made one last stop at a monastery twenty miles away. We're used to waiting on planes, but the Armenian Airlines staff had been given orders not to provide us with food or drink until the pope arrived. Not even water was being distributed. The pope was running late, and as the hours passed the reporters grew testy.

Andreas Englisch lounged in the aisle, his necktie loose around his collar, sweat forming on his brow. As always, he managed to smile at the absurdity of our predicament.

"This is ridiculous!" He caught the attention of a flight attendant and gently informed her that his colleagues might riot unless they got something to drink. The water was apparently still being loaded, she said.

"So what have you got?" he asked.

She paused and went to check, returning a minute later with a bottle of vodka.

"Ah ha!" Englisch said delightedly. Soon many more bottles of vodka were circulating around the plane, emptied into plastic cups and tossed down with the reckless abandon of those who have no more deadlines that day. I am not a big vodka drinker, but I quickly discovered the pleasure of Avshar, an eighty-proof liquor that is produced, I was told, from wheat grown under Mount Ararat. It was Armenia's best, and it was now flowing like a river on our plane. The mood changed from bellicose to jocose. Who needed water, anyway? I don't think we even noticed when the plane took off.

Then Navarro appeared. He had an announcement to make. In one last twist of his spinmeister's baton, he had arranged for the pope to personally greet each of us on the flight back to Rome. As we were brought forward one by one to sit next to the pontiff and chat briefly with him, we would see for ourselves how alert and engaged he was.

Navarro apparently hadn't noticed that half the plane was tanked to the gills. And so it came to pass that John Paul sat listening as a parade of reporters staggered up and, in tones ranging from maudlin to chummy, blurted out vodka-fueled ruminations on life, religion, children and, of course, the papacy. The photo souvenirs were priceless: We looked as if we were the pope's seatmates on the flight, chatting away like old friends. On closer inspection, however, my own photo told the real story: me in animated conversation, the pope smiling weakly as his eyes glazed over.

As a traveler, Pope Benedict has avoided the outposts of Christianity and their cultural quirks. This reflects the focus of his pontificate: After more than twenty-five years of church expansion in places like Africa and Asia, Benedict believes the priority now is to shore up the base. It's no accident that most of his trips have been to Europe. And, unlike his predecessor, he seems to have zero interest in traipsing through shantytowns, saying Mass in the desert or watching native dancers boogie to the beat during a papal Mass.

Benedict set the tone of his travels during his very first trip, when he presided over World Youth Day in Cologne, Germany, in August 2005. These mega-gatherings of young people are sometimes compared to Woodstock, but the only thing they have in common with rock festivals is big crowds. In the Vatican's definition, a "youth" is someone between the ages of sixteen and thirty-five, so the encounters attract a lot of twenty-something Catholics who are already active in local parishes and who are eager to network with other young people like themselves.

The highlight of these international assemblies is always an evening vigil with the pope, followed by Mass the next morning. John Paul II conducted the vigil as a kind of spiritual pep rally, listening to the youths tell their personal stories, watching them dance and joining in their songs. He lightened the mood by kidding and cajoling, twirling his cane, tossing aside prepared texts and generally catching the fun flavor of the event.

As we discovered in Germany, that was not Pope Benedict's style.

The Cologne vigil took place at twilight on a gently sloping hill, as a full moon rose along the horizon. It was heavy on prayer and light on entertainment. From time to time the crowd began chanting Benedict's name as they used to do with John Paul II, but the German pope put his fingers to his lips to gently hush them; it wasn't long before the chanting died out. The program included a few slow and dignified dances by youths from Ghana and India. But the highlight was silent adoration of the Blessed Sacrament, when the attention of nearly a million young people was directed to a consecrated host in a gold monstrance, elevated on a papal platform.

Toward the end of the evening, as a clarinet played a haunting melody, the young people lit candles and waved them from side to side, creating a moving sea of light. On the stage Benedict held his own candle, but didn't move it. Behind him a phalanx of Roman Curia cardinals took their cue from the pope and remained still, like statues. All except for Cardinal Angelo Sodano, who looked up, saw the crowd, smiled—and slowly waved his candle. For singing out of tune like that, Cardinal Sodano, at the time the Vatican's secretary of state, received some behind-the-back criticism. One senior Vatican official told me a few days later, "Sodano looked ridiculous." He said it in a way that implied there might be some career fallout from candle waving.

The young people seemed to take all this in stride. Their T-shirts may have read, "Do it, Ratzi!" but when interviewed at the vigil they quickly adopted a more serious tone and spoke of the importance of rediscovering Catholic identity. They'd gotten the message.

"It was good. People need to be reminded to pray," said one twenty-two-year-old from Spain.

Afterward, tiptoeing through a landscape of sleeping bags, I talked with Gabriela Delgado from California, asking her impressions of this World Youth Day. "It was more religious than political," she told me. "I think that's fine because that's what we really came for."

Benedict is at heart an academic, and he did not set that aside in Cologne. I listened in astonishment when, at the closing Mass, he explicated the Greek and Roman roots of the word "adoration," an etymological lesson that must have gone right past 99.9 percent of his young audience. On the other hand, I was impressed when he compared Holy Communion to nuclear fission, saying the Eucharist was like an "intimate explosion" that sets off a series of transformations. It struck me as creative, and as a journalist for a Catholic news agency I could work with that.

Most *Volo Papale* reporters, however, were not so pleased with the pope's almost exclusive focus on religious themes. When we picked up each day's papal speeches from van Brantegem's hotel room at five a.m., my colleagues groaned as they skimmed the texts. "I can't write a story about the 'power of the Eucharist,'" said one reporter for a major British publication. The secular media were beginning to struggle with this new pope. John Paul II had always seasoned his World Youth Day events with remarks about global conflicts, refugee crises, technological challenges, sexual hedonism or something—anything—that might make a headline in the *Pittsburgh Post-Gazette* the following morning. Benedict seemed to deliberately avoid all that.

Gone likewise were the gestures of enthusiasm and shared exuberance, the papal hugs and line dancing. As Benedict sat motionless on the papal altar in Cologne, shrouded in a gold cope beneath a mushroomlike canopy, an Italian photographer nudged me with his shoulder and said with a grunt, "What are we supposed to do with this guy? He's a mummy."

When Pope Benedict made his first trip to the United States in 2008, major media rediscovered interest in the German pontiff. And for once the pope seemed to be riding high in the headlines. On his plane from Rome to Washington, he fielded a question on priestly sex abuse with a directness and command of detail that got everyone's attention. "We are deeply ashamed and will do all possible that this cannot happen in the future," he said in a soft voice. It seemed so utterly simple, yet none of the Vatican's top people had ever said as much before. Of course, the question on sex abuse came as no surprise to the pope. For this trip, in fact, the Vatican had asked reporters to presubmit their questions. Vatican officials then chose a few and handed them to selected journalists to recite on the plane during the public Q&A. The theatrical ploy left many of us grousing.

The pope arrived at the White House for a star-spangled love fest on his eighty-first birthday. President George W. Bush led nine thousand well-wishers in an impromptu rendition of "Happy Birthday" on the South Lawn. The pope was treated to a mini-pageant of Americana, complete with a fife and drum corps that played "Yankee Doodle." As the pope and president traded speeches, Bush seemed to be trying to reach a little higher than usual. George W., most people would agree, was no intellectual, and though he once claimed he'd read a book by Pope Benedict, he later wisely qualified that by saying he'd read "parts of it." Now, however, as the pope sat and listened a few feet away, the president went into star pupil mode, dishing around philosophical phrases like "dictatorship of relativism" and quoting Saint Augustine—in Latin. The pope's address was a subtle reflection on the founding fathers and moral values. As he ended with the inevitable "God bless America!" the president leaped to his feet and told the pontiff, "Thank you, Your Holiness! Awesome speech!"

The U.S. visit was a logistical nightmare for reporters, who were forced to arrive at events up to six hours early for endless security checks. In theory, the *Volo Papale* journalists were given easier clearance. When the papal plane arrived in New York, the pope was scheduled to speak almost immediately at the United Nations, and I was among a small pool of reporters who were whisked onto a military helicopter awaiting us on the JFK runway. The operation was all very *Apocalypse Now*, and through the chopper's open door we watched the skyscrapers loom and recede. Deposited in lower Manhattan, we boarded a bus that raced up an empty FDR Drive behind the screaming sirens of our police escort. But when we reached UN headquarters, New York's finest wouldn't let us cross the street to get inside. As our handlers pleaded, the city cops dug in. In desperation, we walked west to Second Avenue and marched several blocks north to try our luck on the other side of the UN building. It was hot, and the midtown sidewalks were crowded with people who didn't seem to care about our predicament. One of our handlers sprained her ankle and fell behind, soon absorbed by the crowd. We reached the north doors, our dark suits drenched in sweat, and could hear the papal motorcade arriving around the corner—the event we were supposed to be covering. The guards told us they weren't authorized to let us in; they would call someone in charge. We now risked not seeing the pope at all. It was time for me to break away from the pack, and Andreas Englisch had the same idea. He and I walked over to the doors, where no one seemed to be checking badges very closely, and slipped inside behind some staffers. Down a long hallway we found an elevator. A few minutes later we opened a door and stood in the balcony of the General Assembly Hall, where Pope Benedict was entering to an ovation. I flashed my press pass to a guard standing sentry, but he didn't seem to care.

The purpose of papal reporting pools is to make sure some journalists actually eyeball the pope, as opposed to simply watching the video feed.

Even if nothing dramatic happens off camera, there is always a value, sometimes intangible, in being present, as you get the feel of the event. And now, sitting in the General Assembly balcony as the pope read his speech, I felt a distinct coolness in the hall. The papal text itself was an interesting analysis of the relationship between morality, freedom and human rights, but it was failing to ignite any enthusiasm. Pope Benedict has a habit of burying his applause lines in a monotone, as if he should never have to raise his voice. That makes for dull listening. A key passage of his speech, for example, came when he defended religious freedom: "It is inconceivable, then, that believers should have to suppress a part of themselves—their faith—in order to be active citizens. It should never be necessary to deny God in order to enjoy one's rights." This was one of Benedict's deepest beliefs, his bread and butter, but the crowd did not react; they were half asleep. He had the world's stage, but sounded like an academic in a lecture hall.

In contrast, even Pope Paul VI, who was not one to ham it up, had risen to the occasion when he addressed the United Nations in 1965 and issued his electrifying plea that ended with the words "No more war, never again war!" When Benedict wrapped up his speech, he received a standing ovation, but it was pro forma. A couple of weeks later, I told a Vatican official I thought the pope missed an opportunity at the United Nations, and I got an earful: "You journalists! Did you even bother to read the speech? All you want is emotion and razzle-dazzle!" Clearly we were not getting it from this pope.

In the spring of 2009, I got a call from an excited Andreas Englisch. "Gänswein wants to see us," he said. It turned out that Monsignor Georg Gänswein, the pope's private secretary, was doing some proactive media prep for Benedict's upcoming pilgrimage to the Holy Land. For weeks I'd been hearing that a small group of advanced thinkers in the Secretariat of State were quietly working to head off the kinds of gaffes that had plagued this pontificate from the beginning. Many of these blunders had occurred when the pope was traveling outside the Vatican. He would utter remarks that offended or shocked—on topics ranging from Islam, condoms and abortion to the Holocaust—and his aides would then make things worse with awkward attempts to spin his words or simply change them. Now the pope was preparing to walk through the minefield of the Middle East, visiting Jordan, Israel and Palestinian territories, and Gänswein wanted to identify potential problems. So he summoned three journalists for an off-the-record exchange: Englisch, myself and Rachel Donadio, the *New York Times* Rome correspondent. One fine morning we got into Andreas's car and headed out to Castel Gandolfo, where the pope and his close aides were spending a few days.

We were in an elegantly furnished salon of the papal villa when Gänswein burst into the room, lifting his soutane slightly as he sat on an antique chair. The sandy-haired monsignor, whom CNN was calling "the pope's George Clooney," looked every bit as handsome in person as on TV. He made easy conversation for a while, and then we got down to business. Essentially, he wanted to know what would make this pilgrimage a success, journalistically speaking, and what could make it a disaster. In our opinion, what were the things a pope could not say or do? Where were the booby traps? I had to hand it to Gänswein: He realized that some degree of media sympathy was crucial for a trip like this.

Our answers, however, probably left the good monsignor more confused than ever. Andreas said quite forcefully that when Benedict visited the Yad Vashem Holocaust Memorial, he must address the issue as "the German pope." This would be a historic opportunity to talk about the failings of German Christians in the Nazi period. I did not completely agree, as I believed that Benedict could not come to Jerusalem as a spokesman for the soul of the German nation; his role was more universal now, and his message needed to reflect that. Moreover, I felt that whatever the interreligious and political flash points along the papal itinerary, the spiritual dimension was the key to the success of the trip. That was how John Paul II had won the hearts of people during his own Holy Land trip in 2000—by being, first of all, a pilgrim, and by emphasizing the connections between all believers, whether Christian, Muslim or Jewish. Benedict's challenge, I said, was to not appear as if he were simply mimicking his predecessor. He had to be himself.

Gänswein took it all in thoughtfully, then rose and thanked us and was gone—he had to run, he said, looking at his watch. A guest was arriving and he had to introduce him to the pope.

Two weeks later, we found ourselves at the midpoint of the pope's Holy Land visit. Benedict had, indeed, avoided missteps so far. In Jordan he had adroitly raised the issue of religion and violence, but in a way that encouraged moderate Islamic leaders and insulted no one. He underlined their common belief in God's place in civil society, and won the whole country over when he donned a red-and-white-checkered Jordanian kaffiyeh.

Things got more complicated in Jerusalem, however, where his visit to Yad Vashem was less than a triumph. It turned out, perhaps, that Andreas Englisch was right. I watched the whole event unfold as I stood in a corner of the darkened memorial and could feel things going flat. The pope wore an expressionless mask as the cantors sang and a funeral prayer was read. Then he gave an unusually brief talk, in which he spoke movingly about the tragedy experienced by victims, but said nothing about the historical responsibility borne by Germans or by Christians. He expressed "compassion," not remorse. As the pope's motorcade sped away from the memorial, I joined the pack of reporters who laid siege to Jewish leaders in attendance. While generally appreciative of Pope Benedict's visit, they also expressed disappointment. The pope who grew up in wartime Germany had failed to mention the Nazi perpetrators of the Holocaust. Once again, Benedict's reluctance to share publicly his own personal experience had deflated what should have been an emotional high point of the trip.

At breakfast the next morning, the papal entourage read the reviews and were not happy. "Benedict's Speech Showed Verbal Indifference and Banality" read one newspaper headline. What really rankled Vatican officials was that several articles mentioned that as a teenager the pope had been in the Hitler Youth program. The entourage members discussed it at breakfast, and Monsignor Gänswein remarked that it simply wasn't true—that Joseph Ratzinger had never been an active member of Hitler Youth. Father Federico Lombardi was taking mental notes as he listened to the papal secretary. And thus the seeds of yet another gaffe were planted.

A few hours later I was sitting next to Victor Simpson of the AP in a packed media center, listening to Lombardi fend off suggestions that Pope Benedict had shied away from the "German question" during his Yad Vashem visit the day before. Then Lombardi switched gears and went on the offensive. Without being asked, he began referring to news reports about Joseph Ratzinger's involvement with the Hitler Youth. Some media had quoted the speaker of the Israeli parliament, who described Benedict as a "German who joined the Hitler Youth and . . . a person who joined Hitler's army."

Lombardi said it was important to counter the "lies" that were being spread about Ratzinger as a young man. "The pope was never in the Hitlerjugend. Hitlerjugend was a corps of volunteers fanatically, ideologically for Nazis. The pope was never in the Hitler Youth, never, never, never!" the spokesman said emphatically. I looked at Vic Simpson and saw that he was as slack-jawed as I was. We both knew that Ratzinger himself had acknowledged that he had been forced to join Hitler Youth. We cornered Father Lombardi after the press briefing and reminded him that in his 1997 memoir, *Milestones*, the pope had recounted how he had been involuntarily enrolled in the Hitler Youth program, even though he quickly stopped going to meetings. Lombardi later issued a clarification, saying that what he meant ("Never, never, never!") was that the young Ratzinger had never embraced Hitler Youth or the Nazi ideology. But by then it was too late. The story going out on all the wires was that the Vatican had clumsily and inexplicably tried to deny what was part of the historical record on the German pope's activities under the Nazi regime. It pained me to see Father Lombardi, who was genuinely pushing for more openness in the Vatican, make such a blunder. It was the kind of mistake that arose precisely from the Vatican's decentralized way of handling information—an offhand and misunderstood remark over breakfast had become the latest media fiasco by lunchtime.

In Jordan, the pope had closed out his four-day visit with a trip to the Jordan River, a stop that would showcase the pontiff as pilgrim, walking in the footsteps of Jesus. Our busload of journalists arrived at the river after a one-hour trip from Amman, passing a sign that announced, "The Baptism Site of Jesus Christ." The road looked new, and there were buildings going up. In fact, the Jordanian government had created this place, donating adjacent land to Christian churches with the aim of making it one of the biggest pilgrimage attractions in the region. The government boasted that the site had been recognized as "the real (and only true) site where Jesus was baptized," and Benedict's stop that day would be touted as a papal stamp of approval.

This was no small thing for Jordan. The religious tourism industry is a relatively big source of income for countries in the Holy Land, and to an increasing number of Christian visitors Jordan looked like a safer place to travel than Israel. Jordan's baptismal site brought the pilgrimage competition to a head, because Israel had one, too.

The Gospel says that John the Baptist was living and baptizing people at "Bethany beyond the Jordan," which to the early Christian community must have meant the east bank of the Jordan River, now part of Jordanian territory. Nevertheless, in the long tradition of pilgrimages, a place on the western side of the river was regularly visited as the baptism site and, until the 1967 Middle East war, was crowded with pilgrims. Then it became part of a militarized Israeli-occupied zone and was off-limits unless special permission was obtained. Its venerable Christian churches were deserted and surrounded by signs reading, "Danger: Mines." When Israel caught wind that Pope Benedict was going to be visiting the Jordanian baptism site, it quickly announced a reopening of its own site to the public. But all the attention had shifted to the other side of the river. In PR terms, this was a big win for Jordan.

The Jordanian government had worked very hard to make this happen. In the 1990s it had supported archaeological excavations at Wadi al-Kharrar that uncovered the foundations of five ancient Christian churches and other ruins near a series of river pools once used for baptisms. Comparing the discoveries with biblical texts and the accounts of medieval pilgrims and historians, the experts were convinced that this had surely been a major pilgrimage site in Christianity's early centuries. More recently they had discovered a cruciform baptismal pool that seemed to match descriptions of the very place where John the Baptist led Jesus into the waters of the river. This was the spot Pope Benedict had come to see.

Our journalistic pack arrived two hours ahead of time, and we hiked along the wooded riverbanks in the afternoon heat. It should be noted that the Jordan River is not what it used to be. A pure, rushing waterway in ancient times, it's been reduced by agricultural use to a sluggish brown stream about thirty feet across. The baptism site is on a floodplain where the waters are even more still. As we were led down to the edge of the pool, its stagnant waters appeared uninviting. But in a photograph, the setting would be ideal—the white-robed pontiff standing on the ancient stone steps leading down to the pool where Christ himself began his public religious life.

A huddle of photographers stood in the mud and brushed away flies. I recognized Greg Tarczynski, a well-known photographer for Catholic and other media outlets. He looked excited, as he was in perfect position for a great shot, with the lighting growing more dramatic by the minute. But the pope's arrival was still a half hour away. I put on a "Pope in Jordan" baseball cap against the bright sun and chatted with *Time* magazine's Jeff Israely. I told Jeff this might just be the defining moment of this trip—yes, even before we made it to Jerusalem. The baptismal site, I explained, had to be especially significant to Pope Benedict, who'd set the first chapter of his book *Jesus of Nazareth* at this precise spot. He saw it as the place where God entered human history. Archaeology had made it more real to the modern mind-set: These stones offered tangible confirmation of a biblical event. Now the pope had come to stand on the banks himself, as Jesus once did, and perhaps—if he knew the value of a photo op—to touch the very waters of the Jordan.

A guard with a rifle came running past us at full speed, and a few seconds later the pope's motorcade appeared from behind a knoll. "Motorcade" would be stretching it—he rode at the head of a convoy of electric vehicles that resembled oversized golf carts, along with members of the Jordanian royal family. The carts moved silently along the dirt road, then stopped high above the baptismal pool. Prince Ghazi bin Muhammad chatted briefly with the pope. And then, incredibly, the convoy began moving again. It was over. The pope came all this way and never got out of his golf cart. Never approached the water. Never moved into position for a photograph. The shooters down below had been shut out. Greg Tarczynski, his shoes caked in mud, was shaking his head and laughing. "Never file a picture in your mind before you've taken it," he remarked as he picked up his gear and hustled off to the next event.

We walked briskly for half a mile to a dusty plain where eight hundred people were sitting in front of a pavilion that marked the future site of two new Catholic churches. I looked around: It was the middle of nowhere. The only feature on the landscape was a barren promontory, atop which stood a huge cross. Two flags, Vatican and Jordanian, fluttered in the breeze. Suddenly the crowd erupted: Pope Benedict was onstage. As he basked in the standing ovation, he seemed delighted. He thanked them all, spoke about prospects for their Catholic communities and lingered with them for more than an hour. The pope had already laid several cornerstones for church buildings throughout Jordan, and he was clearly excited that Christianity was showing small signs of a revival in a predominantly Muslim country. I understood now why he had rushed past Jesus's baptismal site to get to these folks: He was more interested in the church's future than its past.

The pope's motorcade left us in the dust, and our press bus was nowhere in sight. As the sun began to set, we slouched in red velvet chairs in the VIP section, waiting for Vik to bark out some instructions. We would be getting back to the hotel very late. Out of the corner of my eye I saw the ever energetic John Allen approaching the empty papal stage. He had been videotaping himself throughout the trip and relaying the tape to CNN for behind-the-scenes commentary. He had no crew, so it was a one-man operation. As John related, he had learned how to use the tiny video camera only a few days earlier, and it was amusing to see him turn it on himself—on the papal plane, at Masses or on our press bus. We laughed, but the print reporters among us also wondered whether we might be doing the same thing in a few months. This seemed to be the future path of journalism, and now it had come aboard the *Volo Papale*. We watched as Allen climbed up on the stage, sat in the pope's gilded throne, held his camera six inches from his nose and interviewed himself. The photographers, amused, took pictures of the scene. It would be the lasting image from this day on the Jordan River.

CHAPTER THREE

NUESTRO PADRE

"CAN YOU GIVE ME a character portrait of Father Marcial Maciel Degollado?"

The question hung in the air for a few moments. It was a Saturday in New York in April of 2005, and rain fell against the windows of a small room inside the Church of Our Saviour on Park Avenue.

J. Paul Lennon, a former priest in the Legion of Christ religious order, weighed his answer carefully. More than forty years earlier, at the age of seventeen, he had been one of eight Irish boys to enlist in Maciel's seminary, studying first in Spain and then in Rome, where the Legionaries had their headquarters. Looking back, Lennon viewed his time in the Legion as a twenty-three-year-long dark night of the soul: the painful severing of family ties, the discovery of the manipulation and falsehoods that were tolerated for the greater glory of the order, the rules designed to suppress any form of questioning or independence, the insistence on Maciel as *Nuestro Padre*, Our Father, the Saint. But Lennon had never accepted Maciel as a father. He grew to despise Maciel's despotic governing style and his penchant for humiliating anyone who challenged his decisions or ideas, even in the meekest manner. Finally, at a retreat in Cotija, Mexico, the Legion founder's hometown, Lennon surprised himself and other Legionaries by confronting Maciel as he gave a sermon to a rapt audience. Maciel was describing the energy and generosity of the new Legion recruits, painting the usual rosy picture, when Lennon interrupted him and asked why he never spoke about all the Legionaries who had left, or who had been exiled and were hurting. This was a taboo subject, and the founder responded by telling Lennon to shut up, that he didn't know what he was talking about. But Lennon came back with names and examples. The argument turned ugly. The members had never seen Maciel defied in this way, and it disturbed them. They listened in stunned silence. Finally another Legionary spoke up, saying they had not come to hear a discussion but to listen to *Nuestro Padre*. Lennon walked out of the room and never returned. He was now one of the outcasts, and he would experience the harsh treatment reserved for former members. The Legion's attitude was summed up in one of the founder's most popular proverbs: "Lost vocation, sure damnation."

Some things had not struck Lennon until many years later: the order's recruitment of pretty adolescent males, for example, and Maciel's clear preference for some of the younger men. In retrospect, it seemed to him that *Nuestro Padre* was an ephebophile, someone attracted to postpubescent boys. But Lennon himself had never been abused in the Legion. As a young seminarian in Maciel's world, he was too naive to have even imagined such things.

"Do you feel there is credence to the accusations that Father Maciel has sexually abused Legionaries of Christ?"

Monsignor Charles Scicluna carried out his inquiry with businesslike efficiency. He listened carefully as Lennon searched his memory. Both were aware that his testimony could tip the scales toward guilt or innocence. An Australian priest who had accompanied Scicluna from Rome sat beside them and silently transcribed the interview on a computer.

"Do you know Juan José Vaca? Do you trust his story? Do you vouch for his integrity?"

Paul Lennon felt a surge of solidarity.

Yes, he said, he trusted Juan José absolutely, and he believed the other former Legionaries who had come forward against Maciel. He knew the accusers had nothing to gain and, in fact, much to lose. In pressing for justice, they were spending their own money and asking for none in damages. Some, especially the Mexicans, risked bringing shame upon themselves even by making the allegations. Lennon felt confident, however, that they were telling the truth. There had been telltale signs—things he hadn't noticed at the time but that, in retrospect, stood out like forewarnings. Why, he asked himself now, had he never guessed what was going on?

He did remember one unusual incident. In 1962, at the age of eighteen, he had the "privilege" of going to confession to *Nuestro Padre* for the first time, as a way of obtaining special graces just before taking his religious vows. Lennon had lived a relatively uneventful and sheltered life in Ireland,

but he felt he had committed two "sins of purity" that troubled his scrupulous conscience and made him feel very much ashamed. One he had confessed to a Carmelite friar in Dublin. Now he confessed the second to Father
Maciel. He recalled that Maciel was kind, absolving him in a fatherly way.
Lennon had kissed the end of the priest's stole as a sign of reverence and
gratitude, happy to be free of that sin. But in retrospect, it occurred to him
that his confession may have saved him. Could the "sin" he had confessed to
Maciel—being sexually accosted by an Irish Christian Brother—have immunized him against abuse? If so, he thought, *O blessed sin!* As the years
went on, Lennon would become convinced that Father Maciel was not an
indiscriminate sexual predator, but one who carefully chose his victims after
factoring in the elements of secrecy, isolation and control. With his confession, Lennon had probably thrown up a red flag to the wary Mexican.

"Did Father Maciel have any strange or unusual habits?"

Lennon paused. He was under oath and wanted to be careful not to make
any unjustified accusations. But in fact, he told Scicluna, he considered Maciel a very strange man. For one thing, he was always getting sick, although
his maladies seemed like hypochondria to Lennon. And when Maciel did
become ill, he would have a younger brother attend to him. One of the things
Lennon still appreciated about his Legion formation was its emphasis on
universal charity, the idea that kindness and affection should be shown in
equal measure to everyone in the community. Maciel, however, had his favor-
ites; this might seem normal enough, but in the Legion the brothers had
been warned repeatedly about "particular friendships." Maciel seemed to
break that elemental rule whenever he wanted, occasionally picking a brother
to accompany him on trips during which they stayed in hotels together.

Seated at a small desk across from Lennon, Scicluna was patient but
encouraging. "Tell me what you know," he said. Scicluna was a genial, di-
minutive man in his fifties, with a round baby face and a thin stratum of
black hair that sat on the back of his head. His voice was pleasant but did
not betray much sympathy with the witnesses—he was not here to win
them over but to take testimony. He had a long list of questions. Lennon
had begun the interview with a few questions of his own, starting with Scicluna's title. The monsignor politely explained that he was number three in
the pecking order of the doctrinal congregation, a "promoter of justice."

And how many promoters of justice are there? Lennon had asked. "Only one," Scicluna answered cheerfully, smiling to himself. Lennon, like most outside the Vatican, clearly had no idea how few people actually worked at the Congregation for the Doctrine of the Faith, the doctrinal command center of the universal church.

Scicluna had placed a small crucifix before Lennon and asked him to swear on the cross to tell the truth. This struck Lennon as a little archaic, but he'd obliged.

Part of Scicluna's job was to determine whether sex abuse allegations against clergy—even those that had taken place more than forty years earlier, like the ones now in question—were substantial or baseless. It was very difficult to prove or disprove claims that old, so the Vatican often had to weigh testimony, recollections and even impressions as part of the fact-gathering process. Maciel had no lack of accusers, and they would be heard. But a man like Lennon could provide an equally important piece of the puzzle. As someone without a particular grievance against Maciel, he could offer a more objective character evaluation of the accused and his accusers. The depositions were time-consuming and probably seemed unnecessary to the accusers, who had already put their testimony in writing. But that was the Vatican's way: procedure, canon law, due process. Justice, but above all prudence. Much was at stake, as Scicluna realized only too well.

Father Maciel, now eighty-five, enjoyed tremendous favor at the Vatican, despite the lingering allegations that he had abused thirty or more of his young seminarians. He had founded the Legion of Christ in Mexico in 1941. A photo from that year shows Maciel, grimacing in the sunlight, surrounded by twelve pubescent seminarians. He established a new seminary in Rome in 1950, impressing a string of popes with his success in delivering vocations and raising money. By 2005 the Legion had become one of the wealthiest religious orders in the church, and perhaps the only one attracting significant numbers of new priests. Frequently, high-ranking Vatican officials would preside over triumphal liturgies to ordain fresh batches of forty or fifty Legionary priests. Incredibly, the order was still building minor seminaries, or "apostolic schools," around the world, designed for boys ages eleven and up who thought they might be called to the priesthood. And in addition to its own seminary in Rome, since 1991 the Legion had been running, at the pope's request, an international seminary for future diocesan priests in more than twenty-five countries. The Legion also had fifteen universities, including two in Rome, and its members had become a presence in the media, both church-run and secular. Its affiliate organization, Regnum Christi, was considered one of the most vibrant and militant lay movements in the modern church. In many ways, the Legion was the church's flagship, and the last thing the Vatican wanted was to see it run aground.

The Legionaries' rising stature and Pope John Paul's personal esteem for Father Maciel had been unequivocally displayed a few months earlier, in the fall of 2004, at a Vatican celebration of the sixtieth anniversary of Maciel's priestly ordination. The ailing Polish pontiff greeted Father Maciel warmly in front of four thousand of his Legionary followers. As Maciel knelt before him, the pope with a trembling hand traced a blessing on his forehead. In words that made some Vatican officials wince, the pope told Maciel that his work had been "full of the gifts of the Holy Spirit." Even more laudatory was a papal letter posted proudly on the Legionaries' Web site, in which the pope said he wanted to join in a "canticle of praise and thanksgiving" for Father Maciel's sixty years of "intense, generous and fruitful priestly ministry." Father Maciel, the pope said, had always been concerned with the "integral promotion of the person."

It would have been hard to imagine a stronger papal endorsement of the man whose future, in a sense, now rested in Monsignor Scicluna's hands.

"Did Father Maciel have special relationships with young Irish seminarians?"

Lennon recalled the unusual mix at the seminary in Rome—it was mostly Spaniards, Mexicans and Irish. He told Scicluna about one of his friends who had been very close to Maciel and who undoubtedly would have known specific details.

The interview was reaching the one-hour mark when a cell phone rang. Scicluna reached into his pocket, but the call had already dropped. From the number that flashed on the screen, he could see that a Vatican official was trying to reach him. It would be nine thirty-seven p.m. in Rome; that could mean only one thing.

A few minutes later Scicluna stepped into the corridor, where the signal was stronger, and returned the call. His hunch was right: The announcement was just being made to the tens of thousands keeping vigil in Saint Peter's Square, and to the world.

Scicluna walked back into the room and said, "The Holy Father has just died. Let's pray for him." The three men recited the Our Father for the repose of Pope John Paul's soul and then closed the interview. The Australian priest printed out the text of the deposition and Lennon signed it. Before seeing him out, Scicluna handed Lennon a small printed card. On one side was a picture of Jesus, and on the other, in Pope John Paul's uneven handwriting, the words "*Mane nobiscum, Domine!*" Stay with us, Lord! The holy card struck Lennon as a tender, old-fashioned gesture of piety. He left the building feeling, as he put it later, sorrowful but unburdened.

That morning Juan Vaca had sat in the same chair and answered his questions with equal candor. But Vaca's testimony had been far different. In appalling detail, it represented the heart of the case against Maciel.

Vaca, the top Legionary in the United States in the early 1970s, was now an adjunct professor of psychology at a college outside New York City. It was Vaca who had written to the Vatican in 1976 and 1978 recounting the alleged abuse and urging officials to take action against Maciel. In 1989, when Vaca left the priesthood, he wrote a personal letter about Maciel to Pope John Paul. Then, in the late 1990s, he helped lead the effort to press the legal case against the Legionary head. When it appeared the Vatican was stonewalling, Vaca went public. In the book *Vows of Silence*, a groundbreaking exposé by Jason Berry and Gerald Renner, Vaca described his own abuse at the age of twelve: "In the bedroom, Maciel spoke of pains in his internal organs. He said, 'Rub me, rub me,' and made a circle on his stomach to show me," recalled Vaca. "I was trembling. I was frightened, but I began rubbing. He said, 'Do it lower, lower.' Maciel got an erection. I didn't know anything about masturbation. I was on the verge of puberty. He moved my hand to his penis. I was terrified. Finally he was relieved and he faked being asleep." That marked the beginning, Vaca said, of thirteen years of abuse.

Vaca was not particularly hopeful during that day's encounter. After being ignored for more than twenty-five years he was wary of this new wave of interest from the Vatican. He wanted to know how serious it was, and when he was introduced to Scicluna in New York, he asked to see some credentials—a letter of appointment, for example, that authorized him to conduct this investigation. Scicluna could not or would not produce it, offering his business card instead.

The interview ran five hours, far longer than scheduled. Scicluna posed questions in what seemed to Vaca like a flat tone, devoid of passion or sentiment. He couldn't quite understand why this Vatican monsignor, both as a priest and as a human being, failed to share his sense of outrage. Toward the end of the session, Vaca looked at Scicluna and asked him bluntly what was going to happen with all this information. He said Scicluna told him: "The church owes the victims a public apology, because we failed to protect you."

The long day and its turn of events left Vaca and Lennon feeling more than a little apprehensive. They had finally obtained a hearing from the Vatican—but at that very moment, the pope had died. What was going to happen to the investigation now? Would it go back on the shelf again? Would Scicluna even be able to file his report? Wouldn't everything be suspended until a new pope had been elected?

After taking depositions in New York, Scicluna did not hurry back to Rome, as most of the Catholic hierarchy in the world seemed to be doing, but, amazingly, missed the papal funeral period entirely. Instead he flew to Mexico City and began interviewing other witnesses—more than twenty-five, according to some accounts—who could help him determine whether to proceed to a church trial against Maciel. By the time Scicluna did return to Rome, with a suitcase full of notes and a list of additional potential witnesses, the pope had been buried and cardinals had begun gathering to elect his successor.

Two things were certain: With the death of John Paul, Maciel had lost his most significant backer. But inside the Vatican, there remained powerful friends of the Legionaries who would do everything in their power to protect the founder's name.

I met Monsignor Charles Scicluna in 2002 while working on a story to explain the Vatican's complex new rules dealing with sexual abuse by priests. On a sunny morning I walked up the double flight of marble steps to the doctrinal congregation's second floor, where an usher led me into a gloomy parlor.

A few minutes later Scicluna rolled into the room like the second leg of a three-cushion billiard shot. A short man with a bounce in his step, he took a seat on a gilded chair, and I noticed that his feet barely touched the ground. In fact, on closer inspection, they *didn't* touch the ground. A native of Malta, he was multilingual, erudite and one of the most respected church lawyers in the business. No wonder the Vatican wanted him on their roster. Yet despite his crucial role in the handling of sex abuse cases, Scicluna was practically unknown outside the Vatican. His only visible mark on the world had been a specialist legal tome published years earlier under the title *The Essential Definition of Marriage According to the 1917 and 1983 Codes of Canon Law.*

Scicluna's body language told me the clock was ticking, so I plunged in with some very direct questions: about how many sex abuse cases were coming into the Vatican, how much confidence they had in Cardinal Bernard Francis Law's handling of sex abuse allegations in Boston and how much the pope knew about the details of priestly abuse. The Maltese monsignor gave me nothing—he wouldn't touch any of those topics. I began to navigate more carefully.

That meeting, like most conversations between journalists and Vatican officials, was on background. With rare exceptions, Scicluna would never speak to me on the record and he always refused to discuss the details of particular cases being handled by the congregation, which were covered by "pontifical secret." His role as a sort of full-time prosecutor at the doctrinal office required him to be *super partes* and super discreet, he explained. Unlike civil courts, the Vatican system operates under strict confidentiality, and Scicluna believed this secrecy ultimately helped weed out perpetrators. Therefore, he stressed, he couldn't divulge information about individuals to reporters.

Monsignor Scicluna also seemed painfully aware that because the number of Vatican experts dealing with sex abuse cases was so small, any leaky faucets would quickly be identified and replaced. What he was willing to do for me was run through the procedural details and explain how, in his view, the church's own legal system and its tough new provisions could meet the still unfolding challenge.

As a canonist, of course, he wasn't happy about shortcut solutions that would circumvent an accused priest's right to a hearing. And yet, more than others in Rome, Scicluna seemed to understand the gravity of the sex abuse scandal—indeed, that it *was* a scandal, and not just a story that had been blown out of proportion by the media. He spoke of the "horrible" crimes committed by clergy against trusting children, and of the sense of betrayal felt by Catholic communities. The church had to act in a new and decisive way, he asserted. He did not try to diminish the problem by citing the high number of good priests, nor did he question the motives of victims who had come forward. He realized that in the handling of this situation, the church had somehow failed its people.

At the time, Scicluna's sense of indignation was probably a minority position in Rome. While genuinely aghast at the scandal's effect on the church's reputation, many at the Vatican felt U.S. bishops were the victims of a well-orchestrated campaign by the media and dollar-hungry lawyers. At an infamous press conference in 2002, Cardinal Darío Castrillón Hoyos, the Vatican's top clergy official, had responded to reporters' questions about sex abuse by suggesting they investigate other professions to see how many were accused of sexual abuse and how much money they paid to victims. Throughout that year, as the accusations against U.S. priests multiplied, the Vatican's own newspaper, *L'Osservatore Romano*, refused to report a word on the problem.

Although Pope John Paul had ultimately addressed the issue—too late and in too general terms, for many people—the blind spot that persisted throughout the rest of the Vatican sometimes seemed surreal. In one ten-day period at the height of the clerical sex abuse crisis, for example, I noted the following developments: A Vatican official published a major book on sexual abuse of children; the Vatican newspaper condemned perpetrators of such abuse and recommended no leniency by judges who sentenced them; and the Vatican denounced sexual exploitation of children by pedophiles, telling a UN-sponsored conference that "the veil of silence . . . has finally been ripped open." Yet none of these Vatican initiatives mentioned priests. It was as if the scandal were occurring on another planet, and not inside the church.

Gradually, of course, even the Vatican had to acknowledge the seriousness of the problem, and although this is not widely known, it later adopted as universal church law some of the stricter measures instituted by U.S. bishops, including the power to defrock abusive priests without holding a church trial.

From the beginning, though, the allegations against Father Maciel seemed to fall into a special category. The Vatican was informed of the initial accusations in 1976, then again at the start of Pope John Paul's papacy in 1978, and again in the late 1980s. Nothing had ever been done.

Some former Legionaries began to suspect that the obstacle was not so much the Polish pope as his personal secretary, Monsignor Stanisław Dziwisz. Known to insiders simply as "Don Stanisław," he was the gatekeeper, the man who ultimately decided which people saw the pontiff every day, which reports arrived on his desk and which letters made it through the chain of subordinates. He had come with John Paul from Kraków, and he evidently had the pope's full trust. With reporters, Dziwisz was genial and unassuming. But insiders reported that he could be ruthless when it came to protecting the pope. It was no secret that Dziwisz was close to the Legion of Christ and Father Maciel; when the pope had made him a bishop in 1998, Dziwisz held a celebratory luncheon for six hundred guests at the Legionaries' Regina Apostolorum university in Rome. The ex-Legionaries pressing the accusations against Maciel had made sure to bring them to the attention of Monsignor Dziwisz. But they began to wonder how much was actually getting through to the pope himself.

By the 1990s eight former Legionaries had accused Maciel of sexually abusing them when they had been teenage seminarians forty or fifty years earlier. Their stories were all similar: Maciel would typically invite students to his room, complain of aches and ask them to rub his stomach, sessions that often ended in mutual masturbation. According to some of the accusers, Maciel at times claimed to have a special dispensation for such acts from Pope Pius XII, as a remedy for chronic pain.

All this became public in 1997, in a story written by Gerald Renner and Jason Berry for the *Hartford Courant* in Connecticut. Their account was shocking. In the eyes of many, Father Maciel became a walking example of how the church protected its own. Maciel denied the allegations, and the Vatican appeared to continue to do nothing about them. In 1998, the accusers filed a formal complaint at the Vatican seeking a canonical case against Maciel. The alleged acts of abuse were too old to prosecute under church law—the statute of limitations had run out—so they tried a different approach. The accusers remembered that, as young seminarians, whenever they would express anxiety about the sinfulness of the incidents, Maciel would absolve them on the spot. That meant Maciel could be tried on a sacramental technicality: giving absolution to an accomplice in a sexual sin, for which there is no statute of limitations.

Still the Vatican did not act. Maciel was untouchable, or so it seemed. In actual fact, however, the case against him was not dead but was just lying dormant until the U.S. sex abuse scandal gave it new life.

As a talking head, Father Tom Williams offered NBC News a pretty decent package: a collar, good looks, reasonable sound-bite skills and a thorough knowledge of the ways of the Vatican. A native of Pontiac, Michigan, Williams had earned a business degree and worked as a cash and investment analyst for ten months before deciding to enter the Legionary seminary at the age of twenty-two. After nine years of study, he was ordained a priest in 1994. Even at this young age, Williams showed leadership qualities and other obvious assets, including fluency in five languages. The Legion decided to keep him in Rome and eventually made him dean of theology at Regina Apostolorum. He was appointed a briefing officer for a Synod of Bishops in 1997, and from that exposure became a regular in the lineup of the ten or so "quotable" priests routinely used—one might say overused—by U.S. reporters in Rome. His transition to video was only a matter of time. He broke into TV punditry during the 2004 presidential election and the same year became a featured contributor to the endless media debate over Mel Gibson's film *The Passion of the Christ.* By the time Pope John Paul checked into the hospital in early 2005, Williams was NBC's go-to guy on matters ecclesiastic, doling out daily wisdom about papal health, conclave rules and the beliefs of the Catholic Church. He spoke a layman's language when it came to church affairs. Like others in his order who did TV commentary, he was not identified on the air as a member of the Legion of Christ—a handy omission, given that the Maciel case was threatening to blow wide open.

Williams had an earnestness that seemed genuine and the kind of clean-scrubbed appeal that made him, briefly, the "hot father" heartthrob of some Catholic bloggers during the pope's funeral. Later the same year, he was featured in Italy's *Panorama* magazine as one of "The Lord's Beauties," priests in Rome who seemed more like Hollywood stars, in the magazine's enthusiastic assessment. In a country where *bella figura* still trumps everything, it was considered shrewd of the church to have a stable of handsome faces to put before the world.

I had known Williams for years, and usually found him ahead of the curve when it came to the political and cultural impact of religion. For example, when Mel Gibson came to Italy to shoot *The Passion of the Christ*, Williams sensed that it would become not only a cinematic blockbuster but also a cultural and religious lightning rod. He and other Legionaries networked with Gibson and helped arrange an old-style, Latin language Tridentine Mass on the set every morning, in effect assuaging Gibson's traditionalist Catholic tendencies. The Legionaries became a kind of bridge between the filmmaker and the Vatican, quietly helping to pave the way for a massive embrace of the film itself by the church.

Although he lived in Rome, Williams also had an ear finely tuned to U.S. politics. He weighed in with the "Catholic perspective" on the 2004 presidential election campaign, and his commentary platform later grew to include the *Weekly Standard*.

Williams was not the Legion's only well-groomed media player. Over at Fox News, Father Jonathan Morris dished out conservative commentary, advising Mexican immigrants, for example, to "learn English and try to get legal." And after Mel Gibson's 2006 drunken tirade against Jews, he declared: "Mel is not an anti-Semite." Morris, who typically delivered his on-air reports standing in front of Saint Peter's Basilica, was often introduced as "direct from the Vatican," although he has no Vatican connection. Fox did not identify him as a member of the Legion of Christ.

The Legion's media tentacles spread in other ways, too. A Legionary priest was named in 2005 to head the Internet Office of the Holy See, a prime piece of Vatican turf. And the free online news agency Zenit, with half a million subscribers around the world, was secretly overseen by the Legion and its lay affiliates at Regnum Christi.

Reporters sometimes joked about the cloned good looks of Legionary priests and the fact that they tended to show up in pairs when invited anywhere outside their religious headquarters (they could police each other if temptation arose). But many of us found Williams truly helpful and forthcoming. There was one topic he clearly didn't like talking about, however: the accusations against Father Marcial Maciel. But inevitably, as Maciel's case turned into a media hazard for the Legion, Williams was called upon to put the best face on the scandal. In April of 2002, when ABC News aired a lengthy and embarrassing report on Maciel, Williams defended the founder and head of his order with the usual arguments: The accusations were made decades after the fact, one accuser had said he had been pressured by others to make the claims and the Vatican had found no substance to them. Williams said he had known Maciel well, having lived with him for ten years, and that the allegations were "patently false." In short, Williams put his own reputation on the line. Those who knew Williams did not doubt his sincerity. But they also knew that Legionaries, in addition to regular religious vows of obedience, poverty and chastity, made a promise to never speak ill of their superior, and to report on anyone who did.

The ABC News report had a kicker, one that shocked some viewers and amused others. Brian Ross, the ABC correspondent, waited one morning outside the apartment of Cardinal Joseph Ratzinger, who would routinely walk across Saint Peter's Square to his office at the doctrinal congregation. When Ratzinger appeared, Ross and his cameras approached him and asked the cardinal why his office had not acted on the accusations against Maciel. Ratzinger, visibly upset at the ambush, said, "You do not ask such questions." After slapping Ross's hand, he told him heatedly, "Come to me when the moment is given, not yet."

That seemingly cryptic remark proved prophetic a few years later.

After gathering dust for years, the Maciel file landed on Monsignor Scicluna's desk in late 2004. The wheels had already begun to turn the previous year, when the doctrinal congregation began to systematically process sex abuse cases. Pope John Paul, in a crucial but unpublicized document, had defined sexual abuse of minors as one of the *graviora delicta*, or "more serious crimes," and had given the doctrinal office authority over all such accusations around the world. Among the cases now working their way through the pipeline was Father Maciel's. Ironically, the turning point came shortly after the gala celebration of Maciel's sixtieth anniversary as a priest. A few days following the pope's public praise, Cardinal Ratzinger decided there was enough evidence to prompt a deeper investigation. There was no announcement or official proclamation of this step. Instead, Ratzinger asked Scicluna to quietly pursue interviews with Maciel's accusers and others in an effort to reach some kind of resolution. Scicluna phoned Martha Wegan, a canon lawyer in Rome who was representing several of the accusers. Did the men still want to proceed with legal action? Scicluna asked her. Wegan posed the same question in a letter to three of the men; the answer in each case was yes.

Scicluna's life was already becoming hectic, though you'd never know it to look at the man, who could be seen sauntering down Via Giulia in the heart of Rome, white earbuds connected to an MP3 player in his pocket. Scicluna liked Mozart and found his music a soothing antidote to the blare of traffic as he threaded his way toward the Vatican each day. The priestly sex abuse cases were monopolizing his time and energy and straining the resources of the doctrinal congregation's thirty-five-person staff. When some bishops in the United States began to complain that Rome was taking months to process cases, Scicluna responded that haste would lead to injustice. He acknowledged that the Vatican was on a "learning curve," working out the details as it went. For example, the congregation had only recently determined that this special category—the "grave crime" of sexual abuse—included not only acts involving physical contact between a priest and a victim, but such things as downloading pedophile pornography.

The congregation had also established that it must sometimes base its judgment on what Scicluna called "moral certainty" of the crime, rather than the existence of incontestable evidence. That was a vital policy decision, especially as Father Maciel came onto the Vatican's radar screen once again. It meant that in cases too old for evidence gathering, if there were several accusations involving the same person and the same pattern of manipulation, the moral certainty would be satisfactorily established.

An even more ominous question hung over Maciel. In late 2002, prompted by the situation in the United States, Pope John Paul gave the doctrinal congregation the power to waive the statute of limitations on sex abuse cases that were especially egregious. That meant much older accusations, even those dating back as many as thirty years, would have to be investigated.

To those who had been following all this closely, the new investigative phase of the Maciel case seemed a prelude to one of two courses of action: a church trial or a whitewash. One of those most surprised by the move was Juan José Vaca, who had been pounding at the Vatican's door for nearly thirty years. Vaca's faith in the system had understandably been shaken, and this new development didn't change that. "My personal feeling at this point is that I've lost all trust in Vatican officials," Vaca said in January of 2005. "Of course we will pursue it, but I don't expect anything to be done."

Within weeks, however, Vaca learned that he and other witnesses would be granted their official hearings with Monsignor Scicluna. Even the doubters could see that, after all these years, the investigation had moved into a higher gear. What had happened inside the Vatican to prompt such a turnaround?

Several factors had come into play. First was the simple truth that Maciel had become an embarrassment at a time when the church was trying to convince the world that it would not tolerate predator priests. Second, the machinery that had been put into place—including Scicluna's appointment as a full-time prosecutor—ensured that the Vatican would slowly but surely process accusations, new and old. Ratzinger did not want unresolved cases sitting on the congregation's shelf.

The third element, however, was perhaps the most significant: the failing health of Pope John Paul and its effect on the Vatican's internal balance of power. Even as papal secretary Monsignor Dziwisz tightened his grip on access to the pope, he discovered that not every decision was being run past him anymore. Many in the Roman Curia were getting tired of treating Don Stanisław as if he were Pope Stanisław.

In other offices in the Apostolic Palace, intimations of the pope's mortality had created a sense of uncertainty. For years the secretary of state, Cardinal Angelo Sodano, with either the pope's explicit backing or his unstated support, had protected Maciel and made sure that no investigation gained traction. But with the pope growing increasingly feeble, the doctrinal congregation was able to move ahead unchecked by Sodano's office. As the pope went in and out of the hospital in February, Scicluna was making plans for his fact-finding trips to the United States and Mexico.

Maciel had to be alarmed at these developments, even if other Legionaries downplayed them. As the order prepared to meet in a general assembly, Maciel decided not to stand for reelection as general superior, having directed the Legion of Christ since its founding in 1941. Father Tom Williams assured reporters that the resignation had nothing to do with the reopened investigation, but was simply because Maciel was eighty-four, too old to serve another twelve-year term.

In late March, on Good Friday, as the pope lay sick in the Vatican, Cardinal Ratzinger presided over the traditional Way of the Cross at Rome's Colosseum. Ratzinger had written the meditations for each station, and as Vatican officials listened in shock, the German cardinal delivered a searing denunciation of the moral failures in the church. The line that everyone quoted in coming days and weeks was: "How much filth there is in the church, and even among those who, in the priesthood, ought to belong entirely to [Christ]." Unlike the frail pope, Ratzinger appeared fully capable of moving against offenders, and ready to do so.

But there were more twists to be played out. When John Paul died on April 2, it triggered an inevitable and unpredictable shift in power. If a Latin American pope were elected, he might be much less eager to act against Maciel; in fact, had the College of Cardinals been polled at the time, a majority would probably have viewed the accusations against Maciel as ancient history not worth exhuming. But when Ratzinger emerged as Pope Benedict XVI on the fourth ballot of the conclave, it must have sent a shudder through Maciel and his followers.

Few people dared to connect Cardinal Ratzinger's Good Friday meditations directly to Maciel—at least in public. But one Italian reporter did. Sandro Magister, who covered the Vatican for *Espresso* magazine and wrote a popular blog, quoted Ratzinger approvingly and said Scicluna's interviews had uncovered even more "filth." "The sequence of recent events seems to have turned against [Maciel]," he wrote in May of 2005. Magister is widely read in church circles, and his column is picked up by a number of Catholic blogs around the world. For the Legion, then, this was a public relations bombshell that could not go unanswered.

A few hours after Magister's article appeared, the Legion had its defensive weapon in place: a one-line fax from the Secretariat of State that stated that Maciel was not presently facing a "canonical process," nor was one foreseen in the future. The Legion immediately sent out a press release proclaiming this good news, along with a forceful denial of accusations by Maciel and a "turn the other cheek" message for his critics: "We hold no grudge against those who accuse us; rather, we keep them in our prayers." Cardinal Sodano was apparently still looking out for Father Maciel.

To the untrained eye, the Vatican statement seemed like a declaration of innocence. What it was, in fact, was the equivalent of a smoke bomb, a diversionary tactic to buy time and deflect attention. Of course there was "no canonical process" under way—for one thing, Scicluna had not yet finished his preliminary investigation, which was needed to determine whether a canonical trial would follow. No trial was "foreseen," the Vatican said, but that, too, exploited a nuance: At the Vatican, most things, including meetings, documents and papal trips, are "not foreseen" until they are officially announced.

In an even more subtle way, pending the result of Scicluna's investigation, the Legion was trying to preemptively narrow the definition of guilt in the public mind. A church trial, according to the Legion's line, would mean the accusations were substantial; anything less would be presented as a Maciel victory over his accusers. Perhaps the Legion already knew that there was strong sentiment in some Vatican quarters for an "extrajudicial" punishment of Maciel, a penalty based on the evidence uncovered by Scicluna but without going through a painful and time-consuming trial. A summary judgment and quick conclusion, it was argued, would deliver justice but spare the church, the octogenarian Maciel and the Legion of Christ further embarrassment.

The Legion's public relations coup had a devastating effect on the men who had waited so long for action against Maciel. "I am outraged," Juan Vaca told the *National Catholic Reporter*. "We are being re-abused." David Clohessy, director of Survivors Network of Those Abused by Priests (SNAP), called the Vatican's action a "transparent whitewash."

Yet the wheels continued to grind slowly forward inside the Vatican. Although Scicluna was becoming more and more sphinxlike, I called him a few months later with a simple question: In spite of the secretary of state's disclaimer, was the case against Maciel still alive? First came the hearty laugh, followed by the predictable "no comment": "When I tell you that I cannot comment on things that are *sub iudice*, you understand what I mean." *Sub iudice*, of course, means "under judicial consideration." In typically oblique fashion, Scicluna had given me my answer.

The judgment finally came in May of 2006. In a terse communiqué the Vatican announced that Father Maciel had been called to live a life of "prayer and penance" and to renounce any public ministry as a priest. The decision was taken by the doctrinal congregation and approved personally by Pope Benedict, after the results of Scicluna's investigation had been reviewed. At the same time the Vatican said a canonical trial of Maciel was being waived because of his advanced age and poor health. Finally, it tossed a bone to the Legionaries, affirming that their work in the church was appreciated "independent of the person of the founder."

For Maciel and the Legion of Christ, this was a serious blow. In effect, the Vatican was stating publicly that the accusations were substantial enough to warrant an extrajudicial punishment. The penalty, in fact, was the same as that imposed on clerical sex abusers in the United States who, because of old age or infirmity, were not dismissed from the priesthood.

And yet, from the Legion's point of view, it could have been worse. Maciel could have been forced to face the accusations in embarrassing detail in a church trial. He could have been defrocked, with no chance of appeal. He could have been excommunicated for his role in absolving seminarians of their "sins." All this might have triggered a deeper investigation of the order and its secrecy. Technically, there was no explicit acknowledgment of Maciel's guilt—and that was something the Legion's PR people could work with. In a statement posted on its Web site shortly after the Vatican announcement, the Legion said Maciel had declared his innocence but, "following the example of Jesus Christ, decided not to defend himself in any way." He would accept the Vatican decision in a "spirit of obedience" and serenity of conscience. If anyone was looking for a sign of contrition here, they found none; instead, the statement offered self-serving spin.

The Legion's PR efforts were pure pretense. A month before the public announcement, in fact, the Vatican had informed the Legion leadership that its investigation had found Maciel guilty of the gravest accusations.

Claiming otherwise, and presenting Maciel as a Christlike figure of suffering, was simply outrageous.

The popular Catholic news agency Zenit—a Legion of Christ operation, although unadvertised as such—had its own characterization of the Vatican's action against Maciel: "The Holy See's statement, released Friday, said it would stop the canonical investigation into allegations against the eighty-six-year-old, Mexican-born founder." In short, the Legion was exploiting a margin of ambiguity.

Not surprisingly, this characterization of the Vatican's decision disappointed Maciel's accusers and left them feeling the system had somehow let them down.

"This was a travesty of justice, a compromise," said Juan José Vaca. "They did not apply canon law. They should have had a church trial—why didn't they? Maciel was invited to a life of personal prayer. What is that? The statement is not punitive enough, and of course the Legion is twisting it and saying, 'You see, Father Maciel was not officially charged.' Just look at their Web site."

José Barba Martín, who had testified to Scicluna that he had been abused by Maciel at age sixteen in Rome, said the church was sending the wrong message to "let him off and invite him to meditate." He wanted Maciel's punishment to fit the gravity of the crime.

Paul Lennon was pleased that the Vatican did take some action, finally, but disappointed that no mention had been made of the victims. "They were just kind of left hanging out there. They had been called liars by the Legion. If you read the Vatican statement, that's still up in the air . . . it allows each party to continue thinking they're right."

Few people would have guessed how difficult it was for the Vatican to go even this far, and what kind of shock waves it would send through Rome. In his own way, Pope Benedict had set a new course.

Under John Paul II, it had been unthinkable to criticize the "new" religious orders and movements that had flourished in recent decades but that often operated with a hidden agenda in a cultlike climate of secrecy. John Paul considered them the future of the church, the engine that could power his cherished "new evangelization." And the Legion of Christ was leading the way. The Legionaries had risen to such prominence that they now expected a bigger share in the running of the church's central administration. They had shown they could deliver—vocations, missionary zeal, influence and money—and they wanted to help hold the reins of power. They had already won key appointments under John Paul, and Pope Benedict was expected to keep up the trend, favoring organizations like the Legion over traditional but numerically declining orders like the Jesuits, the Franciscans and the Dominicans. But in fact the opposite was happening: In his first year as pope, Benedict turned repeatedly to the older orders, rewarding the Jesuits in particular. And now the Legion's charismatic leader had been tarred and feathered.

The public disgracing of Maciel also had some undeniable Old World/New World overtones. Most Latin American bishops defended the Legion, and in Mexico the order was practically a shadow government for the church. I'll never forget the revelation I experienced during a trip by Pope John Paul to Mexico City in 2002. Wandering through the massive building that housed the press center, I mistakenly took an elevator to the top floor, where I caught a glimpse of Father Tom Williams hurrying into an unmarked room. I followed him through the door and came face-to-face with the Legionaries' media operation—a high-tech panorama of people and equipment that was as big or bigger than the media center serving the entire press corps. I was quickly and politely ushered out. Mexico City Cardinal Norberto Rivera Carrera was, not surprisingly, one of the Legion's biggest backers. But with the Vatican decision on Maciel, the "Latin American moment" in the church seemed to have ended.

In addition, many saw Pope Benedict's move against Maciel as a mark against his predecessor, the "great" Pope John Paul II, highlighting one of the late pope's biggest failings as universal shepherd: the handling of sex abuse cases. Jason Berry, the reporter who helped break the Maciel story in 1997, wrote in a commentary in the *Los Angeles Times* that Benedict had cast doubt on his predecessor's judgment: "Historians now must scramble to explain why the late Pope John Paul II, who called for the church to atone for institutional sins by 'the purification of historical memory,' sheltered Maciel for years."

Even some Vatican officials now thought John Paul's unquestioning support for the Legionaries of Christ had been reckless. He had personally ordained their priests, visited their university, brought them into important Vatican offices and, shortly before he died, given them control over an international pilgrim house, the prestigious Notre Dame Center in Jerusalem. Not everyone in the Vatican hierarchy was comfortable with the Legion, and in particular some viewed the order's high departure rate as a red flag. A few bishops, including Cardinal Roger Mahony of Los Angeles, were so concerned about the Legion's secrecy and predatory recruiting methods that they would not allow the order to work in their dioceses. But John Paul would hear no criticism. He was impressed with the Legion's growing influence in education, communication and social services—its "apostolic fervor," as he put it—and once said he was counting on the order to "set the whole world on fire."

Now that Maciel had been marginalized, the question whispered in the halls of the Vatican was a simple one: Would the Legion's fire be extinguished?

Two tremors in 2007 demonstrated that the Maciel affair was far from over. One was hidden from public view inside the Vatican, and the other was played out in a Virginia courtroom.

That June rumors began to circulate that Pope Benedict had quietly ordered the Legion of Christ to do away with two practices that had helped create the Maciel mess in the first place. The first were two "private vows" made by Legionaries, in which they professed never to aspire to a position in the Legion and never to criticize a superior. According to former Legionaries, the private vows were made in secret, usually in front of Father Maciel himself, and included this promise: "No professed religious should ever externally criticize, either by word, in writing or by any other means, any act of governance or the person of any Director or Superior of the Congregation." Anyone who heard such criticism made by a fellow Legionary was obligated to report him. To Maciel's accusers, this vow was an important instrument of control, granting the founder an untouchable status and creating a general cultlike atmosphere.

The second practice quashed by Benedict was that of Legionary superiors habitually hearing the confessions of their subordinates. His accusers, it should be remembered, reported that Maciel had used confession to ensure that his abuse of younger members remained hidden.

This was an important story, but I needed confirmation from someone at the Legion or the Vatican. The Legion wasn't saying anything because, as Father Tom Williams put it, they viewed these as "internal questions." The man to see was the head of the Vatican's congregation for religious orders, Cardinal Franc Rodé. Fortunately, he was an old acquaintance.

I first met Rodé in the late 1980s, when he worked for a now defunct Vatican agency called the Pontifical Council for Dialogue with Non-Believers. A native of Slovenia, Rodé had a keen interest in Eastern European politics and was keeping a watchful eye on developments in Moscow. In 1989, with the Eastern Bloc in turmoil, Rodé invited some of the Soviet Union's top minds to a dialogue in the tiny town of Klingenthal, France. Though most of the encounter was closed-door, I went up to France to cover it. Based on what I heard from participants, I came away with the conviction that glasnost was about to set dramatic changes in motion and that Rodé was astutely positioning the church to make the most of these reforms.

When the Soviet Union disintegrated, Slovenia was among the satellite countries that regained its freedom. Rodé was made archbishop of Ljubljana, his birthplace, and it seemed like a happy culmination of a clerical career. But for some reason, Rodé was not a perfect fit in Slovenia. The few times I spoke with him, he seemed unhappy at the post-communist turn of events. It was a phenomenon happening all over Eastern Europe: His country's citizens were embracing freedom, but not the freedom to believe in God and follow the church. By 2004 Rodé was back at the Vatican, appointed by Pope John Paul as prefect of the Congregation for Institutes of Consecrated Life and Societies of Apostolic Life. His job was to monitor the hundreds of religious orders and institutes, male and female, around the world.

In September of 2007 I went to ask Rodé about the latest rumors regarding the Legion of Christ. I was ushered into the congregation's elegant first-floor receiving room, which looked out onto Saint Peter's Square. At seventy-three, the cardinal was no longer the young Turk. There were puffy bags under his eyes, I noticed, and his face was now framed by white hair.

His eyes still sparkled, though, and he managed a smile. "What's on your mind?" he asked.

Beating around the bush was not a very good strategy with Rodé, so I told him bluntly that I'd heard about Pope Benedict's orders to the Legion, and I'd also heard that the Legionary superior, Father Álvaro Corcuera Martínez del Río, was quietly making the rounds of Legionary houses around the world to explain the pope's decision.

Rodé's eyes lost a bit of their sparkle, but he was still smiling.

"So you want to know: Has there been a decision to suppress private vows in the Legion of Christ? John, on this you will not get one word from me—not one word," he said.

It was a "no comment," but the way he'd phrased it was intriguing. I felt certain that if the rumors were completely false, Rodé would have found a way to let me know. He hadn't done that. And then he went on to deal with the second part of the question.

"As for confession, it would be logical for us to tell any religious order to avoid that practice. It's in canon law. You can't have a religious superior confessing members of the order. That would be an abuse. The person deciding the member's future or making the order's decisions shouldn't be entering into the *foro interno* of the conscience. This is true of all orders, and there should be no exceptions," he said.

Again, Rodé seemed to be suggesting there was something substantial to the reports I'd heard. But he wasn't finished. He didn't want me to leave his office with the wrong impression—the impression that the Vatican was signaling lack of confidence in the Legion of Christ. He leaned in a little more closely and began defending the Legion in no uncertain terms.

"If there's anything dynamic left in the church today, it's them!" he said. "They have the talent, the ideas and the means to carry them through."

He recalled a recent trip he'd taken to Atlanta, where he had addressed some four thousand Legionaries and members of Regnum Christi at their tenth annual "Youth and Family Encounter." Rodé had been mightily impressed. He'd then gone down to Mexico to visit Legionary houses, where he found an incredibly vibrant apostolate. Did I know, he asked, that the Legion now runs twenty-three universities—twenty-three!—around the world? One new Legionary university was geared particularly to the poor, he said, offering young people an educational path out of poverty. The Legion had 490 seminarians in Rome! And when it came to fund-raising, nobody did it better than the Legion.

"They have zeal and energy. They know what they want to do and can raise the money to do it," he said.

The gleam was back in Rodé's eye. In a way, I understood his enthusiasm. Rodé probably spent the better part of his days reading depressing reports about the decline of Catholic religious orders—their lack of new vocations, the need to close their schools, concern about their aging membership and rising pension costs, the wisdom of selling off their property. But the Legion of Christ ran counter to all these trends. It was successful. It grew and thrived. It had money. It even had lay followers. It was an island of success in a sea of trouble. In Rodé's view, that was probably one reason it was under attack.

As I walked out of Rodé's office, I realized that this was one of those important Vatican stories that would be almost impossible to report because no one would publicly acknowledge it. Not only had Benedict disciplined Maciel, but now he had personally intervened to reform the Legion's ways and help prevent such abuse in the future. He had trimmed the Legion's sails, and in doing so had sent one of the strongest signals of his pontificate. The irony was that the world outside the Vatican didn't know it.

When Paul Lennon arrived at his home in Virginia one afternoon in August 2007, he saw a thick packet wedged against his door. He picked it up and quickly recognized from the markings that it was some kind of legal document. He went inside, sat on the couch and had just enough time to unpack its contents when a young woman knocked at his door. Polite and smartly dressed, she told Lennon that it was her job to hand him an envelope that turned out to be a summons to appear in court in one week's time. The packet, he later discovered, was a complaint drawn up by the "Legion of Christ, Inc.," and as he read through the more than forty pages of legalese, Lennon realized they were suing him in order to shut down his Web sites, RegainNetwork.org and ExLegionaries.com. ReGAIN had become a kind of central clearinghouse of criticism of the Legion, and the ex-Legionaries site was a discussion board where many former members told their stories.

The complaint alleged that Lennon had stolen "personal and proprietary" documents from the Legion and disseminated them online in an attempt to maliciously damage the order. The documents in question, listed in an appendix, were the foundational publications of the Legion that circulated among its members: its constitution, its norms, twelve volumes of letters from Father Maciel and even a book called "Etiquette and Social Formation" used in seminary programs. It struck Lennon as ironic that the Legion was arguing that dissemination of these materials had caused the order "irreparable harm." It seemed like a self-indictment and, in a sense, pointless: How could documents that had already seen the light of day now be hidden away again behind this archaic notion of privacy? But the tone of the complaint and its addenda were quite serious. The Legion was asking for pretrial seizure of the documents as well as their "return" in hard copy or electronic format, the deletion from Lennon's Web sites of any information that derived from them and a permanent injunction against their use in the future. Although Lennon possessed only copies of these documents and no originals, the complaint listed their "fair market value" as at least $750,000. The suit also aimed to identify "conspirators" who had posted information about the Legion using Web pseudonyms. Lennon sighed deeply as he turned page after page of requests, motions and exhibits. This was censorship, pure and simple. And it would not be easy to fight.

Lennon knew he needed a lawyer, so he immediately made a few phone calls. What he heard was disheartening: The lawyers wanted between $20,000 and $70,000 as a deposit before even touching the case. He didn't have that kind of money; at the moment, ReGAIN had $400 in its bank account. So Lennon went to the first court appearance representing himself. The judge told him to get a lawyer as soon as possible, and in the meantime to hand over any of the Legion's "documents" in his possession.

Lennon eventually found a lawyer willing to work for a modest fee, and they began filing an endless series of briefs with the court, including a motion to dismiss the complaint. In November of 2007 they appeared in court, but instead of resolving anything it only set in motion a new round of discovery and depositions. Lennon was meanwhile trying desperately to raise money for his cause, and not finding it easy. He passed the hat online with a series of YouTube videos, which generated a trickle of contributions ranging from $10 to $1,000, most of them modest donations from individual Catholics.

As the weeks turned into months, it became clear that the Legion's strategy was to bury him in legal fees, and Lennon realized it would probably work. Worse, from the outset Judge Lisa Bondareff Kemler seemed inclined to go along with the thrust of the Legion's complaint. In January of 2008, at Lennon's second court appearance, she ruled that the conspiracy motion could go forward and ordered him to turn over documents and reveal the names of third parties who had posted forbidden material on ExLegionaries.com. For Lennon, the hearing was a disaster, and he had already run out of money; he had spent the $20,000 raised so far and owed another $9,000. His lawyer was talking seriously about a settlement.

Dispirited, Lennon came home one night in late January and, checking his e-mail, learned that Father Marcial Maciel had just died.

The news of Father Maciel's death spread quickly in Rome, yet there was something typically secretive about the way that even this development was handled by the Legion of Christ. For one thing, no information about the cause of death was made available. Maciel had died on January 30 at age eighty-seven in the United States, but the Legion did not say exactly where; some reports said Houston, others Florida. In Rome everyone wondered whether Maciel's longtime friends in the Vatican would appear at the funeral and try to rehabilitate his image. But the new director general of the Legionaries, Father Álvaro Corcuera, announced on the order's Web site that, in keeping with Maciel's wishes, "the funeral will be celebrated in an atmosphere of prayer, in a simple and private manner." In other words, there would be no public eulogies, and no parade of cardinals or Vatican officials.

The big question was whether Pope Benedict would send a condolence telegram to the Legion. Such gestures are routine, and in the case of so prominent a figure would have been obligatory except for Maciel's ambiguous status when he died. This was, after all, a man who had founded one of the most dynamic religious orders in modern times. As the days passed, however, it became clear that the pope had no intention of glossing over Maciel's transgressions with a postmortem message. The Legion's usual Vatican supporters were strangely quiet as well. At the Legion's headquarters in

Rome, there was no activity at the Church of Our Lady of Guadalupe, where Maciel had many years earlier constructed an elaborate mausoleum as his final resting place. In fact, his body would not be coming to Rome. A week after his death, with little fanfare, Maciel was buried in his hometown of Cotija, Mexico. Ultimately, the Vatican would not mark his passing with even a single word.

In March of 2008 Paul Lennon sent an e-mail to ReGAIN supporters informing them with sadness of his "legal defeat." He simply could not afford to keep fighting the Legion of Christ, Inc. The lawyers were already preparing a settlement, and he knew that under its terms he could not discuss the lawsuit. A few days later he removed his YouTube videos about the suit and sent out another e-mail declaring, "My lips are sealed." The ExLegionaries .com site was shut down. The excerpts from the offending "proprietary documents" were removed from the ReGAIN Web site. The site continued to function, but the criticism of the Legion now lacked the corroborative bite of the founder's own words and policies. At the end of it all, Lennon's legal bill amounted to just over $40,000, and he felt fortunate that most of that amount had been raised through contributions. Thank God, he thought, that the Legion had not pressed for damages and its own legal fees.

Lennon had not given up, however. For years he had been putting together notes for a book, a personal memoir and exposé, detailing his experience in the Legion. He had shopped around for a publisher and not gotten very far but then discovered that he could affordably self-publish with BookSurge. Over the next several months he completed his project, and in August his four-hundred-page paperback went on sale under the title *Our Father, Who Art in Bed: A Naive and Sentimental Dubliner in the Legion of Christ*. Lennon's tale was less about sexual abuse than about mind control. He described in detail the cultlike atmosphere fostered by Maciel and the psychological isolation he'd suffered when he'd dared to question the founder's methods and practices. Lennon had invested about a thousand dollars in publishing the book, and on a good day he sold two or three copies; at that rate, he told himself, he would probably not lose money on the venture. The important thing was that he was keeping public attention on a scandal the rest of the church seemed willing to quietly forget.

✦ ✦ ✦

In February of 2009, a year after Maciel's death, the foundations of the Legion of Christ suddenly began to tremble. Rumors percolated in e-mails and soon appeared in Catholic blogs—blogs that had arisen during the sex abuse scandal and its aftermath, and were unsympathetic to perpetrators of any stripe—that Father Corcuera, the Legion director, was quietly visiting the order's centers in the United States and revealing to their communities some shocking facts about *Nuestro Padre*, specifically that Father Maciel had once had a mistress, possibly a very young woman, and had fathered a child. A few days later the Legion headquarters in Rome confirmed those reports and said the order was acknowledging the scandal as part of a "process of purification" desired by Pope Benedict XVI. As the days went by, other high-ranking Legionaries came forth to express their sense of suffering and surprise at the discoveries. Father Tom Williams, who had once so adamantly defended Maciel on the basis of having known him personally for many years, now said that the Legion was removing the founder's pictures from its walls. In the United States, Legion spokesman Jim Fair said the order had learned only recently of "inappropriate" behavior by Father Maciel, that public examination of the details would serve no cause, that the order would continue its ministries and that Maciel would never be renounced by the Legion of Christ. "It's one of the mysteries of our faith, that someone can have tremendous flaws but yet the Holy Spirit can work through them," Fair stated. In other words, the show must go on.

Once again, however, the Legion's self-serving public statements belied the truth. Legion of Christ officials had known about or suspected Maciel's misdeeds for several years. In 2006, for example, Father Luis Garza, the second-in-command at the Legion, noted the presence of a woman with whom Maciel was rumored to have had an affair. Garza did some investigating and by September of that year he was certain that Maciel had fathered a child. More evidence trickled in, and by 2008 top Legionaries had a fairly complete picture of *Nuestro Padre*. They just didn't tell anyone.

But while the Legion now presented its public acknowledgment of Maciel's misdeeds as a courageous and painful act of self-examination, some former members suspected that its officials were essentially sacrificing their dead founder's reputation in order to save the corporation. Nowhere was there any hint that the order itself bore any responsibility for a cover-up; on the contrary, the Legion's highest officials were portraying themselves as victims of Maciel's duplicity. And while the Legion was admitting to the founder's extramural heterosexual affair—he was human, after all—it refused to touch the more serious allegations that Maciel had turned his own seminary into a pedophilia camp. In essence, it was pleading guilty to the lesser charge.

The Legion insisted that it was dealing with the problem internally, "as a family." Father Paolo Scarafoni, the Legion's spokesman in Rome, said that "with prudence and charity we are informing our members and trying to help each other overcome this situation. What is important is not to renounce the great mission that we have."

As the statements kept coming, it became obvious that most Legionaries were reciting from the same script. And in fact, the conservative blog *American Papist* soon published a "talking points" memo that had been sent out to key members of the Legion and its lay affiliate, Regnum Christi, complete with sample questions and answers. It read like a catechism of damage control:

What do you have to say about Father Maciel?

To our surprise and pain, we recognize that some of our founder's behavior was incompatible with his priestly condition. We are deeply sorry for the offenses he committed and we ask pardon for the scandal this has caused. . . . Even so, we can't forget that our founder was the instrument that passed on, in all its integrity, the charism God gave him and the Church approved. For that, we are forever grateful to him.

How do you explain Father Maciel's behavior?

It's very hard to understand. We are not able to grasp it fully, and we probably never will. It's part of the mystery of human behavior, and involves moral and psychological factors, circumstances, etc. It's especially hard to mesh all the good that we knew about him with the facts that are emerging now. At any rate, he has already passed away.

Were the superiors aware of these facts?

The superiors had no evidence of these facts, and they suspected nothing.

And how was that possible?

We all trusted our founder; it never occurred to us to be suspicious of his behavior. Frankly, with 20/20 hindsight we see that we should have been more alert to possible signals. But the superiors acted unsuspectingly; they never knowingly collaborated with his misdeeds or covered up the situation once they found out.

Strangely, even as the Legion professed its shock and sadness at the founder's weaknesses, its Web site clung to the official hagiography: "The [Legion's] specific charism is to know, live and preach the commandment of love that Jesus Christ came to bring us with his Incarnation. From the first years of the foundation, Father Maciel has transmitted this charism with his testimony of life and through tireless preaching and writing."

Meanwhile, new allegations leaked out, now concerning money. The major media were now paying attention to priests who had left the Legion years earlier. Father Stephen Fichter, an American ex-Legionary who was once the order's chief financial officer, told the *New York Times* that whenever Maciel left Rome, "I always had to give him $10,000 in cash—$5,000 in American dollars and $5,000 in the currency of wherever he was going." Fichter added, "As Legionaries, we were taught a very strict poverty; if I went out of town and bought a Bic pen and a chocolate bar, I would have to turn in the receipts. And yet for Father Maciel there was never any accounting. It was always cash, never any paper trail." The spending money was the tip of the iceberg, according to some rumors coming out of Mexico City, which spoke of money laundering on a grand scale.

All this made it more difficult for the Legion to finesse the situation by making a limited confession, professing shock and ignorance, and moving on without Maciel. But it was a fine line the Legion was trying to walk on the question of the founder's continued influence in the order's life: While they were taking down his pictures, his writings remained as the foundation of the Legionary formation program. That didn't make much sense, but they were in a bind. The Legion had built its whole raison d'être on Maciel, and without him it would lose what is known in the church as its "charism," a distinctive spiritual gift that gives religious orders their identity. At that point, it might have been more judicious to disband the order and reorganize it—a thought that had already occurred to Vatican officials and even some former friends of the Legion.

Soon after the allegations were made public, I called Cardinal Franc Rodé for an interview on these points, but he indicated that he'd decided to give only one interview on the issue: to the *National Catholic Register*, a newspaper controlled by the Legion of Christ. Rodé, the overseer of religious orders, was continuing to work behind the scenes to protect the Legion's enterprise. The Legion could also count on the support of Cardinal Angelo Sodano, the retired secretary of state and now the dean of the College of Cardinals, who had ordained forty-nine new Legionary priests in Saint Peter's Basilica only a month earlier. No other order was producing vocations as successfully, which helped account for the Legion's continued backing in some of the Vatican's highest offices.

But the fulcrum had gradually been moving in the debate over the Legion, and critical voices, primarily from the United States, were now given more weight. Among them was that of Archbishop Edwin O'Brien of Baltimore, who flew to Rome in February of 2009 and met with Father Corcuera at Legion headquarters. O'Brien had asked for full disclosure of the operations of the Legion, which ran an academy in the suburbs of Baltimore, and he wasn't getting the answers or cooperation he wanted. In the wake of the disclosures about Maciel, O'Brien announced loudly and clearly that he wouldn't recommend that his faithful have anything to do with the Legion or its lay association. "It seems to me and many others that this was a man with an entrepreneurial genius who, by systematic deception and duplicity, used our faith to manipulate others for his own selfish ends," he said.

The writer George Weigel, seen by many as the voice of conservative Catholicism in the United States, called for a full outside audit of the Legion, carried out not by Cardinal Rodé's congregation or other Roman Curia offices but by someone who answered only to Pope Benedict. Weigel castigated the Legion leadership for self-serving statements that only confirmed the organization's "institutionalized culture of defensiveness." He even dared to suggest the unthinkable: that the Legion might best be dissolved.

What may have alarmed Legion of Christ leaders even more than these high-profile critiques was the fact that Catholic media and the Catholic blogosphere had both turned very hostile. Catholic bloggers are in general very conservative and might have been expected to be less critical of the Legion. But the opposite was happening. Typical was an essay posted on the blog of the Catholic weekly *Our Sunday Visitor* by Kevin Keiser, a moral theology student, who urged accountability instead of talking points: "This is the time for concrete words and concrete actions. This is not the time to use terms like 'purification' or any overly abstract word in public statements. This is not the time for giving a spiritualized account of what the Will of God is trying to achieve by this turn of events, and still less a time to refer to it as a 'miracle,' or a 'mystery' that needs to be 'processed.'" The Internet became a meeting ground for U.S. Catholics scandalized by the Legion, including many lay members of Regnum Christi. As an internal revolt, it was small scale, but it was unprecedented in the Legion's history. Despite being informed by Legion officials that there was no need to exhume the sordid details of Father Maciel's shortcomings, they wanted to know. They wanted to make sure there hadn't been a cover-up. They wanted to examine again the accusations of pedophilia, well aware that the Legion continued to run a variety of youth activities. They wanted names, dates and numbers. They wanted clarity and full disclosure.

What Legion officials didn't seem to comprehend, despite all their insistence on Maciel being only human and a flawed instrument in the hands of God, was that the relevant issue was not about being sinful, but about being deceitful. They had underestimated the depth of outrage and sense of betrayal. The formation books packed with Maciel's teachings now read like a litany of hypocrisy: "Purity of heart . . . is so foreign to the licentiousness and cult of sex all around us." "We should never lie for any reason whatsoever. . . . Lips that lie are abhorrent to Yahweh."

All this raised the question: How can a man who was humanly, morally and psychologically bankrupt have a positive charism?

That issue was taken up by Edward N. Peters, a respected canon law expert whose blog is widely read among Americans at the Vatican. In a series of posts he pointed out that Maciel's actions, had they been discovered in his lifetime, would probably have warranted not only expulsion from religious life but also penal dismissal from the clerical state, something unthinkable for the founders of healthy religious orders. Peters ridiculed the argument that Maciel nevertheless bequeathed a valuable charism that must endure, arguing that it was just as likely that Maciel had established a religious order to assure himself of "ample access to sexual targets and unaccountable funds." In any case, what was this presumed charism of the Legion that had to be protected in these times of trial? To Peters, the Legion's charism was virtually indistinguishable from the Maciel persona. And therein lay the contradiction: "What can one say, with a straight face, about a religious institute that must scramble to remove, forever, its founder's pictures from the walls hardly a year after laying him in the grave?"

There were two striking features about the reaction to this latest chapter of the Maciel scandal. The first was that, in former centuries, questions about the future of a religious order would have been quietly discussed within the Vatican, without the involvement of laypeople. But in this case, Maciel and the Legion had become the center of an open and acrimonious debate among Catholics.

The second element was that the outrage had found public expression, particularly in Maciel's native Mexico. Although pilgrims still came to Maciel's hometown of Cotija and prayed at his grave, Mexican media were reporting on the scandal on an almost daily basis. In the United States, where for years coverage of Maciel had largely been confined to the pages of the *National Catholic Reporter*, criticism now poured in from all sides of the Catholic spectrum. In Rome, Legion officials were tracking public sentiment carefully and concluded that they could weather the storm. One thing that worked in their favor was that, with few exceptions, Vatican higher-ups did not want publicity about this scandal any more than the Legion did. Even if the Legion did have to be brought to heel, it could be done without radical measures and without a public fight. To a good number of Vatican officials, the calls for transparency and full accountability were typical of moralistic (and legalistic) Americans, but not necessarily helpful for the universal church. Some even suggested that probing into the details of Maciel's failings was leading people to the sin of "detraction"—revealing a person's secret faults when no proportionate good can result. As one Vatican official put it, "We have a two-thousand-year history of not airing dirty laundry. You don't really expect that to change, do you?"

In March of 2009 I got a tip that the Legionaries of Christ and all their related institutions would be the subject of an apostolic visitation. The term "visitation" is a Vatican euphemism for "investigation." While it's always a serious matter, it doesn't necessarily bring disaster for those being investigated. In some cases, it's a harmless way to clear the air after doubts or suspicions have been raised about a religious order or diocese, almost a public relations operation. In others, it's a genuine shakedown, a prelude to drastic action by the pope. The Legionaries hoped for the first scenario—a kind of collective examination of conscience, followed perhaps by a reorganization and a new sense of mission detached from the person of Father Marcial Maciel Degollado.

The Vatican was clearly cooperating with the Legionaries in their attempt to put the best possible spin on things. In a letter Cardinal Tarcisio Bertone, the Vatican secretary of state, characterized the visitation in typical Curia language: "The Holy Father is aware of the noble ideals that inspire you and the fortitude and prayerful spirit with which you are facing the current vicissitudes, and he encourages you to continue seeking the good of the church and society by means of your own distinctive initiatives and institutions." Translation: *You've done some very good things, and we're not going to throw all that out the window.* "In this regard, you can always count on the help of the Holy See, so that with truth and transparency, in a climate of fraternal and constructive dialogue, you will overcome the present difficulties." Translation: *There's probably a solution here, but we will be dictating it.* "In this respect, the Holy Father has decided to carry out an apostolic visitation to the institutions of the Legionaries of Christ through a team of prelates." Translation: *Prepare for a period of penitence.*

The team of prelates, I later learned from Legionary sources, was made up of five bishops who were given geographical assignments. In the United States the call went to Denver Archbishop Charles Chaput, who would later be named a cardinal and transferred to Philadelphia. As a "visitator" his task was to interview past and present members of the Legion, visit their seminaries and religious houses, and try to piece together a picture of the order's spiritual health and power dynamics. Chaput soon found himself bombarded by hundreds of lengthy letters and e-mails from former Legion priests and seminarians and their families, and he had to put out a public announcement asking for "brevity"—a paragraph or two, if possible—in these over-the-transom testimonies.

Officially, the Legion welcomed the visitation. From its headquarters in Rome, Father Corcuera, whose position was looking less and less tenable, issued a statement inviting all the Legionary priests and lay members of Regnum Christi "to thank God for the help that the Holy Father is offering us and to welcome the visitors with sincere charity and faith as representatives of the vicar of Christ."

But already Corcuera was seeing key people depart, part of what some insiders called a "quiet exodus" from the Legion of Christ. In the United States, Father Thomas Berg, executive director of the New York–based Institute for Ethics and the Human Person, announced he was leaving the Legion and would become a priest of the New York archdiocese. He did not go silently, however. After denouncing the "disastrous" response by the Legion of Christ leadership to the Maciel mess, he charged that the core issue in the order was the promotion of conformity and unquestioning submission that allowed Maciel to build a "cult of personality" and cover for his misdeeds. Berg's broadside echoed criticism murmured for years in some U.S. church circles, but now it was coming from one of the most respected Legionaries in the country. With his departure Father Berg seemed to be saying the Legion was irreformable.

Meanwhile, Archbishop Chaput and the other four visitors were having a hard time keeping up with fresh rumors and revelations about Father Marcial Maciel Degollado. News media in Mexico and Spain reported that at least three, and maybe five, additional individuals were claiming to be Maciel's children, and some were suing the Legion of Christ for inheritance rights. Other reports said the acknowledged daughter of Maciel and her mother had been supported by Legion funds for years, and that the mother had been a minor when her relationship with Maciel began. If true, it would be difficult to believe that other high Legion officials had been unaware of the situation.

In January of 2010 the Spanish newspaper *El Mundo* published another bombshell, a long article that described Maciel's pathetic and bizarre final hours. The article reported that by the time he died in January 2009, Maciel had at least five different identities. As Raúl Rivas, he was the lover of Norma Hilda and the father of her daughter in Madrid. While he lay dying in Florida, the newspaper recounted, Maciel's personal secretaries were ordered to liquidate these identities and associated properties, trust funds and bank accounts scattered all over the world, secret personal assets estimated to be worth close to $30 million. Sorting it out quietly, without public scandal, challenged even the Legion's crisis management abilities. In Maciel's final days, Norma Hilda and her daughter (also named Norma) showed up at Maciel's bedside, eager to take care of him. Maciel, instead of sending them away, told his aides, "I want to stay with them." The appearance of Maciel's lover and daughter so alarmed his aides that a call immediately went out to the Legion's headquarters in Rome, and soon the order's top officials were huddled in Maciel's room in Jacksonville, Florida—along with the two Normas. And an exorcist: Some of Maciel's assistants felt that his sudden rejection of all things religious might be the work of the devil. Toward the end he refused to confess his sins, despairing of God's forgiveness, and when a fellow Legionary tried to anoint him with holy oils, he shouted, "I said no!"

While sexual advances on seminarians could be kept secret for decades, these transgressions were different: They were committed outside the Legion's walls and the repercussions were outside its control. The bedside spectacle in Jacksonville was the final act of Maciel's undoing, his utter disgrace. Yet still the Legion kept dissembling. The official announcement that Father Maciel had gone to his "heavenly glory" came from Father Corcuera, who said simply that *Nuestro Padre* had died in front of an image of Our Lady of Guadalupe after writing his last words on a piece of paper: "*Et verbum caro factum est.*" And the Word was made flesh.

In March of 2010, on a popular Mexico City radio show, Blanca Estela Lara Gutiérrez described how, some thirty years earlier, at the age of nineteen, she had come to know Maciel's alter ego Raúl Rivas in Tijuana. Rivas told her he was a private detective and a sometime CIA agent who wanted to have a family. Their son José Raúl was born two years later. They were a couple for twenty-five years, and their two children (as well as another child from a different father) called him Dad. Maciel was absent for long, unexplained stretches, and when he was around, the family failed to pick up on clear signs of his double identity.

"When we were eating breakfast, there were some people who would say, 'Good morning, Padre,' and we had orders to withdraw ourselves," Omar, his second son, told Mexican media. "We never asked ourselves why they called him 'Padre.' We supposed it was because he had many children."

The masquerade was revealed in 1997, when the family saw Father Maciel on the cover of the Mexican magazine *Contenido*, with a story detailing the Legionary seminarians' allegations of sexual abuse. Confronted by his family in a phone call, Maciel denied the accusations and sent them enough money to buy all the copies of *Contenido* in Cuernavaca, where they were living. Blanca Lara believed Maciel's protestations of innocence until the day in 1999 when her son José came to her and said that, beginning at age seven, he had been abused by his father. Omar came forward with a similar story. Maciel responded by sending them both to Spain for psychological treatment.

His sons told Mexican journalists that before Maciel died, he had promised them that an inheritance had been placed in a trust fund, but there was no sign of that now—and the Legion of Christ had been of no assistance, they added.

The Legion of Christ responded to these disclosures by telling the press that, in essence, the Lara family's story was about money. In a statement posted on its Web site, the Legion provided details of a meeting between its procurator, Father Carlos Skertchly, and José Raúl, who had asked the Legion for $26 million—$6 million in fulfillment of his expected inheritance and $20 million in compensation for his sufferings. Couched in the language of compassion ("We share the suffering and pain of the members of the family, understanding the difficult circumstances that they have lived and are living"), the Legion played hardball. Father Skertchly's letter to José Raúl, no doubt written on the advice of the Legion's lawyers, was posted online: "On January 8 in the afternoon, I received your phone call, in which you confirmed your request, affirming that 'if you give me the money, I will keep quiet about the truth.'" The statement went on to say that the Legion could never "accede to your request for money in exchange for silence."

"We will never accept petitions of this sort, which are also illicit," it continued. "We prefer to seek and face the truth, no matter how painful it may be."

By depicting itself as the victim of extortion, the Legion hoped to take the edge off the increasingly sensational revelations about *Nuestro Padre*. Its survival instinct had kicked into gear, precisely because, with each passing day, it felt more and more cornered.

In March 2010, as the Legion's visitors prepared to submit their findings to the pope, the sixteen top officials of the Legion of Christ and Regnum Christi met in Rome. They knew their future was at stake, and the rumors coming out of the Vatican were not good. The general expectation in Rome was that the Vatican planned to decapitate the Legion and send in proxies to run the order and its $25 billion empire. Faced with being stripped of all their power and influence, after long discussion the officials decided to try a new tactic. It was time to disown *Nuestro Padre*. Until this moment, even while acknowledging Maciel's mistress or mistresses as the result of an unfortunate human failing, the Legion had carefully avoided any mention of the more serious accusation that he had sexually abused young seminarians for years. Now, in a statement that appeared on its Web site, the Legion's top brass admitted that "these acts did take place" and apologized to Maciel's accusers for failing to believe them. It was a desperate act of contrition, designed to demonstrate to the Vatican that the order's existing leadership was ready to turn the page. Their statement pledged a new attitude of cooperation with local bishops, more transparency in Legion operations, accountability at all levels and safety for minors in all its institutions.

Tensions were high when the five bishops reported back to Pope Benedict at the end of April 2010. The event turned out to be a surprise on several fronts. First, the meeting lasted one full day and spilled over into the next, as the pope brought in the three Roman Curia cardinals who would do follow-up work: Cardinal Bertone, the Vatican secretary of state; U.S. Cardinal William J. Levada, head of the Congregation for the Doctrine of the Faith; and Cardinal Rodé, the Legionaries' booster who oversaw religious orders. These were men who presumably would not go out of their

way to dismantle the Legion of Christ. But the Vatican, at the pope's request, also released a statement that summarized the visitors' findings
and hinted that the Legion could be gutted.

The statement represented a hardening of the Vatican's official verdict
on Father Maciel. It castigated him for his "most grave and objectively immoral conduct" and said he had committed "true crimes" that reflected "a
life devoid of scruples and of authentic religious sentiment." It said that
most Legionaries didn't know about his conduct because Maciel was a master of deceit, able to skillfully "create alibis and obtain the trust, confidence
and silence of those around him." This line seemed to exonerate ordinary
members of the Legion but implied that those whose "silence" was "obtained" would also have a day of reckoning. In a nod to Maciel's accusers,
the Vatican statement expressed the pope's gratitude to those who, "although in the midst of great difficulties, have had the courage and determination to demand the truth." Finally, it said that Maciel's moral bankruptcy
required the Legion to redefine its core mission and to change its authori-
tarian and secretive ways of operating.

To the Legion's leaders, the communiqué read like an indictment, and
the most shocking line was this: "In fact, the disappointment about the
founder could place in question the vocation and that nucleus of charism
that belongs particularly to the Legionaries of Christ." That left open the
possibility that the whole operation might indeed have to be dissolved, at
least in its present form. And to make sure the Legion understood it was no
longer controlling the situation, the pope announced he'd be naming his
own commissioner to run the order until final decisions were made.

Reaction was swift. "It looks like they are calling for a refoundation of
the Legion," Monsignor Scicluna told me after I read him the communiqué
over the phone. He sounded pleased and perhaps a little surprised. Sandro
Magister, whose blog had led the charge against Maciel in the Italian media, called the Vatican's judgment "severe and unprecedented" and predicted there would be no indulgence shown to Maciel's allies in the Legion.
The *New York Times* reported Pope Benedict had moved to "rein in" the
order. The respected Jesuit commentator Father Tom Reese said the pope
had "finally imposed martial law" on the Legion of Christ.

Officially the Legion "welcomed" the Vatican report, but behind the scenes its politburo, led by Father Corcuera, scrambled into action. A memo from the order's regional heads a few days later—quickly leaked and published by Magister—outlined how Legion officials should spin the media coverage: The Legion would undergo revision, not refounding; the charism would be tweaked, not scrapped; the pope expressed his appreciation for the Legion, not his disdain. Their key talking point on the Vatican communiqué was its assertion of their own innocence: "When it says that 'most of the Legionaries were unaware of this life [of Maciel],' this means that the majority knew nothing, including those who are currently in command of the Legion." The memo confirmed to critics that the self-preservation instinct still reigned inside Legion of Christ headquarters.

Father Tom Williams, the media-friendly talking head, also tried to do some preemptive damage control. In an interview with a U.S. Catholic weekly, Williams portrayed himself as one of the innocents: "Father Maciel was always very discreet, and in the ten years I lived with him I never witnessed anything but exemplary religious behavior. Maybe others did, but I certainly didn't. I don't believe that Father Álvaro knew anything about Father Maciel's immoral behavior, either, and I have no reason to believe that any of our current leadership was aware of this. I know that for people outside the Legion this can seem unbelievable, but for those on the inside it's just the way it was."

A few weeks later Pope Benedict named the commissioner who would take interim control of the order, Italian Archbishop Velasio De Paolis. De Paolis was a canon law expert, whom I had interviewed several years earlier about the emerging sex abuse scandal in the United States. At that time, like many at the Vatican he had seemed primarily concerned about protecting due process for accused priests. This was not a man, I said to myself, who would come in like a commando and start dismembering the Legion of Christ. He would take his time, and he would try to make certain that no good priest was lost in the process. In fact, De Paolis—who was made a cardinal a few months later—carried out his task in slow motion. It took him months to set up a five-man "outreach commission," which was tasked with listening to grievances from abuse victims and determining the proper response from the Legionaries of Christ.

In Washington, Paul Lennon was intrigued by that announcement until he read the small print: The commission would not hear grievances from victims who had gone to court. To Lennon this smacked of a ploy aimed at neutralizing legal action against the order: "The Legion's message is clear: *Be nice to us and we will be nice to you.*" But why should Maciel's victims jump through more hoops? he asked. And why should they expect justice from a commission that included two key Legionaries under Father Maciel? "I say go to your local church and civil authorities and sue the Legion's ass!" he proclaimed on his blog.

De Paolis, meanwhile, had announced that reform of the Legion might take "two or three years or even more" and would require the establishment of at least three commissions. It seemed as if the pope's strategy was to keep the Legion of Christ under close watch forever.

In effect, Benedict was trying not to kill the patient with the cure. He saw Maciel as an immoral man who nevertheless had managed to create something good—which made him a "mysterious figure," as the pope remarked in his 2010 book, *Light of the World*. He wanted to "save what could be saved" among the Legion's priests, seminarians and lay followers without causing undue trauma to the church. Dismantling such a thriving religious order was not something a pope did without qualms; it was a bit like sacrificing one's own son.

Benedict had other motives for moving so cautiously. For one thing, the scandal now directly involved the Legion's allies in the Roman Curia—several of whom, according to a new report by Jason Berry, had been receiving large cash gifts over the years from Legionary officials. Any drastic action against the Legion of Christ would force those murky dealings into the open.

There was a final reason Benedict hesitated to deliver a decisive blow to Maciel's minions, one that became obvious as soon as the depths of the founder's depravities were confirmed and publicized: The scandal highlighted the failings of Pope John Paul II. This was a black mark that came into focus just as the much beloved Polish pontiff's sainthood cause was approaching the first big hurdle, beatification. It was increasingly apparent that John Paul had for many years turned a blind eye to credible accusations, preferring to trust an organization that flattered and applauded him, that delivered funds for the church's good works and that brought fresh vocations into the priesthood. Was it coincidence that the push for Pope John Paul's beatification, which had seemed so close to completion only weeks earlier, now appeared to run out of steam? Was this really the time to beatify a pope who had mishandled such a high-profile case of sex abuse? In the eyes of the world, if Maciel was evil incarnate, John Paul II was his enabler.

Such doubts were aired even inside the Vatican. That was apparent in an offhand remark a leading Roman Curia official made to me as we discussed the Legion's disgrace.

"It's a very sad story," he said. "And guess who let it happen? *Santo subito.*"

By the time Cardinal Velasio De Paolis arrived at the Basilica of Saint Paul Outside the Walls, the church was already packed. It was Christmas Eve 2010, and De Paolis was ordaining sixty-one new Legionary priests—an annual event that highlighted the Legion's tremendous ability to produce vocations. For Legionary officials, this year's ordination Mass was a symbol of continuity: The order's work went on, despite its trials and tribulations. And having De Paolis preside was a good PR move, for if the man charged with "reforming" the order was ordaining sixty-one new members, could things really be that bad?

De Paolis vested carefully in the sacristy of the immense basilica, allowing a small radio microphone to be slipped over his left collar. The Legion was intent on recording everything today and using the video and audio to publicize the event. De Paolis could not blame them for that. Sixty-one new priests in a single year, in a single religious order, was a new record, and no one else could come close to those numbers. Someone handed De Paolis a miter, embroidered with a design of Christ as the Good Shepherd. He slipped it carefully on his head, and a few moments later an organ pealed out the notes of the processional hymn invoking the Holy Spirit.

Behind a long line of altar boys bearing three-foot-tall candles, behind the sixty-one candidates and the other concelebrants, the cardinal walked up the main aisle, holding a pastoral staff in his left hand and vaguely blessing the congregation—families, most of them Latin American—with his right. Among today's ordination group were twenty-eight Mexicans, still the vocational breadbasket for the Legion. The whole church was singing, and it was impressive. *"Effonderò il mio Spirito su ogni creatura, effonderò la mia gioia, la mia pace sul mondo."* An invocation of joy, peace, the Holy Spirit. That was the tone for this day, De Paolis thought. It was not a day for recriminations or mea culpas.

A camera crane operated by a Legionary technician swooped down above the congregation, dipping close to the upturned faces of young people. Their images were visible on giant TV screens placed along the side aisles. De Paolis walked up to the altar, past potted poinsettias and baskets of yellow roses and white lilies. As to be expected, the Legion had appointed everything with great care. Appearances meant something.

When the cardinal rose to deliver his homily, it was the moment the Legionaries had most feared: Would he mention Maciel? The Vatican investigation? Would there even be a Legion of Christ in a year or two?

De Paolis stood at the lectern and commenced what was not a particularly pleasant task. At heart, he was a canon lawyer, more at home with a library full of law books than a roomful of people. He was not a polished public speaker, and he adopted that high, loud tone of preachers who fear losing their audience. But there was no chance of that today; the congregation was hanging on every word.

His sermon reviewed the role of the priesthood, from ancient pagan times to modernity, how the New Testament priesthood differed from that of the Old Testament. The homily began to have a Wikipedia feel to it, but there was a gold nugget for his listeners when the cardinal paid tribute to the unusually large number of priests he would ordain that day. "You come from every part of the world, and in a sense you represent the whole church. You are a great number, sixty-one, and today that's a cause for amazement when we see the scarcity of vocations." His words lit up the faces of the Legionary officials seated in the front row. De Paolis was praising them! Not a hint of chastisement. Not a mention of Marcial Maciel Degollado. These new priests, De Paolis said, were proof that the Holy Spirit was still alive in religious orders. "Your religious family is a gift of God to the church."

As he wound up his twenty-three-minute oration, it became clear that De Paolis was not even going to allude to the Legion's uncertain future. And for the Legion, that could only be good news. "Jesus told his disciples: You won't be left orphans, I'll be with you always. And in a special way this happens in the priesthood." De Paolis was clearly sending a signal: The Legionaries would not be abandoned or suppressed.

When the cardinal finished, the congregation seemed to breathe a collective sigh of relief. The candidates went up to De Paolis one by one for the "laying on of hands," a key element of the ordination rite. De Paolis never actually touched their heads—he held his hands an inch or two above their heads.

The cardinal showed the same reticence later in the Mass, when each new priest came forward to be embraced by the ordaining celebrants. They hugged the Legionary superior, Father Álvaro Corcuera, as a child might hug his father, holding him close and laying their heads on his shoulder. De Paolis watched expressionless; that was not his way. The cardinal hugged them much like a wrestler would meet an opponent, gripping their shoulders and holding them firmly at arm's length. After squaring off with all sixty-one, he was feeling physically tired. He stood on the altar and tapped the tips of his fingers together impatiently. The liturgy was now going on three hours.

When the final procession ended, the Legionaries and their families were clearly grateful, and the Legion would feature their comments in a video that was quickly posted on its Web site. "This is a day so big it is hard to comprehend," said one proud father. "We are happy and we thank God. Having your son become a priest is an unmerited blessing," a mother proclaimed. A few days later, Pope Benedict would give them a special greeting at his weekly general audience, confirming the widespread impression that the Legionaries' worst days were behind them.

It was January 2011, a Friday, and the Vatican press office was humming with excitement. Instead of the usual dozen or so regulars, at least fifty journalists stood waiting for the release of the Vatican's official bulletin of announcements. Phil Pullella of Reuters paced around the press room, smiling nervously. For his own entertainment, he occasionally yelled out *"Bollettino!"* and watched the entire pack of reporters dash madly to the front desk. Each of these false alarms only added to the oddly lighthearted mood that day.

I sat in our CNS booth and tweaked the story I had prewritten. We all knew what was coming: Pope Benedict had just approved a decree stating that a miracle had occurred following prayers to Pope John Paul II, which meant he could now be beatified. Despite the howls of protest this would bring from abuse victims, Benedict, it appeared, had never really considered delaying John Paul's beatification. The reason the sainthood cause had stalled in recent months was due to another matter altogether: The Vatican had some nagging doubts about the miracle.

From the beginning, Sister Marie-Simon-Pierre's story had seemed too good to be true. A member of the Little Sisters of the Catholic Motherhood in France, she was diagnosed in 2001, at the young age of forty, with Parkinson's—the same disease that afflicted Pope John Paul. As she watched him deteriorate in his final years, she thought to herself: "That is me in years to come." When John Paul died in 2005, her condition worsened, and the members of her religious order began praying to the deceased pontiff, asking him to intervene with God to heal her. By now she was struggling to walk, write or carry out everyday functions. On June 2, exactly two months after the pope died, she said a prayer to John Paul and went to bed. The next morning she woke very early and discovered that she could move and walk normally. "I was sure I was healed," she said. Before long, she returned to work at a maternity hospital in Paris.

The Vatican faced a problem, however. What if this was only a temporary improvement? How would it look to the world if the "miracle nun" who advanced Pope John Paul to the beatification altar suddenly had a relapse? Or what if the original diagnosis had been mistaken? It was unheard of for Parkinson's to strike so early and then just disappear. What if—the thought crossed some minds—the nun had imagined her malady or, worse, faked it? An in-depth investigation was ordered, and the Vatican's team of medical experts moved quietly into action. They took their time, reviewing every aspect of the case. They interviewed doctors and the nun herself, and then reported back in late 2010. Everything checked out. There was no reason *not* to approve this healing as miraculous.

Pope Benedict read the reports himself and made his decision quickly. As the pontiff saw it, he really had no alternative: To suspend John Paul's beatification now would effectively allow his predecessor's twenty-six-year pontificate to be permanently branded by the sex abuse scandal.

Meeting with the head of the saintmaking congregation that morning, Benedict signed the decree without hesitation. And now, as the digital clock in the press room flipped to noon, piles of documentation were suddenly unloaded in front of the journalists. I read through the pages and pages of official testimonies and reflections on Pope John Paul. Pope Benedict would preside over the beatification himself on May 1.

On a 50cc *motorino*, the ride out to the Pontifical University Regina Apostolorum is a long one. But on this particular evening in April of 2011, taking a taxi was out of the question. Traffic was backed up for miles on the Via Aurelia as hordes of Romans fled the city on the eve of beatification weekend. I wove in and out of the gridlock with ease, using long stretches of the empty oncoming traffic lane. In Rome, a *motorino* is the only way to fly. By the time I reached the Legionaries' university on the outskirts of the city, the evening light was glancing off the buildings and the surrounding fields were glowing pink. I went inside toward the auditorium, where the Legion had prepared a multimedia extravaganza in honor of the soon-to-be Blessed John Paul II.

The first thing I noticed was that none of my journalistic colleagues had bothered to show up. The beatification brought hundreds of reporters to Rome, but they were apparently busy doing other things. I had expected the Legion to keep a low profile for this event, given that additional documentation had surfaced revealing that the Vatican had known about the accusations against Maciel for decades. The Mexican magazine *Proceso* had just published a copy of a 1956 letter from Father Maciel to the cardinal-prefect of the Vatican's congregation for religious in which he responded to what he called "slanderous accusations" of pedophilia and drug addiction. The accusations, according to the documents unearthed by *Proceso*, had come from prominent Mexican church officials, including Cardinal Miguel Darío Miranda, the primate of Mexico. At that time, Maciel had been given a two-year suspension for medical treatment, and was reinstated as head of the order. The Vatican's earlier investigation was well known, but it had supposedly centered on Maciel's addiction to painkillers. What the new documents showed was that accusations of sexual abuse of minors by Maciel were already part of the record at the Vatican—some fifty years before the Vatican finally acted. It was impossible, critics said, that Pope John Paul had not been informed of all this.

The Polish pope's beatification brought the issue back into the spotlight, but dissenting voices were not given much attention. For the media, the beatification was a feel-good story. And, strangely, some of the Legion's most familiar faces were back in the public eye. Father Tom Williams, the TV commentator who had dropped out of the limelight for two years, was quoted in a widely distributed story defending John Paul: "His life was scrutinized in minute detail and the result was what people had expected: John Paul was a truly holy man." In an interview with the British magazine *The Tablet,* Williams exonerated the late pope on the Maciel affair, and absolved himself at the same time: Neither he nor the late pope, Williams said, had any idea what had been going on. This was hardly a reflection on John Paul's saintliness, he added, explaining, "We make errors of judgment all the time." Williams even opined that perhaps it was providential that Father Maciel's depravity had gone undiscovered for so long, because if all this "had come out thirty or forty years ago, the Legion would have been destroyed immediately."

(A year later, in May of 2012, Father Williams acknowledged that he had once had a relationship with a woman and had fathered a child. The admission stunned his TV fans, but not his Legionary superiors, who had known about it for at least seven years. They had urged Father Williams to lower his public profile, but Williams ignored them; his media career was peaking at the time, he was teaching morality to Legionary seminarians and he was churning out popular books like *Spiritual Progress* and *Knowing Right from Wrong: A Christian Guide to Conscience.* When his past was finally divulged by an ex-Legionary, Williams apologized and withdrew for what was termed "a period of reflection, prayer and atonement.")

Unlike Father Williams, the Legion's other big media star, Father Jonathan Morris, had quietly left the order and was working as a priest for the Archdiocese of New York. In an interview with *National Review Online* three days before John Paul's beatification, Morris asked forgiveness for the way he had dismissed reports of Maciel's crimes. "I didn't believe the accusers, and I told other people they shouldn't believe them either. I am deeply sorry for that. Thank God, people with knowledge of the truth didn't give up on their cause," Father Morris said. Now the priest was back on Fox News for the beatification.

At the Vatican, I noted a subtle difference in the planning for this papal liturgy. In the past, the Legion would furnish dozens of priests and seminarians to assist at the Mass. The Vatican's liturgical planners had apparently decided that, under the circumstances, such a large contingent might invite unwanted notice.

All of which made the Legion's multimedia tribute to John Paul more intriguing. Inside the main university building, references to Father Maciel had long been removed. It occurred to me that this might be the only religious order in the world whose founder had become officially invisible. I passed the time surveying literature stacked up on tables in the entryway, an array of Legionary publications about John Paul II. One volume on "John Paul the Great" closed with a quotation extolling the spiritual qualities that made the pontiff a saint. The quotation came from Marcial Maciel Degollado, who, the booklet explained, was able to grasp the importance of prayer in the life of a holy man. It was inevitable, I supposed, that the Legion's scrupulous efforts to erase all signs of the founder would miss a few.

Inside the auditorium a final rehearsal was taking place. Onstage were thirty students from a Rome elementary school run by the Legionaries, dressed in elegant uniforms but looking as if they'd have rather been running around outside. The director was leading them one final time through their performance, which closed with a procession into the seating area, where, before a portrait of the late pope, they chanted in unison: "John Paul II, we love you!" In their hands, they held long-stemmed white roses, a symbol of purity and innocence.

CHAPTER FOUR

BONES

"Go back."

The digital images skipped in reverse on the monitor until the top of an open truck appeared. The freeze-frame showed it was full of wooden pallets.

"Never mind."

The video continued, at triple speed. This was decidedly an odd assignment for the Gendarmeria, the Vatican's police force. Following a tip from Italian police, they were reviewing security footage shot in early 2003 by one of the cameras above the main gate to Vatican City. They were looking for big trucks pulling an open load.

What impressed the security team was how many vehicles passed through the gate in a typical day. The traffic was near constant, from the time the gate opened at six a.m. until it closed at eleven p.m. In recent months there had been recurrent rumors that the Governatorato—the Vatican City governor's office—was going to make some employees park outside the walls, to keep the tiny city-state from going into gridlock. The rumors would always bring howls of protest from the workers, and nothing ever happened. But the cops now understood there was legitimately a traffic problem. Or so it seemed in fast-forward.

On the monitor appeared a truck filled with dirt. In one corner was a white smudge, perhaps a piece of cement.

"Zoom in."

The blown-up image revealed a pattern, a texture of rectangular stones. It was a mosaic.

An officer moved the zoom over the rest of the debris, revealing several slabs of decorated travertine, the kind you'd find in a cemetery. "When did this go out?" asked the astonished officer.

A colleague checked the tape list. "Three days ago."

"Where to?"

"Someplace near the airport. A landfill."

Six months earlier, in the late summer of 2002, Cardinal Edmund Szoka was looking down at an engineer's drawing of the new Santa Rosa underground parking lot. Three levels deep, it would provide more than two hundred badly needed parking places in the congested northeast corner of Vatican City—the "urban" part of the city-state, where the drugstore, printing press, post office, bank and supermarket drew thousands of vehicles each day. The blueprints were impressive. Along the western perimeter of the site were 226 circles, which represented massive cylindrical posts that would be sunk into the ground for support. The entire area would be perforated and filled in with concrete to shore up the sloping terrain. Only then would the excavating commence. It was a huge job, but, in Szoka's view, one that needed to be done. His realm was being overrun with cars.

As president of the government of Vatican City, Cardinal Szoka, a transplanted American, was chief executive of the world's smallest state. In the hillside headquarters of the Governatorato, he lived and worked far above the hustle and bustle of lower Vatican City. Facing him was the back of Saint Peter's Basilica, a graceful curving shell designed by Michelangelo. Szoka thought it was more beautiful than the facade, and it was a shame so few people got a chance to see it. Behind him were the immaculately trimmed Vatican Gardens, dotted with fountains and crisscrossed with narrow service roads. It was quiet here, almost bucolic. The governor's building itself was a five-story structure that housed Szoka's apartment and the working offices needed to keep the ministate fully functional: finance and accounting, utilities, maintenance, sanitation and security.

One of the cardinal's secretaries entered with a pile of papers, heralding another busy day. Like almost all of the city-state's sixteen hundred employees, she was a layperson. On her way out, she told the cardinal that the *ingegnere* needed to see him.

Szoka nodded, unsurprised at this piece of news. The *ingegnere* was Massimo Stoppa, whose full title was *Dottore Ingegnere Cavaliere di Gran Croce*, enough to fill a large brass nameplate on his office door down the hall. Stoppa directed the powerful Department of Technical Services at the

Governatorato and would probably be bringing more news from the construction zone. The Santa Rosa lot was Stoppa's pet project, one that Szoka fully supported. But there had already been problems.

The Vatican Museums had an archaeology department, and its experts were convinced the parking lot site was some kind of Pompeii waiting to be discovered. They wanted to do some test digging in the area. That was a red flag to *ingegnere* Stoppa, who knew that once the archaeologists got into any site, they never left. He was bound and determined not to let that happen, which in theory wouldn't be difficult: Because the museum answered to the Governatorato, Stoppa was counting on Cardinal Szoka to hold the line.

At age seventy-five, the silver-haired Szoka wasn't looking for more battles; he had witnessed enough of them inside the Vatican walls. He heaved his curved frame out from behind his desk and went to the window, where he looked out on the Governatorato parking lot and smiled wanly. It was finally empty, and he could see all the way to the topiaried papal crest on the other side of the blacktop surface. This was one of his victories.

Parking and traffic had been Szoka's bête noire ever since he'd arrived at the governor's mansion. He was determined to move cars off the landscape, and to do so he'd already inaugurated one underground parking facility on the south side of the Vatican hill, where Governatorato employees were now forced to leave their vehicles. It was only a few steps from the office complex, but the employees—almost all of them Italians—hated it. It seemed to them that this American cardinal had a bit of the *fanatico* in him; why would anyone want to clear out a perfectly serviceable aboveground lot? Was there something beautiful about bare asphalt? It was especially odd that a war on cars was being led by someone from the onetime automobile manufacturing capital of the world, Motor City.

Szoka, a Michigan native of Polish descent, had been archbishop of Detroit, where his insistence on balancing the budget had put him on a collision course with the people in the pews. In 1989 he had to close or consolidate thirty-three parishes because the archdiocese couldn't afford to keep them running. There was an outcry, but to Szoka, it was simple economics: You couldn't pay the bills with Hail Marys. And of course, time proved him right. With the decline of the local auto industry, Detroit was shifting demographically, and Catholics were moving out. Just as in business, there was a time to expand and a time to contract, and a good bishop knew when to do both. But the parishioners never forgave him, and the public criticism stung.

A few months later, in 1990, Pope John Paul summoned him to Rome and placed him in charge of the Vatican's budget office. Dropping a fiscally responsible U.S. cardinal into the Italianized world of Vatican finances was one of the pope's wiser management decisions. By curbing spending and publishing annual financial statements, Szoka ended a string of budget deficits that were slowly bleeding away Vatican reserves. In 1997, as his reward, he was handed the reins to the Vatican City State. Although it is the sovereign territory of the Holy See and its administrative apparatus, the Roman Curia, Vatican City is regarded as a separate entity. Ultimately it answers to the pope, but it generally operates on its own authority, its own budget and its own turf.

Cardinal Szoka quickly made a mark in his new job. He redesigned the entrance to the Vatican Museums, busting a large new opening through the Vatican walls. He increased security, setting up a system of surveillance cameras that filmed nearly every square inch of Vatican City's 109 acres, with two police officers watching the monitors twenty-four/seven. He wired Vatican City with fiber optics and standardized the city-state's nine different computerized bookkeeping systems. In one of his most controversial moves, he banned smoking in all Vatican offices and corridors, leading to deep grumbling from many of its employees.

Most of all, Szoka kept his eye on the bottom line. He discovered that despite its reputation for wealth, the city-state had less than a year's operating budget in reserve. Its investments were mostly in dollars, and the dollar was taking a big hit from the euro. Vatican City had to finance its own operations through meager commercial revenues (primarily taken in from the Vatican Museums), the sale of coins and stamps, and profits from the supermarket and other shops and six gas stations. With no margin for financial error, Szoka began looking for new ways to generate income. He didn't have to look far. On the other side of the Governatorato was the Vatican's empty three-story train station. Since most supplies these days came in by truck, not rail, Szoka was able to transform the terminal into a high-end, duty-free department store. Shoppers with a Vatican pass—including employees and their families—could now pick up Armani suits, Swiss watches and Cuban cigars. It was not the Mall of America, but in Szoka's view it added a nice touch of free enterprise to an otherwise dull landscape.

Szoka had an even more ambitious design for the new underground parking lot. Once it was built, he would breach the Vatican walls one more time and create a new gate that exited directly to the busy Roman piazza on the other side. The preserve-everything crowd wouldn't like that, but the shortcut through the walls would free Vatican City from the rush-hour traffic snarls at the end of the working day.

The cardinal watched as a green bird flitted down from the hillside. It looked like one of the parrots that had taken up residence on the hill above the Governatorato. There had been only two in the Vatican Gardens when Szoka arrived here, and now there were more than thirty. When he walked through the gardens, the cardinal would marvel at their huge nests with the ingress holes underneath. Now that cars were kept out of the area, the birds could often be heard chattering beneath the pines.

The cardinal heard a knock. *"Eminenza."*

Ingegnere Stoppa was at the door. Thick jowled with a bulbous nose and overgrown eyebrows, Stoppa held a folder under his arm.

"We've finished," Stoppa said, looking pleased with himself as he pulled out a report and laid it on the cardinal's desk. "There's nothing."

Szoka glanced at the papers. Instead of allowing Vatican Museums experts in, Technical Services had decided to drill its own test samples into the Santa Rosa terrain. Here were the results, and they were negative: No artifacts, no tombs, no surprises. If anyone objected to the project, the Governatorato now had the paperwork to answer them. Szoka didn't understand the procedure involved, but he figured Stoppa had covered all the bases. The *ingegnere* was like a bulldog, and he didn't like it when someone tried to take away his bone.

Stoppa had weathered these storms before. Eleven years earlier, when he oversaw construction of a five-story clerical hotel inside Vatican City, every environmental group in Italy had protested. The ecologists were upset because, for a handful of Rome apartment dwellers, the new building eclipsed the view of the back of Saint Peter's Basilica—the same view Cardinal Szoka liked so much. Visitors to Stoppa's office would find his desk strewn with maps and photographs proving that the hotel, the Domus Sanctae Marthae, was actually lower than many of the Italian buildings in the neighborhood. Stoppa ridiculed the environmentalists' concerns, and in return was attacked in the press. When Italian politicians demanded the project be halted, it was simply too much for Stoppa, who insisted that the construction was ultimately a matter of sovereignty. The building was completed and, as he predicted, the whole brouhaha was soon forgotten.

Stoppa realized that the parking lot posed a trickier problem. The critics in this case were in-house professionals, not the outside radicals of the Italian Green Party. And an archaeological objection was a bit more difficult to finesse. But now he had a report, and he hoped it would function as an insurance policy.

"*Bene, bene*," Szoka murmured, though a nagging doubt hung in his mind. Personally, he was convinced that if modern development projects were held hostage to relics of the past, society would soon stop functioning. But he also knew that in previous situations like this, Italians tended to side against developers; the mentality here was to protect and conserve antiquity at all cost. The main thing was not to get caught in a public battle, because the Governatorato would inevitably be painted as the bad guy.

Stoppa had taken one more precaution to make sure that didn't happen. He had informed the Vatican Museums that their personnel were prohibited from setting foot in the construction site.

On a sunny February morning in 2003 the phone rang in Giandomenico Spinola's office.

"The director wants you down at Santa Rosa. He'll meet you there at ten o'clock."

Spinola paused. "That's off-limits for us."

"Not anymore," the voice informed him.

In a vague way Spinola had been expecting the call. As chief archaeologist for the Vatican Museums, he was one of several people who had warned against excavating the site without first making systematic test soundings in the area. But he also knew how things worked in the Vatican: The decisions were made not in the museums but in the Governatorato, where the Department of Technical Services ruled. The bulldozers had gone in a few weeks earlier, and when the wind was right Spinola could hear the destructive grinding from his museum office on the hillside above.

The night before, Vatican Museums director Francesco Buranelli had received a phone call at home, offering a tip. It must have been a significant one, because Buranelli now wanted Spinola to meet him down in the forbidden zone. *They must have dug something up,* Spinola thought. He'd probably be handed some broken pieces and asked to reassemble them.

He walked out a private exit of the museum and from the belvedere on the north side caught the sunlit panorama of Rome. Already spring was in the air. Spinola, forty-two, moved at a brisk pace. He was a trim man with sandy hair and a thick mustache, and his tweed jacket and bright green tie set him apart from the aging corps of Vatican functionaries. He had been hired as director of antiquities and paleo-Christian art in 1993 after a career that included excavations throughout the Mediterranean and Turkey. Spinola soon learned, however, that he'd be allowed to do very little digging in Vatican City. In urban areas, archaeology typically thrives on new construction—it's the window of opportunity into the subterranean record. But whenever a building project began in Vatican City, the engineers did their best to keep the archaeologists out.

Spinola lit a cigarette as he strolled past the Fountain of the Galea, where a sailing ship spouted water out its sides, and continued along the path next to the Vatican warehouses, far from the crowds of tourists who packed the museums. It was strangely silent here; that seemed fitting for a place that two thousand years earlier had been a graveyard. Archaeologically this corner of the Vatican was a potential gold mine. Spinola had studied the early maps of Rome, and there could be no doubt: The whole tract, which stood right next to the beginning of the ancient Via Triumphalis, the Triumphal Way, was an extended tomb area.

Two millennia earlier the Vatican hill was a wild place, with steep overgrown ravines and claylike soil that discouraged building. It lay outside the city gates, and two roads ran around it: the Via Cornelia on the south and the Via Triumphalis on the north. The ancient Roman government had allowed tombs to be built next to both roads, and the cemetery near the Via Cornelia became famous as the supposed burial place of Saint Peter. Archaeologists of later centuries would have their doubts, but the Emperor

Constantine pretty well settled the question when he built the first basilica over an area that was venerated as Saint Peter's grave.

With no such illustrious tomb of its own, the Via Triumphalis cemetery had been forgotten and had come to light only piecemeal, beginning in the sixteenth century, when footings were sunk for the northernmost wing of the Vatican palaces. Then, in 1930, below the Fountain of the Galea, more tombs were uncovered but quickly buried again beneath a modern warehouse building. Spinola had managed to excavate an additional small section near the fountain in the 1990s, revealing tombs that dated to the time of Augustus. The most important finds, however, were made in the 1950s during excavation for the Vatican's first underground parking lot. A small section of the graveyard was preserved, hinting at much more that still lay belowground to the north—precisely the territory that Technical Services had earmarked for the new parking facility. The engineers had promised to call the archaeology office if they discovered anything interesting. That was a polite way of saying, "Get lost."

Now, as Spinola approached the construction zone, he could see that the area had been thoroughly torn up. The bulldozers were turned off today—which was odd, he thought. He walked through a fence gate and saw Buranelli and the foreman waiting for him, along with officials from Technical Services. They all looked nervous, and Spinola soon saw why. Lying in a pile, heaped casually to one side, were several Roman funerary markers. Next to them was a marble altar decorated with rams' heads and birds; one of the rams' heads had been clipped, and the altar edges bore the fresh scars of a bulldozer's blade.

"Where did these come from?" Spinola asked. But his hosts were already leading him to the answer, in the western corner of the excavation. When he looked out over the devastated landscape before him, his heart sank. Stumps of marble tombstones were strewn across the site, scattered by the earthmoving machinery. In the muddy tire tracks he could see small remnants of mosaics and terra-cotta urns. Despite the upheaval, he could make out a vague topography: a ridge that ran up the hill, broadened in areas to accommodate family tombs. At the bottom of the incline was standing water, where everything looked destroyed; higher up, perhaps, they could still salvage something. This was not just a small cluster of graves; it was extensive, probably four thousand or five thousand square feet. In the center were the brick walls of what looked like a columbarium and other small mausoleums, shorn off at an angle by the bulldozers.

Buranelli was arguing with the foreman, vowing to halt the work. Spinola wondered bitterly: "Why didn't they stop? Why didn't the engineers call us?"

They had sliced through a city of the dead.

The war drums were beating loudly that March, and for the Vatican press corps the coming Iraq invasion was the only story in town. An ailing Pope John Paul II had sent envoys to President Bush and Saddam Hussein, convened diplomats at the Vatican and even hosted Tony Blair in an effort to head off the inevitable. It was a good story, but little else was on the pope's agenda, which meant the *vaticanisti* were growing hungry for some other news.

I sat in our booth in the Sala Stampa and began updating an article on the Vatican's fears that war in Iraq would be seen as a Christian invasion of a Muslim country. Our other most popular feature that week had been a piece on Vatican efforts to evangelize the yachting society at the America's Cup race in New Zealand.

So the rumors of a new discovery beneath Vatican City were quick to catch our attention. The report going around was that the bulldozers had unearthed some ancient graves. The hint of scandal was that some of the artifacts might have already been carted off and hidden somewhere in Rome. It sounded like a case of tomb robbing on a large scale, right under the pope's window. Like many suspected scenarios involving the Vatican, this one was too clever by half. It didn't seem to occur to people that developers inside the Vatican, like developers everywhere, had no interest in stealing old inscriptions and didn't really care if a bunch of ancient tombstones ended up in a landfill.

I remembered a similar discovery a few years earlier, when the Vatican had decided to allow construction of a five-story underground parking lot on a historic hill near Saint Peter's Square. Technically that site was outside of Vatican City, but access was through the grounds of a Vatican-owned college. One evening Slovakian Cardinal Jozef Tomko, who lived at the college, took me to see the excavation hole. It was vast and deep and looked like the entry to hell. I later learned the bulldozers had cut into an ancient Roman villa on the hill, with frescoed paintings of birds, masks and monsters. Archaeologists speculated that it might have belonged to Agrippina, the mother of the Emperor Caligula. After much debate authorities decided that the parking facility was too important to sacrifice; the artifacts were cleared out, cataloged and forgotten in the back room of a Rome museum. They had gone from one form of oblivion to another.

The supposed new discovery at the Santa Rosa site would be harder for all of us to report on, because it was inside the Vatican. I discussed the matter with our two other CNS reporters, Cindy Wooden and John Norton, and we all agreed that this was the kind of story people loved: the ultimate "secrets of the Vatican" tale, with intrigue and ancient tombs. But we needed a source, because the Italian media reports were wildly speculative. And we needed a photo, which the Vatican would never allow us to take.

"I know someone who might be able to help," Norton said. "Jen Cole. Her apartment looks right into the Vatican from Piazza Risorgimento. Maybe she'll let me take some pictures."

A religion teacher at Marymount International School, Jen Cole had come to Rome as a volunteer during the Great Jubilee of the year 2000, and like many before her had fallen in love with the city. The chance to live in Rome during the final phase of Pope John Paul's pontificate probably sealed her decision to stay. She was a committed Catholic, and John Paul was quite simply her hero. About a half dozen roommates and apartments later, she found herself living in the shadow of the pope's own apartment. From the fourth floor, she had a room with a unique view—a view that peered directly over the Vatican walls. For weeks she'd been a spectator of the parking lot construction, which unfolded below her in panoramic detail. As she worked out on a treadmill in front of her picture window, she watched its progress: the fencing off of the site, the demolition of the small existing buildings, the arrival of a huge crane that stood sentry above everything and most of all the continuous digging. The noise would begin early in the morning, and her alarm clock was now a jackhammer, followed by the grinding gears of heavy machinery and the crashing of rubble being dumped into trucks.

As time passed, Jen came to recognize the workmen and their routines. They took lots of breaks, to smoke or drink coffee or eat *panini*. On these occasions she noticed that she had become a figure in their landscape, too. As she exercised next to her window, the workers would smile and wave at her. They could see her only from the waist up, and not the treadmill, which probably made for an amusing sight. Sometimes they would mimic her, moving their arms back and forth in mechanical rhythm. Jen didn't mind; they were all entertaining one another. Then one day construction abruptly came to a halt, and the workmen disappeared.

When he reached the roof of Jen's building, Norton saw that the big machinery had been moved out, and the tomb area could be clearly recognized. From above, it looked like the last brownie in the corner of a stainless steel baking pan, a dark brown mound tucked incongruously into an expanse of concrete and wire mesh footings. A few people were crawling on its surface, surveying its contours. Sections of the parking lot's poured foundation were being used as a staging area, where experts had carried buckets of dirt and were now sifting through them carefully. Norton took a panoramic photo, and when it was blown up we all stared in amazement: We could see several half-buried sarcophagi and what looked like many other smaller artifacts sticking out of the ground.

The photo moved on our wire that afternoon. It was the first visual evidence that there was something behind the rumors, after all.

The newspaper *La Repubblica* lay across *ingegnere* Stoppa's desk, open to the Rome *cronaca* pages, where a headline proclaimed: "Tombs Don't Stop the Bulldozers: 'We Need the Parking Places in the Vatican.'" As he read the article a second time, Stoppa grew more and more irritated. All those details, which must have come from the Vatican Museums people, had been rolled into a ball of journalistic invention. The newspaper was reporting nothing less than the methodical looting of the Santa Rosa site. Latin inscriptions and tombstones being hauled away by the truckload! They even quoted a truck driver who said they'd unloaded the archaeological plunder in a "big room" somewhere in the city. Pure fantasy!

It had not been a good month for Technical Services. When the first

pieces were removed from the ground—a couple of antique marble markers—
Stoppa had ordered them set aside. As long as the findings were small scale,
he figured they'd just hand them all over to the Vatican Museums at the
end of construction. But the pieces began piling up. Then a marble inscription had been found in the landfill near the airport, and Italy's Nucleo Tu-
tela Patrimonio Artistico—the archaeology police—suspected it had come
from the Vatican's excavation site. The Italian police must have alerted the
Vatican police, and at that point the problem began to spin out of control.
It was bad enough that the Vatican Museums director had gotten involved,
and now it was in the papers.

The day before, a reporter had called the Governatorato, snooping
around about the archaeological finds. Cardinal Szoka was in the hospital
for a series of intestinal operations, leaving Bishop Gianni Danzi in charge.
Danzi agreed to be interviewed, thinking he could deflate the story before it
appeared in the newspaper, but instead the article made him appear to be
the classic small-minded bureaucrat. Stoppa read the bishop's quotes again:
"Sure, we found some things during the excavation, but I don't think they
were that important. . . . We really need this facility. It's getting so hard to
drive around Vatican City and find a place to park."

Even worse than Bishop Danzi's poor performance was a sidebar article, an interview with Archbishop Francesco Marchisano. Marchisano
headed a minor pontifical commission that promoted protection of the
church's artistic patrimony; its ineffectiveness had been demonstrated all
too clearly when, in 1995, fourteen Renaissance paintings were stolen out
of the commission's own offices in Rome. Just recently Pope John Paul had
named Marchisano head of the Permanent Commission for the Protection of Historic and Artistic Monuments of the Holy See. It was an insignificant advisory panel, but apparently Marchisano was unaware of the
fact. He announced to *La Repubblica* that he was going to convene the
commission to investigate the Santa Rosa site and make some decisions.
Marchisano had even suggested the site might be preserved for future
visitors!

Stoppa knew what had to be done. They would put out the word that
the scope of the discoveries had been exaggerated. Then they would reas-
sure people that every artifact would be dug out, dusted off and put where

it belonged—in the Vatican Museums. After a quick archaeological harvest, construction would resume. The bulldozers would soon be back at work.

Spinola was now up against a deadline. He and his staff of antiquities experts at the museum had been told to wrap up their excavation of the tomb site. Normally, archaeologists might take years to dig out such a place, documenting every square inch. But the Governatorato had decided that any additional delay would cost too much. So the team of two archaeologists and five assistants worked as fast as they could, hauling out dirt by the bucketful as they peeled layers off the mound with shovels, picks, trowels and brushes.

The first thing Spinola noticed about the tombs was how well they had been preserved. Normally, an ancient Roman site yields mere bits and pieces from the past, because it has already been destroyed—by urban renewal, looting, neglect or just the passage of time. But here they were finding intact graves, buried but relatively undisturbed. Some of the tombs still had votive oil lamps placed on their marble ledges; others contained the ceramic funeral vases that held balsamic fragrances. Whatever happened here had happened very quickly. It reminded Spinola of Pompeii, except that instead of raining ash the tombs had been buried in dirt. Or, more precisely, mud. Judging from the grade of the Vatican hill at this precise spot, mud slides must have been common in ancient times. From what Spinola could tell, sometime in the second century a huge mud slide had enveloped this whole sector, covering up tombs and making them impossible to unearth. Abandoning a burial place would have constituted a rare and dramatic event, because funerary rights of relatives of the dead were enshrined in Roman law. But clearly this lower stratum of tombs had been untouched since the slide.

In Spinola's view that made this site unique among Roman cemeteries. As they dug deeper, the discoveries became even more stunning. Some tombs were simple hollowed-out ditches covered with tiles, confirming that the burial ground had been open to poor families as well as to the Roman upper class. In many of the more elaborate burial chambers, the team found terra-cotta tubes leading up to ground level, through which relatives would pour ritual offerings of milk, wine or honey. There were classic columbaria, covered huts with a series of wall niches, each with an urn that still held the cremated remains of the deceased. Spinola watched as his assistants carefully brushed the dirt from a small stucco sculpture in one of the niches and revealed, incredibly, a three-headed dog and two male figures. It was a mythological scene that would have been known to every Roman of the time: the Trojan hero Aeneas stealing past Cerberus, the hound of Hades, watchdog of the underworld. The team then uncovered a mosaic pavement with the drunken Dionysius leaning on a satyr, a perfectly preserved miniature bust of a Roman matron and her high coiffure, numerous frescoes, biographical inscriptions and, in some cases, entire skeletons accompanied only by the trinkets and jewelry of the funeral ceremony.

After a few weeks of digging in a single small family tomb, one of the white-smocked assistants let out a cry of amazement. The others hurried over and found her standing above a marble bust of a young boy with particularly fine and beautiful features. As Spinola later recalled, the archaeologists were struck by the boy's expression: the sweetness of youth veiled with a certain melancholy. As the inscription told them, Tiberius Natronius Venustus had exited this world after four years, four months and ten days, sometime during the first part of the first century.

Not far away, the team excavated an amphora. When they lifted it out, they discovered beneath it a rare statuette of a sleeping slave placed above a small, meager tomb. Dressed in a tunic so short that it left no doubt about his gender, the slave was shown curled up on a lantern and holding a pouch of food. The archaeologists debated its meaning. Was this the tomb of the slave himself? Or was it the tomb of the master, whose slave was represented here to accompany him on his final journey to the underworld?

In many cases the inscriptions on tombstones were long and informative, an abbreviated version of our own newspaper obituaries. Sometimes the life stories were illustrated by symbols, as in the case of Alcimus, a servant of the Emperor Nero, who worked as the stage set designer at the Theater of Pompeii in central Rome. On the side of his stone marker were carved representations of the chisel, compass and level that Alcimus used to build the sets. On the other side of the burial mound was found the tombstone of Clemens, a horse trainer for the Venetae faction down at the Roman racetrack, and of Grathus, a plumber who kept the fountains running in the sacred wood in Trastevere. Spinola grew more excited by the day—this kind of biographical data was extremely rare on any dig. As he pointed out, they were uncovering not only stones and pottery fragments, but bringing Rome's "population of the dead" back to life.

"It's like seeing a good poker hand unfold card by card," Spinola told his friends. But the Vatican Museums' team was playing against the house: The Governatorato was following the excavations with mild interest and considerable irritation. The archaeological team would often look up from their work to see Bishop Danzi peering down at them, shaking his head.

"You need to get this stuff into the museum. That's where it belongs," Danzi would tell the archaeologists.

"But museums are full of these kinds of artifacts," they would answer. "What makes this site special is that it's still intact."

"I need the parking places," would be Danzi's inevitable reply.

As the weeks went on, the project's engineers grew impatient, too. One day one of them walked to where the team was excavating and sprayed a red line on the wall with a can of spray paint.

"What's that?" the team asked.

"That's where we start demolishing in ten days," he said.

And then Spinola's crew made a find that can only be described as serendipitous. The area involved, Tomb VIII, was the largest family burial chamber that had been unearthed, and it had already yielded six marble sarcophagi. The tombs emerged slowly as the dirt was scaled down centimeter by centimeter, revealing spectacular sculpted designs. One bore a fine relief of the Calydonian boar hunt, peopled with Greek heroes. Another, the sarcophagus of a noblewoman, was decorated with an unfinished portrait framed by winged victories; below her, two cupids rowed a boat between Tellus, goddess of the earth, and Okeanos, god of the sea. But the group's attention was now focused on the last tomb that had come to light, an oval sarcophagus whose lid was decorated with leaping dolphins. The inscription told them it had held the remains of a young Roman knight who had died at the age of seventeen. As the team sifted through the dirt and uncovered the rest of the sarcophagus with small trowels and brushes, two figures emerged on either end. One was a bearded philosopher, not unusual on Roman tombs. The other was a woman who held her hands up in a pose of prayer. Spinola watched as the workers' fine brushes revealed more details: Behind the praying woman was carved a small bird in a tree. He felt a twinge of excitement. Until now, all the funerary objects they had found on this small hillside were pagan, multiple figures of and emblems referring to the divinities of ancient Rome and Greece. But this looked different. It suggested that the young Roman knight may have been a Christian. And if this was a Christian tomb, Spinola realized, it changed everything. Perhaps the bulldozers could be stopped, after all.

For centuries church leaders have argued about the importance of what comes out of the ground in Rome and how much should be preserved, enshrined or ignored. Early Christian tombs, however, have a special place in this debate. The most famous Christian burial places in Rome belong to Saints Peter and Paul, the city's patron saints, and the rediscovery of their tombs owes much to the determination of two popes: Pius XII and Benedict XVI. In both cases the politics of the bones make for fascinating true stories that few visitors ever hear.

On a rainy day in early 2007, I met Tom Bissell under the colonnade of Saint Peter's Square. As we hustled to our appointment in the Fabbrica of Saint Peter's, he explained a little about the book he was writing, on the tombs of the Apostles. It was to be a travel book, one of Bissell's specialties, and the idea was to visit the tombs of the twelve Apostles, from Saint Matthew's supposed resting place in Kyrgyzstan to Saint Andrew's tomb in southern Greece. As a winner of the Rome Prize, Bissell was at the American Academy in Rome for a year to work on the project, and naturally he planned to examine the tomb of Saint Peter. Bissell had no idea how to break through the Vatican bureaucracy and get close enough to the tomb to actually write about it, so he asked me to help. I knew that a letter to the proper authorities might eventually get him in before he left Rome in a few months, but if you know someone in Rome, you don't go through the regular channels. I happened to have a friend in the Fabbrica. I picked up the phone, and within minutes we had set up an appointment for a personal tour of the tomb with Pietro Zander, the head archaeologist of the necropolis beneath Saint Peter's Basilica.

No story better illustrates the perils of Vatican archaeology than the excavation of the tomb of Saint Peter. The digging was commissioned in 1939 by Pope Pius XII, and it lasted eleven years. It was an inside job, in the sense that the chief archaeologist was Jesuit Father Antonio Ferrua, aided by three colleagues, and the actual excavation was done by the *sampietrini*, the basilica's all-purpose workmen. Overseeing it all was Monsignor Ludwig Kaas, a German who was serving as the administrator of Saint Peter's Basilica. Several feet beneath the modern basilica lay the floor of the original church built by the Emperor Constantine. Ferrua's team used this lower level as a staging area, breaking through the floor and systematically removing the landfill underneath, building sustaining walls as they went. What they uncovered deep below the basilica was the original Roman cemetery, complete with small family mausoleums, frescoes and carved sarcophagi. When they finally came to the area where Saint Peter was believed to be buried, directly below the main altar of the basilica, they encountered an early *edicola*, or small tomb monument, encased in a bigger Constantinian marble monument and topped by a medieval altar. Smaller tombs were arranged around this one, in what could only have been a sign of reverence. Clearly, this was the tomb of Saint Peter, the first pope. When the tomb was opened, however, the evidence was less clear-cut. Many bones were removed from the area, but none seemed to constitute a complete skeleton. In 1950, as the excavation ended, Pope Pius XII summarized the findings in a dramatic radio announcement just before Christmas: "The tomb of the Prince of the Apostles has been found," he announced. He then turned to a "secondary question," the actual relics of Saint Peter, and said that despite the discovery of human bones, "it is impossible to prove with certainty that they belong to the apostle."

Our two-hour tour with Zander focused on the tomb and not the bones. I had been through the necropolis area before, but even for me the underground geography was a little confusing. Bissell was getting the full-immersion treatment, and his notebook looked as if it might be too small for the task. The air down here was moist and heavy, and the path narrow. We walked along a dimly lit Roman road past family sepulchres, glimpsing the stuccoed and frescoed representations of Greek, Roman and Egyptian gods, a virtual pagan pantheon. After painstakingly describing every archaeological twist and turn, Zander took us into a chamber with a view of a wall. Inside a tiny niche we could glimpse the tops of some clear plastic containers. Bissell listened as Zander explained, once again, how the *edicola* pieces discovered here matched the description by the ancient historian Eusebius. Only when I pointed to the tops of the nineteen Plexiglas containers did Bissell realize that they held the relics of Saint Peter. Or did they? Zander wasn't mentioning them and, half hidden in the dirt wall, they seemed almost an afterthought to this tour. So Bissell asked our guide point-blank: Are those Saint Peter's bones? Zander gave a diplomatic answer, quoting Pope Paul VI's Latin phrase *quae putantur*—the bones "which are thought to be" those of Peter. But Bissell and I wondered aloud the same thing: If the original archaeologists were so uncertain about what they had pulled out of the earth, how did these bones come to be resting here, encased and fastened with the papal seal?

Zander sighed and explained that the papal archaeologists had carried out their work with unfortunate speed. He didn't want to get into the details of the real story, because it wasn't pretty. Yet it was fascinating.

Some fifteen years after the excavation of the tomb area below Saint Peter's was completed, an Italian epigraphist named Margherita Guarducci began studying the results of the dig. The more she learned, the more she became convinced that the graffiti near the tomb—dismissed as insignificant by the original excavators—held complex and important evidence. She saw sketches of what she considered a telltale phrase scratched into a red plaster wall: *Petr eni*, which she read as an abbreviation of *Petros enesti*, Greek for "Peter is here." She was astonished to find that this particular graffiti had not even been mentioned in the official final report on the excavations; apparently, it had come to light only after the work was completed in 1950.

Motivated in part by her fervent faith, Guarducci conducted a deeper investigation, interviewing the *sampietrini* who'd done the actual digging. She was told that Father Ferrua had removed the *Petr eni* inscription and was keeping it in his room at the Jesuit residence near the Vatican. Guarducci also discovered that there had been bad blood between Ferrua and Monsignor Kaas, the overseer of the basilica. Kaas, who was not an archaeologist, feared that the human bones in the cemetery were not being treated with respect. So every night, after the archaeologists had gone home, he would patrol the excavation area with an assistant, Giovanni Segoni, and collect bones out of the freshly dug earth. The two men put them in boxes and hid them away in a storeroom. Kaas died in 1952, but Guarducci managed to talk to Segoni, who casually led her to a room that still held boxes of bones. In one box labeled "Graffiti Wall Area" were bone fragments large and small. Guarducci convinced Pope Paul VI to allow scientific testing on the bones; the tests showed that some of them belonged to an older, robust man, and that they had been wrapped in a purple cloth with gold trim— clearly a sign of special treatment. It wasn't long before she had declared them to be the bones of Saint Peter, and Pope Paul VI seemed to accept her conclusion. In 1968, he announced that further study had identified the bones "in a manner that we can consider convincing."

All this triggered protests from archaeological scholars and from Father Ferrua, who bitterly criticized Guarducci and her methods. Guarducci defended herself by going on the attack. She began to speak of a plot by ecumenists to "minimize and cancel the tangible presence of Peter in the Church of Rome" and said that her findings were kept secret during the Second Vatican Council because "it would have bothered the Protestants." She soon found herself persona non grata at Saint Peter's. In a sense, Guarducci had won her case with the pope, but not with the archaeological world.

The Guarducci matter explained why Pietro Zander was almost reluctant to talk about the bones to Tom Bissell and me. For church scholars and professionals like Zander, the story was an embarrassment: The supposed bones of Saint Peter had been surreptitiously dug up by a meddling monsignor when the archaeologists weren't looking; then they were thrown into a box and forgotten for more than a decade; then they were rediscovered by accident and became the focus of a feud between church experts. The whole affair did not inspire confidence in the Vatican's ability to exhume its own history, and it is little wonder that none of it is mentioned in the Vatican guidebooks. In fact, visitors who tour the necropolis beneath Saint Peter's are invariably impressed with the excavated cemetery but are often heard muttering on their way out: "So are they saying those *are* really Saint Peter's bones?"

I was curious to know what Bissell had made of all this. Had the visit to underground Saint Peter's enlightened him?

He observed that Zander had wriggled out of questions about the bones' authenticity.

"It's obviously important for the church. But it seemed to me he was being very gently evasive," Bissell said with a laugh. "I noticed that whenever the question came up he began smiling."

In June 2009, at the close of a jubilee year in memory of Saint Paul, Pope Benedict XVI was celebrating vespers at the Basilica of Saint Paul Outside the Walls on Rome's ancient Via Ostiense, and he spoke enthusiastically about the church as the traditional site of Paul's tomb. Then he surprised everyone by stating that pilgrims should come to the basilica with the knowledge that the sarcophagus below the main altar, "by the unanimous opinion of experts and an undisputed tradition, holds the remains of the Apostle Paul."

I had been following the pope's remarks and did a double take. Saint Paul's tomb was indeed thought to lie below the main altar, but it was inaccessible beneath centuries of architectural buildup, and no one knew what, if anything, was inside.

The tomb itself, a rough-hewn piece of white marble that could be glimpsed through a narrow channel from above, had been identified as Saint Paul's only three years earlier. Incredible as it seems, for centuries the burial place had been forgotten. Everyone knew there was supposed to be a tomb under the altar, but no one had bothered to conduct the most basic archaeological survey. Then Giorgio Filippi, a mild-mannered expert from the Vatican Museums, began ferreting around the church.

I had heard about Filippi's sleuthing in 2005 and arranged to meet him one afternoon inside Saint Paul's. The basilica was practically empty, and Filippi showed up late but with an inexhaustible supply of information. In his three-piece suit, goatee and glasses, he looked like an eccentric and had the enthusiasm of a mad scientist. I asked one question, and he was off on a two-hour-long description of his archaeological quest, a painfully detailed narrative that culminated in the discovery of the marble tomb.

What was inside the sarcophagus? I wanted to know.

The question put him off; it was as if I were suggesting, and perhaps I was, that unless he could produce the bones of Saint Paul, or a reasonable facsimile thereof, his whole enterprise could be called into question. With a pained expression on his face, Filippi explained to me the difference between searching for a historical tomb and searching for an individual's bones. This was not a relic hunt to bolster the claims of the faith or tantalize public opinion, he said. He was a professional, and his archaeology was scientific. His conclusions would rest on an analysis of the evidence, not an ossuary jackpot. The bones—that was something journalists ask about.

I looked appropriately contrite.

Anyway, he added, they had tried to X-ray the sarcophagus from above, to no avail. A video probe appeared impossible. To dig out the tomb would require the destruction of the entire altar area, so it would remain where it was. If some people were left wondering about the bones, that was their problem, Filippi said with some finality.

But now, four years later, Pope Benedict had simply waved aside the margin of ambiguity: Saint Paul's bones were in the sarcophagus. How could he have been so sure?

The answer lay in an unadvertised archaeological adventure commissioned by the German pope. In May of 2007, several Vatican experts had slipped quietly into the basilica around midnight. Using a special extended drill, they reached the marble slab that covered the sarcophagus and bore a tiny hole through the top. Then they slipped a microsurgical probe through the opening, taking pictures and collecting evidence samples. It was one fifteen a.m. when they pulled up fragments of human bone material. The technicians were under orders not to "disturb" the relics, so they worked slowly and methodically, extracting bits and pieces with surgical-type tweezers. They retrieved wool and linen fibers covered with gold or dyed in royal purple and indigo, precious materials indicating the burial of an important person, and small organic crumbs that turned out to be grains of incense.

Once the secret expedition was over, the hole was sealed up and the discoveries were sent for analysis. Carbon-14 dating of the bone fragments gave the Vatican what it was looking for: The bones belonged to someone who lived between the first and second centuries. That was sufficient for the archaeologists to state that their findings did not contradict the tradition that this was, indeed, Saint Paul's tomb. So *were* these the bones of the saint? Ulderico Santamaria, director of the diagnostic laboratory at the Vatican Museums, put it this way: "As a person of science, I stop at the objective data, which only give indications." But Pope Benedict had no such hesitation, claiming the remains definitively for Saint Paul. Having been presented with one of the most remarkable modern discoveries in church history, second only to that of Saint Peter's tomb, he was not about to let science have the final word.

In the spring of 2003 the exciting discoveries were continuing down in the Santa Rosa parking pit, but a question mark hung over the whole operation. The Governatorato was still insisting that the archaeologists vacate the premises. A meeting of Archbishop Marchisano's Permanent Commission for the Protection of Historic and Artistic Monuments of the Holy See was convened. Buranelli, the Vatican Museums director, was a key member of the commission and laid out his arguments for preserving the archaeological area. *Ingegnere* Stoppa responded with facts and figures: Saving the ancient cemetery would mean the loss of between fifty and one hundred parking places, and a huge cost overrun. The whole facility would have to be redesigned. Despite Stoppa's objections, the commission decided to voice general support for the Vatican Museums. But as Stoppa kept pointing out, the commission was merely advisory. It was Cardinal Szoka who would have to evaluate the situation and make a final decision—but Szoka was back in the hospital for more tests, and no one knew when he'd be out. That left Stoppa with the delicate job of quietly lining up allies in the Vatican hierarchy. Ecclesial politics, however, was not Stoppa's strong suit; he was, after all, only a layman, and in situations like this you needed a red hat. As the bureaucratic impasse continued, the Vatican Museums team kept digging.

In his small office, Giandomenico Spinola sat in front of a computer screen looking at the latest photo documentation from the dig. The sarcophagi were stunning, but even more unusual were the photos of a hillside area dotted with *tubuli*, the libation cylinders leading down to unexcavated graves. The more the work proceeded, in fact, the stronger the argument grew for leaving this portion of the cemetery unexcavated. Archaeology is itself a form of destruction, and Spinola realized that nothing like this had

survived anywhere else in the world. He winced when he imagined the bulldozers cleaning it out.

Spinola's office was packed with oddities and cast-off artifacts. A painted
tin Egyptian coffin sat on his desk, the kind sold to schoolkids as pencil
containers. A rosy chunk of Greek marble was a paperweight; he had picked
it out of the rubble when the Vatican builders had blasted through the thick
walls of an ancient tower to expand the Vatican bank a few years earlier.
His wall was hung with faded prints and maps, many of them purchased at
Rome's Sunday morning flea market at Porta Portese. None of them had
much value. On hundreds of occasions in his career, Spinola could have
walked off with precious antique objects from the cultures and civilizations
of the past, but that, of course, was unthinkable for a professional. Only
once had he succumbed to temptation. While working alone at a site on
Rome's Caelian Hill, next to an ancient Roman cistern, he found an exqui-
site gold ring with a sapphire. He reported the find to his superiors and said
he'd deliver it early the next week; in the meantime, he let his girlfriend
wear it for four days.

Spinola and other archaeologists took advantage of Italy's building
boom in the 1980s to do dozens of "preconstruction" excavations. Many of
the sites were remarkable, but the digging had to be done quickly. Then,
after the *tangentopoli* scandal of payoffs and bribes was uncovered in the
early 1990s, the construction industry went into a crisis and the archaeological field day ended.

Spinola learned at an early age that good archaeology is often a combination of opportunism and creativity. Sometimes the rules have to be bent.
On his office wall was a framed clipping from a Rome newspaper, yellowed
with age, that chronicled an unadvertised chapter of his life story. In 1981,
as an archaeology student, he'd heard about a three-room frescoed Roman
house beneath the Aventine Hill, kept under lock and key like so many
finds overseen by the government's archaeological ministry. Spinola figured
out a backdoor way into the site, however. Late one night, armed with flash-
lights, he and three other students lifted a manhole cover in the middle of a
residential street and reached the ancient *domus* through the city's drainage
system. They marveled at the frescoes, took photographs and reemerged
from the manhole to find themselves surrounded by dozens of machine-

gun-wielding policemen. It was a period of terrorism in Italy, and the cops weren't taking any chances. Spinola and his friends were let go with a warning but kept their photos. If there was a lesson learned, it was that archaeology sometimes means taking risks.

As he scanned through the digital photos from Santa Rosa, Spinola returned again and again to one particular image: the sarcophagus of Publius Cesilius Victorinus, the young Roman knight. He zoomed in on the figure of the woman on the left. Her hands were held up, palms facing outward, in the classic posture of prayer. But what kind of prayer? Early Christians prayed this way, but so did Romans when they stood before the shrines of their gods and goddesses. Moreover, the coffin lid had an inscription that began *D. M.* for "Dis Manibus," the standard dedication phrase to the gods of the underworld. That clearly indicated a pagan tomb, like the others in the same burial chamber, which, after all, had a floor mosaic of a drunk Dionysius.

And yet . . . what if? What if the woman did represent a Christian, and what if the bird in the tree behind her represented the soul? And what if the scrolls held by the male figure opposite, seemingly a philosopher, were not symbols of ancient learning but of Scripture? What if the leaping dolphins on the sarcophagus lid evoked not the pagan voyage of the dead but the soul's emergence from mortal life? That interpretation was a stretch, but a case *could* be made that this young man was an early Christian, and that this tomb's ambiguous iconography reflected a transitional stage in Rome— a time when pagan symbols were being repurposed to reflect Christian doctrine.

The theory was not archaeologically convincing, but the people Spinola had to convince were not archaeologists—they were church leaders. A few days later Spinola's group decided on what he would later describe as a "stratagem": They would do an end around the Governatorato and appeal directly to the secretary of state and, through him, to Pope John Paul II. Without exactly doctoring the intelligence, they would emphasize the exciting discovery of a Christian tomb. The argument was simple: What appeared to be the Vatican's most ancient Christian site outside the altar area of Saint Peter's was about to be destroyed, all in order to create a few more parking places. Wasn't it worth saving?

+ + +

By now Pope John Paul II was in poor health and moved around his apartment in a modified wheelchair. Occasionally he ventured into the back
rooms of his fifth-floor residence in the Apostolic Palace, and from his
kitchen window he could see the big crane standing sentry above the Santa
Rosa parking lot. So when it was explained to him what had been unearthed there, he knew what was involved. The pope generally left such
matters to the Governatorato and kept out of the city-state's bureaucratic
details. But he also recognized that people held popes responsible for what
was built and what was destroyed under their pontificates. Even today, for
example, Pope Julius II is remembered at the Vatican as the pontiff who
demolished the original Saint Peter's Basilica. When he authorized the
construction of the new church, Julius allowed his architects to simply tear
down the old one. The fourth-century Constantinian basilica had held
scores of tombs of bishops, cardinals, popes and saints, and inevitably some
of their bones were scattered or misplaced. Five centuries later, that's what
people remembered.

Pope John Paul was shown pictures of the recent discoveries: a sculpted
baby's head, a family tomb with mythological stucco designs, an epigraph
written by a widow to her dead husband. Then, the most interesting find,
the figure of a praying woman. It was the tomb of a young man, he was told,
and it appeared to be Christian.

In early spring Massimo Stoppa learned that there was "movement" on
the Santa Rosa issue at the highest levels. Then word came down quietly
from the secretary of state's office that the archaeological zone should be
preserved. For Technical Services it was a worst-case scenario, but there
was really no appeal. Stoppa told his architects to come up with a revised
design that worked around the necropolis. In the end he would lose fifty-
five spaces, at an added cost that would bust the year's budget. For Stoppa,
now a year from retirement, it would be his last big project inside Vatican
City.

Cardinal Szoka, finally out of the hospital and back at his residence at
the Governatorato, took the news more philosophically. He'd had a feeling
the battle had been lost when the papers started writing about the archaeological discoveries. Now the "convergence of views" had been articulated

from on high, and Szoka would not fight it; the cemetery would be preserved. As always he consoled himself with the bottom line: 155 parking
spaces had been added below the Vatican landscape.

In early 2007 I walked through the Saint Anne's Gate of Vatican City,
flashed a press pass at the Swiss Guards and talked my way past the police
checkpoint inside. I took a right turn and wandered past the post office and
the supermarket, beyond the pharmacy, to a semideserted spot flanked by a
new two-story building. A gas pump stood deserted in the late morning
sunshine. I walked down into the covered parking lot and gazed at the rows
of gleaming automobiles under fluorescent lights. There was a brief roar as
another car pulled out from the lower levels, leaving behind a fresh odor of
exhaust. The place was filled to capacity.

Then I walked through a door at one end of the lot, past a uniformed
guard, and was transported about eighteen hundred years backward in
time, into a cavernous roofed area that smelled of damp earth. The necropolis, still a work in progress, had been "museumized" with metal walkways
arching over hillside tombs, excavated crypts and uneven mosaic floors. A
dozen scholars were paying a visit, one of hundreds of groups that had reserved a tour of this unique discovery. I tagged along, listening as Giandomenico Spinola explained to the visitors the challenges of documenting an
archaeological site that had already been bulldozed. Along the walkways
were flat-screen computers with interactive diagrams and photos and multilingual texts describing the cemetery landscape. Down in the pit a woman
in a white smock was shoring up a brick pile that held a tilted tombstone in
place.

As Spinola led the group through the necropolis, I chatted with Leo-
nardo Di Blasi, another Vatican archaeologist who had logged hundreds of
hours here over the last four years. He recalled the tense days of 2003, the
bitterness at seeing the early destruction and the satisfaction when they
learned the site would be preserved. After four or five months, he told me,
the team decided to stop digging. They were painfully aware that the more
they exhumed, the more context they destroyed. There were certainly earlier tombs beneath the exposed layer of the hill, but to unearth it all would
defeat the purpose of preservation, so they stopped. For the next three years

they cleaned and restored the site, documented all the finds and published articles. Crumbling mosaics were removed to the Vatican Museums' restoration facilities and reassembled, *tessera* by *tessera*, then returned to their tombs. Microclimate technology was put in place to keep the area at the proper humidity and temperature.

In the summer of 2006 Di Blasi was overseeing the placement of the metal walkways, one of the last tasks to make the place visitor-friendly. To secure the structure they had to sink anchors in the ground, and the first sounding had struck something unusual. Di Blasi watched as a flat terracotta tile was exposed, the kind that often covered a tomb. This one was about three feet by three feet. They worked all morning to dig it out, and by the afternoon were ready to lift the cover and see what lay beneath. Di Blasi called Spinola over to watch. As the tile was gently removed, they saw that the cavity below it was still preserved. Inside lay the skeleton of a year-old child, the tiny legs bent, the rib cage seemingly as fragile as a bird's. The child had been buried with two ceramic cups, which lay to the side. Di Blasi noticed something else. He leaned over and dusted away the earth at the end of the right arm. It was an egg, a goose egg, perhaps. Was it used as a toy? A rattle? No, the hollow eggshell was undecorated and unperforated. Its function, Di Blasi concluded, was allegorical. The parents had buried their baby holding a symbol of rebirth. Nearly two thousand years later, the archaeologists had brought the child's story back to life.

CHAPTER FIVE

CAT AND MOUSE

THE SILVER MERCEDES took a final turn on the road to Castel Gandolfo and began threading its way toward the back door of the papal villa. The car approached the unmarked gate, where the Vatican's security contingent was waiting to escort it. Bishop Bernard Fellay, sitting in the backseat, smiled to himself. *So far, so good.* He had insisted they be allowed to enter through a secondary entrance in order to avoid the press, which had predictably gathered outside the ornate main doorway of the villa. The reporters would be frustrated, but such was life. For all its faults, the Vatican still understood discretion.

It was late August 2005, and Fellay was on his way to see the new pope, accompanied by Father Franz Schmidberger, his cohort and consigliere on this mission. Their driver was now following a security vehicle with SCV plates: Stato della Città del Vaticano. The Vatican City State was not bound by the Vatican walls, but extended even to this hundred-acre enclave in the Castelli Romani, one of more than two dozen parcels of real estate designated as extraterritorial Vatican property. Gazing out the window, Fellay smoothed his soutane and saw the villa's rolling pastures give way to manicured landscapes. Then the papal palace came into view, a modest three-story building. On top was a distinctive hump, the dome of the Vatican's astronomical observatory.

Schmidberger pointed out the Swiss Guards and a crew of papal gentlemen assembled up ahead. Was all this for them? It appeared so. When the car pulled into the cobblestoned courtyard, they all engaged in a brief protocol performance: acknowledgments, gestures and salutations. An archbishop materialized and guided them up the villa's central stairway. It was Bishop Fellay's first time inside the villa, his first time this close to Pope Benedict, and he was happy to see that at least some of the pomp survived. This was, after all, the residence of the supreme pontiff, the head of the church; the protocol reminded people of that. What a shame, he reflected, that the Vatican had suppressed several of the palace guard units—another mistake engendered by the Second Vatican Council.

The two men arrived at the villa's main floor and were shown through a series of rooms, some of them looking down on Lake Albano, a bowl of blue in one of the collapsed volcanoes that form the Alban Hills. Fellay checked his watch; they were right on time for the eleven-thirty audience. But the pope, it seemed, was running late. They'd have to wait.

At first glance Fellay and Schmidberger could have been brothers: the same receding hairline, graying at the temples, the same steely eyes and ramrod posture. But Fellay made a less severe impression than his confrere; when he smiled, his face spread into a muffinlike oval, with a big dimple in the middle of his chin. As head of the Society of Saint Pius X, the traditionalist order founded by the late Archbishop Marcel Lefebvre, Fellay was technically a rebel. Today, however, in the heart of the papal court, he felt the strong pull of the church's universal center. At forty-seven, he was twelve years younger than Schmidberger and less experienced in dealing with the Vatican; his face betrayed the excitement of a first audience with the pope.

Both men had mixed feelings about being here. They had asked for the meeting to offer a sign of goodwill toward the new pope. Fellay, though, did not intend to beg for anything. He felt he would be negotiating from strength—in numbers, in vocations, in his order's solid faith—and with the knowledge that Pope Benedict would like nothing better than to reconcile with the Lefebvrists and close this painful chapter of church history. The pope was clearly sympathetic toward them on liturgical matters, Fellay thought. But what about all the rest of the post–Vatican II changes in the church? And what about the pope's past dealings with the group?

More than seventeen years earlier, in 1988, when Archbishop Lefebvre stood on the brink of schism, Pope John Paul II had asked Cardinal Joseph Ratzinger to lead a last-ditch effort to keep Lefebvre and his followers in the fold. Although Ratzinger was authorized to make concessions, he discovered, to his deep disappointment, that the Lefebvrists had an unbending rejection of the teachings of the Second Vatican Council—on ecumenism, liturgy, interreligious dialogue, collegiality among bishops and religious liberty, just to name a few. If the council represented the church's opening to the world, the Lefebvrists wanted to close the door again. They saw the council and its aftermath as a long and painful betrayal of the faith.

The crisis of 1988 was precipitated by Archbishop Lefebvre's announced plan to ordain a bishop to carry on his work. At eighty-one, he wanted to protect his legacy, and the best protection lay in firming up the organization's own hierarchy. Lefebvre's Priestly Society, known commonly as the SSPX, had been formally dissolved by the Vatican in 1975 but was thriving in Switzerland. Lefebvre had violated any number of Vatican instructions, but ordaining a bishop against papal orders was a much more serious matter. As Cardinal Ratzinger told the group in 1988, it would be viewed as "schismatic," and the punishment for everyone involved would be excommunication. Lefebvre and his aides—including Father Franz Schmidberger—did not seem intimidated by this threat.

Despite Lefebvre's intransigence, Ratzinger had nearly pulled off a reconciliatory coup. As the ordination ceremony approached, he designed a protocol that seemed to give Lefebvre and his followers a sweet deal: a degree of autonomy as a religious order, permission to use the pre–Vatican II Tridentine Mass and Vatican-approved ordination of an SSPX bishop. In return the Society was asked to promise its fidelity to the church and the pope, to accept the validity of the new Mass and to engage in a "nonpolemical" study of the reforms of the Second Vatican Council.

An objective observer would have said the SSPX had won the most meaningful concessions, and in fact Lefebvre signed the protocol in Ratzinger's presence, which was then forwarded to Pope John Paul for final approval. But the next day, after a sleepless night, Lefebvre had second thoughts. He smelled a trap, he told his aides, and decided to renege on the agreement. He announced he would go ahead with his planned ordination, with or without papal approval, except now the number of new bishops would be three. The actual number turned out to be four, ordained on June 30, 1988, at the SSPX headquarters in Écône, Switzerland. The ordination made headlines around the world and thrilled Lefebvre's hard-line followers. Pope John Paul was crushed at this act of disobedience, and the Vatican immediately announced the excommunication of Lefebvre and his new bishops. Bernard Fellay, a thirty-year-old

Swiss protégé of Lefebvre, was the second youngest of the four bishops illicitly ordained that day.

Given past history, then, today's meeting with the new pope was nothing short of amazing. To many in the church, Fellay represented disloyalty, so it was no wonder that Catholic liberals were aghast.

After waiting some forty minutes the two priests were led quickly into a small, simply furnished chamber. Standing at his desk was Pope Benedict. The pope, his tuft of white hair crowned by a zucchetto, smiled and greeted them individually, recognizing Schmidberger at once. Bishop Fellay's strongest ally stood on the other side of the room: Cardinal Darío Castrillón Hoyos, a Colombian who had for years tried and failed to broker a deal between the Vatican and the Lefebvrists. Cardinal Castrillón flashed a smile and regarded his guests with hawklike eyes. He had put his influence with Benedict on the line and wanted to finally see some progress. The three took their seats before the pope, who sat down behind his desk and immediately began speaking in French. Fellay had hoped to converse in the pope's native German, as a sign of deference to the pontiff, but French it would be.

Thirty-five minutes later, an aide opened the door, signaling that the audience was over. As he stood to leave, Fellay felt the meeting had gone as well as it could have. The pope had been cordial, there had been no arguments and some proposals were left on the table.

True, the pope had rather glided over the specific accusations that Bishop Fellay had made in a letter to the pontiff a few days earlier. The letter had characterized in dramatic terms what the Society viewed as the church's deterioration, referring pointedly to Pope John Paul II's "silent apostasy"—the Lefebvrists' catchall term of denunciation against the late pope. It was John Paul himself who had first used the phrase "silent apostasy" to describe the weakening of the faith in Europe, but the Lefebvrists had turned the expression against him, charging that his brand of ecumenism and interreligious dialogue had aided and abetted this wholesale apostasy, or turning away from truth. Fellay's letter had gone on to quote approvingly from Pope Benedict's famous sermon a few days before his election, which described the church as "a boat taking on water on every side." The letter's not so subtle point was that if Ratzinger would only stay true to his convictions, he would find himself on the same page as the Le-febvrists.

To illustrate the ecclesial and liturgical deterioration, Fellay had appended to his letter a collection of "scandalous" photos from Masses around the world. For years a conservative organization called Traditio had been building an online photo gallery of liturgical offenses, a kind of "hall of shame" that documented liberties taken with the post–Vatican II Mass. The photos showed African liturgies using what appeared to be pagan masks or voodoo costumes, priests celebrating Mass with Doritos or peanut butter cookies instead of the traditional host, a "puppet liturgy" in which a ventriloquist priest celebrated Mass through a dummy, and various other Masses featuring clowns, jugglers and even a stand-up comedian. One notable photo recorded a "cheesehead Mass" in which Archbishop Timothy Dolan, then of Milwaukee, wore, instead of a miter, a cheddar-colored hat shaped like a wedge of cheese. (In actual fact, Dolan had donned the headgear for a moment during his sermon, to get a laugh.)

Fellay's letter seemed designed to introduce a tone of righteous indignation in their papal audience, but Benedict had remarked simply that there was no need to discuss these matters in detail. Evidently the pope did not want this meeting to turn into a liberal-bashing session.

Benedict did listen, however, as Fellay and Schmidberger cataloged some of the ongoing projects of the SSPX—often undertaken against the objections of local bishops. One example cited by Fellay was the lawsuit the Society had initiated two years earlier in Argentina that had succeeded, temporarily, in stopping the sale of contraceptives. Incredibly, he informed the pontiff, their action was labeled "terrorist" by the Archdiocese of Córdoba! They told the pope how in Lucerne, Switzerland, the SSPX had denounced a gay pride procession that ended up in a Catholic church, an event that met with total indifference on the part of the local bishop.

These telltale episodes formed a prelude to three specific requests that Fellay and Schmidberger now placed before the pope: full freedom for their order to celebrate the Tridentine Mass, withdrawal of the 1988 excommunications and the accusation of schism against the Lefebvrist bishops, and establishment of a reentry "structure" for the SSPX—one that would preserve its status as a traditionalist order and give it some autonomy from local bishops.

The most urgent request, the provision that the Lefebvrists hoped would launch a rollback of the liberal era in the church, was general permission to celebrate the Tridentine Mass—the Latin liturgy that had been used for four centuries before the Second Vatican Council, the liturgy of generations of Catholics who had followed along in their missals, the liturgy that had been unceremoniously replaced by Pope Paul VI with the "new Mass" of 1970. One of the distinctive characteristics of the Tridentine rite was that the priest celebrated Mass facing in the same direction as the congregation, toward God. Liberal critics always got this wrong, in Fellay's view, by arguing that the celebrant had "his back to the people." Didn't they care about a priest's turning his back on God?

Pope John Paul had approved limited use of the Tridentine rite, but traditionalist groups had to obtain their local bishop's permission to celebrate it. Those bishops often refused, fearing that offering the old Mass would at best confuse their faithful and at worst divide local parishes along liturgical fault lines. Now Fellay was requesting something far more radical. He wanted the Vatican to declare that the Tridentine Mass could be used anywhere and anytime, because no one had ever had the authority to abrogate it. The pope himself, back when he had been cardinal, had once said as much in a book. Was it too much to ask him to acknowledge that now?

The pope, to Fellay's relief, did not close the door on the issue of the Tridentine rite, or even on setting up a special status for the SSPX. But he was soon veering in another direction, emphasizing some basic principles, such as unity with Rome and respect for the teachings of the Second Vatican Council. He made it clear that the "spirit of the council" and the changes Vatican II introduced were not optional—even if, of course, they must all be understood in the light of Tradition. In short, whatever liturgical and organizational concessions he might be willing to make, the pope was not about to create a dissident cell that would have license to undermine the council's legacy or the Vatican's policies. Nor, despite Cardinal Castrillón's eagerness to move forward, could the pope promise Fellay and Schmidberger a timeline—even for such a straightforward act as freeing up the Tridentine Mass. Benedict seemed to hint that he wanted the world's bishops on board, but Fellay knew that that alone could be a dealbreaker. The bishops would object, as they always had. The question was, would the new pope make them accept his decision?

All this churned in Fellay's mind as he and Schmidberger walked back through the villa's sumptuous rooms, escorted by the archbishop, when Fellay suddenly stopped. "Wait!" he cried aloud. "We forgot the blessing." They had left the pope in his studio without making the most elemental request: that the pope bless them. Fellay turned to their escort to ask whether they could go back, but the archbishop told them it was too late.

The car was waiting for them down in the papal courtyard, ready to take them the scant two miles to the SSPX residence in the nearby town of Albano. Outside the papal villa's main entrance, the journalists would be whimpering when they learned they'd been circumvented and that Fellay had no intention of meeting with them before returning to Switzerland. But the moment was just too delicate to risk a media firestorm.

A few minutes later, as they turned into the Albano driveway, a flash went off on the right side of the car: An alert Reuters photographer had managed to take a picture, after all. It went out on the wire with a caption identifying a smiling Bishop Bernard Fellay as he returned from his top secret meeting with the pope.

"That's not Fellay. That's Schmidberger!"

The reporters huddled; agencies checked their files. In fact, the photo *was* of Father Schmidberger; the two priests did look alike, after all.

A corrected caption moved on the Reuters wire, but not before conservative Catholic blogs around the world had picked up the photo and immortalized the error in cyberspace. The blogs were already feeding furiously on the pope-Lefebvrist meeting, which they saw as a litmus test of the new pontificate. But ultimately they had to rely on the reporters on the scene, who in this case had embarrassingly little information.

Back in the Vatican press office, a brief official communiqué was being parsed for hidden significance. The crux was in two sentences: "The meeting took place in a climate of love for the church and of desire to arrive at perfect communion. Although aware of the difficulties, the will to proceed step by step and in a reasonable time frame was demonstrated."

The Vatican seemed to be attributing a spirit of goodwill to Fellay, which bode well for the Lefebvrists. But talk of advancing in stages was a red flag to some of Fellay's own supporters, whose greatest fear was being strung along by Rome in an endless game of "beat the Vatican"—a game they felt they could never win.

Later the same day Fellay published his own statement on the SSPX Web site, expressing his hope that "the Holy Father might find the strength to put an end to the crisis in the church by 'restoring all things in Christ.'" Fellay's strategy, in fact, was to present his order's grievances not as a small problem that could be solved bureaucratically, but rather as the catalyst for a new and necessary "pontificate of restoration" for the entire church. The SSPX, in effect, wanted to be seen as easing Benedict away from the feel-good pronouncements of his first few months in office and toward what he'd obviously been preparing for his entire life: an uncompromising return to Tradition, and the undoing of Vatican II.

Reporters trying to make sense of all this felt as if they were reading tea leaves. Because writing about philosophical differences over the Second Vatican Council would produce deadly copy, they needed an issue, a demand, a single cause on which to focus. That was served up a few weeks later, when it came out that Fellay had indeed asked for restoration of the Tridentine Mass and that the pope was seriously considering the matter.

I called one of my usual sources on matters Lefebvrist, one of the many Vatican officials who trade anonymity for being able to vent on the phone. It gets lonely in those Vatican offices, and a reporter's call is often the highlight of the day. I call this source the Warbler; he delivered his information in long, liquid trills.

"If the Great Minds here think they can trust these people, they're in for a rude awakening. We've been down this road before. They get to the brink, and then paranoia sets in. They're fanatics. I'm convinced they're a sect, and when they do come back they'll need deprogramming, because otherwise they're useless. They're troublemakers."

The Warbler was just getting started. I sat back and listened to a thirty-minute performance.

"I personally think if we'd met this mad Lefebvrist propaganda head-on eighteen years ago we'd be in a better position now. But basically we've done nothing to counter it. And as a result, they consider the old Mass their property. Well, it's not their property. It belongs to the church.

"Now that is where our new pope may be going. He's certainly not operating under any illusions with the SSPX, after dealing with them in 1988. So if he broadens permission on the Tridentine rite, he'll be breaking the Lefebvrist monopoly on it.

"But that still leaves the SSPX orbiting around out there. You can give them the Mass. But it won't satisfy them. They'll always keep upping the ante. Now they want the bishops cut out of the loop—so no one has to get the bishop's permission to use the old rite. How can you just bypass the bishops? And what else would this incite? You could have a handful of people in every parish start making all kinds of noises, saying, 'We told you all along to schedule a Tridentine Mass; now here it is in print—*do it!*' Then what? We don't exactly have policemen to send down to take care of these things."

Despite the Lefebvrists' reputation for having friends in high places at the Vatican, most officials I spoke with had a deep mistrust of the SSPX and, to be honest, no particular nostalgia for the Tridentine Mass. They also knew that a real reversal on ecumenism or interreligious dialogue would simply not happen, nor was it desirable; the church could not, as the Lefebvrists seemed to want, go back to treating non-Catholics as the enemy and non-Christians as infidels. On a more personal level, many of these Vatican officials were veterans of John Paul II's organizational team and felt affronted by SSPX leaders' sarcastic and open disdain of the late pope.

Cardinal Francis Arinze, a conservative Nigerian who headed the Vatican's liturgy congregation, told me bluntly that the church could not offer the Lefebvrists a reconciliation-at-any-price deal. "The pope cannot disown Vatican II in order to make the Lefebvrists happy," Arinze said, leaning in for emphasis.

At the end of 2005, however, in a pre-Christmas speech to members of the Roman Curia, Pope Benedict hinted that while he could not "disown" Vatican II, he could at least correct it. The pope made no mention of the SSPX or the Tridentine Mass, but he did present the Second Vatican Council as a problem that needed a solution. Naturally, he did not take on the council or its landmark documents directly; where the church had gone wrong, he suggested, was in "implementation" of the council. And the results of this implementation, he said, had been disastrous. Ever the historian, the pope evoked Saint Basil's famous description of the confusion that followed the fourth-century Council of Nicea: As in a naval battle in the dark, the raucous shouting and incomprehensible chatter "has now filled almost the whole of the church, falsifying through excess or failure the right doctrine of the faith."

As the pope read the text in the frescoed Clementine Hall, the Curia cardinals began stirring in their gilded chairs. This not so subtle attack on the church's direction over the last forty years neatly divided the post–Vatican II church into two factions: those who misconstrued the council as a clean break with the past and those who understood it as part of an ongoing renewal of the church's unchanging mission. Benedict described this division in what would later become a catchphrase among his most ardent supporters: the "hermeneutics of rupture" versus the "hermeneutics of continuity." "Hermeneutics" is a scholarly term referring to the principles of interpretation, and the pope used it deliberately to lend his words authority. His speech, which would be read and reread in coming months, essentially announced a backing away from some of the post–Vatican II innovations. But which ones? Certainly it was laying the groundwork for a major shift, but virtually no one among his own Roman Curia listeners had a clear idea of what that would mean in practical terms.

Several weeks later, in February of 2006, the pope called a meeting of twenty top Roman Curia heads and asked them to review a possible reconciliation scenario with the Lefebvrists. Normally, when there's a foregone conclusion at the Vatican, journalists can spot it coming. Influential cardinals give interviews presenting the case, and soon it builds to a coordinated chorus of acclamation. But on this occasion the Curia members were not singing in harmony. They were unusually quiet and guarded on the topic, and did not sound very hopeful about reaching an agreement with Fellay. There was, however, one vociferous exception.

Cardinal Darío Castrillón Hoyos was a man who might have been pope. Back in the late 1990s all it took was a long article by fellow Colombian

Gabriel García Márquez, the Nobel Prize–winning author, to send Castrillón into the upper ranks of the *papabili*. The article was widely read by journalists, who at the time were desperately trying to fill up their "top ten" lists of papal candidates. The portrait drawn by García Márquez and others was flattering: Castrillón was a theological conservative but a pastor of the people, a voice for the weak, a man who had once donned civilian clothing to enter the home of drug lord Pablo Escobar and ask him to confess his sins. A bishop in Colombia's coffee production center of Pereira for more than twenty years, Castrillón was said to walk the streets of the city at night to look after the safety of beggars, children and prostitutes. His sharply worded sermons were credited with stopping the killing of street people in Pereira, and he built a reputation for social courage. When he was called to Rome in 1996 to head the Congregation for the Clergy, it seemed to offer him a chance to build up his credentials as a papal contender with experience in the Roman Curia.

But once at the Vatican, Castrillón's pastoral side began to be eclipsed. Like nearly everyone there, he spent most of his time in his office, dealing with paperwork or holding closed-door meetings. Contact with the press and public ended, and he became one of the Vatican's shadow figures. When he did show up in the media, his new position tended to underscore his conservative views, particularly on liberation theology. Then came the sexual abuse crisis, and with it Castrillón's chances of becoming pope evaporated overnight.

Early in 2002, at the height of revelations about priestly sexual abuse in the United States, Castrillón had a rare appearance in the Vatican's press hall. As he came into the roomful of reporters, he made the sign of the cross—the first time I had seen that happen. It was as if he were entering the lion's den.

Vatican press conferences are 90 percent scripted, and the cardinal knew the day's game plan. He would present the pope's annual letter to priests, which meant delivering a long speech and fielding a few questions. The pope's missive this year, however, contained a reference to the sex abuse crisis—which meant the topic was fair game for reporters, and that Castrillón would be in for a grilling. The press relished the chance to talk to the man responsible for the world's clergy. On the other hand, the occasion offered the Vatican a unique opportunity as well: By addressing questions head-on, acknowledging failures and vowing to clean up the mess, Castrillón could single-handedly swing public relations momentum in the Vatican's direction.

What happened instead was a worst-case scenario for the Vatican. Castrillón's face betrayed a sense of haughty annoyance from the moment he took his seat on the dais. He glanced sharply at his audience from behind oversized silver-rimmed glasses and began reading his speech, which referred only obliquely to sexual abuse. When he finished, I asked the first question, a straightforward one: What steps did the Vatican plan to take to ensure that priestly sex abuse would not recur in the future? Instead of answering, Castrillón scribbled some quick notes and announced he would take more queries on this topic before responding. Consequently, one after another, reporters asked the obvious: Would the Vatican support a "zero tolerance" policy for priest predators? Did Cardinal Bernard Law of Boston have the Vatican's support? Why wasn't the pope speaking publicly about this scandal, instead of making indirect references in a published letter? The cardinal's characteristic smile had now become a smirk. Although Castrillón kept making notes on more than a dozen questions, in the end, explaining that he didn't want to take any "risks," he pulled out a two-page prepared statement and read it. It was a defensive message, peppered with sarcastic asides, which insisted that the church had always been severe with pedophile priests, "even before it ended up on the front pages of international newspapers," and that it didn't need to take lessons from others. He cited a U.S. study that estimated only 0.3 percent of priests were pedophiles. (In fact, later studies showed that 4 percent of priests had been accused of sexual abuse of minors.) He questioned whether other categories of professionals—doctors, teachers or journalists, for example—might not have similar hidden problems and wondered why no studies were being done on them and "the money they have paid to the victims." In any case, he said, priestly sex abuse reflected the "pan-sexuality and licentiousness" of the dominant culture.

Perhaps his most peculiar remark was when he noted that most of the reporters' questions had been asked in English. "That in itself is an X-ray and offers an outline of the problem," he observed. Some took this as a suggestion that clerical sexual abuse was an Anglo-Saxon issue—not one that concerned the entire church—though, from the cardinal's perspective, it seemed more as if "the problem" was the exaggerated interest shown by English-language media.

Even for a Vatican press corps that was used to being stonewalled, this performance was frustrating. When Robert Kaiser, a sometimes cantankerous and always entertaining correspondent for *Newsweek,* shouted out to the cardinal, "Could you please answer our questions!" an irritated Castrillón replied: "I listened to your questions. I hope you will listen to me when I'm speaking." For many reporters, Castrillón now epitomized the cover-up mentality and confirmed their suspicion that the Vatican was incapable of appreciating the depth of damage caused by sexually abusive priests.

Even inside the Vatican, some officials were shaking their heads at Castrillón's blunder. His name quickly disappeared from *papabili* tote boards, and three years later, when the next papal conclave was held, Castrillón was one of five cardinals singled out as "morally unacceptable" by SNAP, the Survivors Network of Those Abused by Priests.

By then, however, Castrillón had stopped talking about sex abuse and had turned his attention to another problem dearer to his heart: making peace with the Lefebvrists. Besides heading the Congregation for the Clergy, Castrillón was president of the Vatican's Ecclesia Dei commission, a unit formed in 1988 to reintegrate followers of Archbishop Lefebvre. The idea behind Ecclesia Dei (Latin for "the Church of God") was that the many priests and good Catholics who had blindly followed Lefebvre would one day want to come back to Mother Church. The commission could make that happen, brokering deals with small groups of disaffected Lefebvrists around the world. But in truth, the deals were few, and as the years went by the commission did less and less. Its tiny office was staffed by only three people.

In the year 2000, however, a strange thing happened, and it caught Cardinal Castrillón's attention. In the middle of that summer, Bishop Fellay arrived in Rome with several thousand of his followers for a Holy Year pilgrimage.

◆ ◆ ◆

I recognized Bishop Fellay by his pectoral cross, which hung on two wide silver loops of chain. This ultratraditionalist was much younger than I had expected, only forty-two at the time. It was August, it was hot in Rome and Holy Year 2000 was in full swing. Fellay stood in the midday sun in front of the Basilica of Saint John Lateran and amiably answered my questions, occasionally blotting his brow with a white handkerchief. A Holy Year visit by a group of excommunicated Catholics? Wasn't that kind of like crashing the party?

"We don't think of ourselves as outsiders in Rome. Our presence is a kind of proof that we are Catholics and that we want to be Catholics," Fellay said.

And anyway, he added, they didn't consider themselves "schismatic" or excommunicated. The Lefebvrists had always questioned the validity of the excommunication, he explained, and even some Vatican officials agreed with them.

If their pilgrimage wasn't a provocation, I asked, was it designed to open a dialogue with the Vatican?

Fellay did not sound too hopeful about that. There was little prospect for resolving their differences, he said, as long as the Vatican insisted that the SSPX accept the revised Roman rite for Mass.

Were they impressed with the Vatican's Holy Year festivities?

Fellay paused to measure his words. The moment was significant, he said, and his group didn't want to be prevented from celebrating one of the church's oldest traditions. That said, however, he couldn't help registering his disapproval of Pope John Paul's Holy Year efforts to reach out to other Christian churches and apologize for the sins of church members over the last two thousand years.

"This begging for forgiveness has cast a great shadow on the church," he said.

Later that day Bishop Fellay celebrated Mass on the dusty Oppian hill across from the Colosseum, stating in his sermon that church Tradition (which was always spelled with a capital "T") was being "crucified" by more than thirty-five years of Vatican-mandated changes. "We ask the Holy Father to give us back the Mass," he told his congregation. Nearby, on a grassy mound above the sumptuous Golden House once inhabited by the Emperor Nero, hundreds of people lined up for open-air confessions.

The highlight of the pilgrimage was a procession into Saint Peter's Basilica and through the Holy Door. Although their visit was not on the Vatican's official agenda of Holy Year 2000 events, the Lefebvrists were allowed to enter Saint Peter's and pray, as long as they didn't celebrate Mass. They took their time lining up, and the gathering in Saint Peter's Square was an impressive sight. Marching behind more than two hundred priests were about five thousand lay members who carried rosaries, prayer books and banners as they chanted a litany of saints in Latin. From the many Vatican offices facing the square, monsignors peered from windows. It reminded older prelates of the Holy Years past, when pilgrims arrived at Saint Peter's with an air of penitence—not shuffling in shorts, pointing and gawking like tourists, sipping from their water bottles. That, too, had been part of Bishop Fellay's plan. He was here to remind people how faith was genuinely expressed: not the scripted Holy Year circus drawn up by Vatican planners that relied on mega-liturgies and papal appearances on the Jumbotron screens, but a more personal and pious experience motivated by deep faith. Winding slowly through the square, the Lefebvrists won some sympathy among Vatican officials that day. As public relations, it was a brilliant move.

As the SSPX group walked back downtown from Saint Peter's, some of them passed a nondescript building where a uniformed porter sidled up to them and said, "You gave us a strong lesson." He was, in fact, the doorman for Cardinal Joseph Ratzinger and other top Vatican officials. Fellay heard about the remark, and took it as a sign.

Among those peeking from his window was Cardinal Castrillón Hoyos. He decided to invite the four SSPX bishops to dinner; three of them showed up. Throughout the meal Castrillón was so gracious that he made his guests uneasy. He spoke on and on about how close they were, playing down their differences and telling them, "Your fruits are good. Hence, the Holy Spirit is there." Fellay listened in amazement. The cardinal seemed to be trying to diminish the problem, almost to the point of saying there was no problem. Fellay decided to be specific, and asked Castrillón about his views on the Mass. "I am not an expert," the cardinal replied. In other words, he wouldn't be drawn into a debate over liturgical rules and errors.

Castrillón kept assuring the bishops that there was actually so little that separated them: They believed in the same God and the same Eucharist. Here his Lefebvrist guests began to demur, and a short while later English Bishop Richard Williamson cooled off the atmosphere by declaring to the cardinal, "Your Eminence, it's two religions." Castrillón seemed taken aback but would learn in coming years that Williamson was by far the most uncompromising of the SSPX bishops, and the most distrustful of the Roman Curia.

Castrillón's performance had not, in fact, done much to inspire confidence in the others at the table. Fellay recalled the cardinal's telling them at one point, "I don't want the Roman Curia to know what we speak about." *So that's the level of trust* inside *the Vatican,* Fellay thought to himself.

Nevertheless, within weeks Castrillón had designed a new tentative plan to bring the Lefebvrists back into the fold. It was based on two elements that would become familiar over the next several years: allowing wider use of the Tridentine rite ("Give us back the Mass") and reintegrating the SSPX as a personal prelature, a semiautonomous status like that enjoyed by Opus Dei.

Pope John Paul II had little patience with the Lefebvrists and even less eagerness to reinstate the Tridentine Mass. He saw both issues in terms of obedience, or rather disobedience. Archbishop Lefebvre had broken his heart by defying his order in 1988, but, more important, inflicted a wound upon the church. The Tridentine rite was the Lefebvrists' perennial rallying cause, and the pope's position was clear: Once they fully accepted the new Mass and the other changes of Vatican II, then and only then would he consider letting them celebrate freely with the old liturgy.

Cardinal Castrillón was lobbying hard for a deal and used every means at his disposal. A few months after the Holy Year pilgrimage, a Catholic magazine with connections to Castrillón, *Trenta Giorni (Thirty Days),* published an interview with Bishop Fellay. It was full of positive comments from Rome, and Castrillón went around showing it to Vatican officials, including the pope. In fact, the cardinal was using the interview to lay the groundwork for a meeting between the pope and SSPX leaders. For his own part Fellay was surprised when he opened his copy of the magazine and found that all his negative comments about the Vatican had disappeared. The interview had been sanitized for Vatican consumption.

"I have shown the pope your interview in *Thirty Days*, and he has given me the mandate to solve your problem," Castrillón told Fellay proudly.

"I'm sorry," Fellay replied, "but this article is not fair to the reality." Castrillón explained that it didn't matter, and Fellay then understood: It had been a ploy to get discussions moving.

At the end of 2000 Castrillón scheduled a first major meeting with Fellay in Rome. Fellay had by now decided that playing hardball was the only way to deal with the Vatican, and told Castrillón that whatever might be proposed, the SSPX was going to "continue the fight against liberalism, modernism and Freemasonry." Castrillón later quoted that line in a report he gave to Pope John Paul; when the pope read it, he pointed to the statement and said, "That's us! That's us!" What he meant was that he felt his own pontificate was fighting a similar battle, but that sentiment only illustrated the actual gulf between him and the Lefebvrists.

Fellay took a similar hard line with Castrillón about the Mass. Not only should the Lefebvrists be able to use the Tridentine rite, but the new Mass should be recognized as wrong—what was specifically Catholic in the liturgy has been removed from it. Castrillón flinched. "No, we cannot say so because the pope has approved it," he said. Fellay then went on to attack the Vatican's policies on religious liberty, collegiality, the changes made in the new Code of Canon Law, telling Castrillón bluntly, "We don't trust you— not you personally, but Rome." Fellay later said he was astounded that the cardinal had endured it all. "I threw a lot of punches and I was really amazed to see how much he was able to absorb and still continue in a pleasant way. I really admired that."

At the end of their meeting, Castrillón made an offhand remark about preparing an agreement to sign. Fellay told him that that would be impossible at this stage, but Castrillón seemed undaunted. Fellay left the Vatican pondering the consequences of the encounter and determined not to be rushed into anything. Then, later that night, he got a call from an excited Castrillón saying they were to meet with Pope John Paul at eleven o'clock the next morning: The pope had made time for them right before his general audience. Fellay begged off; things seemed to be moving too fast. He told Castrillón he had to catch a plane to Switzerland at noon, and important business awaited him back home. He couldn't change his schedule, because all the other flights to Zurich were fully booked. "I'll take care of that," Castrillón said, and within an hour had found Fellay a seat on an afternoon flight.

Castrillón and Fellay showed up at the Apostolic Palace just before eleven the next morning, but there was a problem: Apparently the cardinal had gotten the time wrong. The general audience began at eleven; they were supposed to have arrived twenty minutes earlier. "Where have you been?" the pope's secretary, clearly upset, demanded. "The Holy Father is waiting for you. Saint Peter's Square—fifty thousand people—is waiting for the pope, who is waiting for you! It's already been a quarter of an hour!" They were led to a private chapel in the papal apartment, where the pope joined them. All three knelt in silence before the Blessed Sacrament for two minutes. Pope John Paul recited the Our Father in Latin and turned toward his guests. He asked Castrillón if he'd been able to discuss matters with Fellay, and Castrillón said he had. The pontiff then wished them a happy new year, blessed them both and handed Fellay a rosary. *That was it*, thought Fellay. *Not much.* The pope had set aside twenty minutes for them, but they had missed the window of opportunity.

A few minutes later, the cheers from pilgrims in Saint Peter's Square reverberated up into the small office where Castrillón and Fellay were now conferring with the pope's secretary. Castrillón had in his hands a written report on his discussions with Fellay the day before. This apparently was the "agreement" Castrillón had spoken about so expectantly. He had hoped to give it personally to the pope, but now he would have to leave it with the papal secretary. Fellay, however, asked to see the text, and immediately wanted to make some changes. Castrillón was a little dismayed but told the pope's secretary to write down Fellay's clarifications. Things quickly got bogged down.

"If I understand you well, you would like to keep some of your traditions," the secretary said.

"No!" Fellay replied. "All of them!"

When they finished, Castrillón proudly took Fellay to a window of the Apostolic Palace. They looked down and saw the pope, a tiny figure in white, blessing the vast crowd in Saint Peter's Square. It seemed to be the cardinal's way of saying, This is the universal church, and you can be a part of it. But Fellay had mixed feelings about the whole affair, and a sense that he was surrounded by smoke and mirrors.

Cardinal Castrillón kept up the pressure after Fellay had returned to Switzerland, telling him the pope wanted things settled by Easter. But on Good Friday Castrillón phoned to tell him that progress had stalled in the face of too much opposition from bishops. That didn't surprise Fellay; he had heard that French Cardinal Jean-Marie Lustiger had gone personally to the pope and warned him that if he allowed the SSPX to work freely in France, sixty-five French bishops would "enter into disobedience." The stakes were that high.

Over the following year the goodwill generated by the Holy Year pilgrimage slowly dissipated. Castrillón stopped calling. It seemed to Fellay that the dance was over. The aging pope seemed to have concluded that a deal with the Lefebvrists was not worth the risk.

But Castrillón had not given up.

The Basilica of Santa Maria Maggiore is a strange and beautiful place. It's the best preserved of Rome's ancient basilicas, built in the fourth century on the Esquiline hill after a miraculous snowstorm in August supposedly traced the outline of the church. The basilica honors the Virgin Mary and was constructed upon the site of a former pagan temple dedicated to the fertility goddess Cybele, whose male followers would ritually castrate themselves, dress in women's garments and take on female identities. The church was rebuilt in the fifth century and remodeled in Renaissance times, its ceiling gilded with the first gold that Columbus brought back from the Americas. When the morning light reflects off the mosaics along the nave, the church looks like a giant jewelry box. Today it is the burial place of popes and a popular stop for pilgrims.

The basilica has always had a connection to what is sometimes called the *Roma nera*—the "black" Roman network of aristocratic families that has survived from the Middle Ages. Fiercely Catholic, these families enjoyed positions of privilege in the church and had strong connections to the Vatican. In the mid-1960s they viewed the Second Vatican Council—

correctly—as another threat to their already fading grandeur. Some of the chapels in Santa Maria Maggiore preserve that former influence in an almost timeless fashion; the most sumptuous is the Borghese Chapel, decorated with lapis lazuli and agate, which houses the famous icon of the Virgin Mary known as *Salus Populi Romani,* or "Health of the Roman People," an image that is believed to have saved the city from plague.

In the spring of 2003 an Italian group close to the old Roman nobility asked to celebrate the Tridentine Mass in Santa Maria Maggiore. That gave Cardinal Castrillón an idea. The request itself was not particularly noteworthy, but if he—a Roman cardinal—celebrated the Mass, it would be. No cardinal had gone to a major Rome basilica to celebrate the old rite since it had been replaced with the new Mass in 1969. It would outrage the liberals, but it would underscore an important point: that the Tridentine Mass still belonged to the universal church. That was the basis of Castrillón's argument to Pope John Paul II: In one stroke the church could reclaim part of its Tradition and hold out an olive branch to the Lefebvrists. John Paul warily agreed.

And so it happened that on a Saturday afternoon in May 2003 Santa Maria Maggiore began filling up with an unusual mix of people. The old families were there, the women dutifully donning black mantillas; the uniformed Knights of the Holy Sepulchre in their white capes; and rows of seminarians, abbots and members of religious orders, many of them toting their worn missals from forty years earlier. But among the congregants were youths in jeans and casually dressed middle-aged Catholics, some of whom seemed to observe the proceedings as if they were watching a parade of vintage automobiles. They snapped photos as Cardinal Castrillón led the entrance procession down the main aisle beneath a ten-foot-tall cross, surrounded by a thick cloud of incense. His elaborate lace surplice added a touch of elegance; hanging from his arm was a maniple, a cloth band whose use had been suppressed in the modern liturgy. As Gregorian chant echoed through the basilica, the procession passed a chapel holding the tomb of Saint Pius V, who had codified the Tridentine Mass in the 1500s.

In the front row facing the altar perched five cardinals, their red birettas placed carefully on top of the wooden kneelers. None was noteworthy, with one exception: Cardinal Bernard Law, who had resigned in disgrace from the Archdiocese of Boston a few months earlier. His presence was odd, but should have been a clue to journalists, who would be shocked a year later when Law was named the archpriest of Santa Maria Maggiore, a comfortable and prestigious position in Rome.

The Mass, preceded by a recital of the rosary and a litany of saints, lasted two hours, which by itself may have quenched some of the nostalgia among those in attendance. The highlight was Castrillón's sermon, which was designed to carry messages all the way to Switzerland:

"The so-called rite of Saint Pius V cannot be considered extinct."

"The old Roman rite retains its right of citizenship in the church, in the multiformity of Catholic rites, both Latin and Eastern."

When people came up for Communion, they knelt at the rail and stuck out their tongues. No one asked for Communion in the hand, another innovation that had found its way into the post–Vatican II church.

For many who attended, the new Mass was where the church had begun to unravel back in the 1960s. It was not just that Latin had been replaced with the vernacular; the new liturgy reflected a revolution in the way the Catholic community worshiped God. For one thing, the celebrant was turned around to face the people, emphasizing the communal aspect of the Mass. For traditionalists, when the priest faced the people, he became an emcee, and the temptation to entertain was strong. No wonder modern priests felt they had to tell jokes and liven up the "audience." The focal point had become the celebrant, not God.

After Vatican II, tabernacles were moved off to the side, a sign to traditionalists that the community was celebrating itself, and no longer the presence of Christ on the altar. Beautiful high altars were smashed into bits, statues of favorite saints were tossed out and anything old was swept out the door. For many Catholics over the age of sixty, those painful memories were still alive.

And what was the result? Mass attendance had fallen to record lows, and fewer and fewer young men wanted to be priests. Couldn't the Vatican see that it had reformed the church right down the drain? For the traditionalists, the Tridentine Mass was the link to a glorious past, the sacred fire they kept burning for a time when church leaders would wake up and see the damage around them.

As he processed out of Santa Maria Maggiore, Castrillón was pleased with himself. He had sent a message to Fellay, but, more important, to the Lefebvrist faithful around the world. This liturgy assured them that they had a home in the modern church and that they didn't have to give up the old Latin Mass. If a Vatican cardinal could celebrate the Tridentine rite in Rome, weren't they all of the same faith? And wasn't it time for reconciliation?

But if traditionalists were intrigued, liberal Catholics were alarmed at what they considered "Tridentine creep." It seemed to confirm their suspicions that Pope John Paul intended to widen use of the old rite, even over the objections of the world's bishops.

The progressives had already become distressed a few days before the Santa Maria Maggiore event, when the Vatican confirmed that it was now giving priests permission to celebrate the Tridentine Mass in a below-ground chapel of Saint Peter's Basilica. For years the Vatican had been aware that small groups of traditionalists had been clandestinely holding Tridentine Masses against basilica rules. They would check in with the sacristy, proceed to an assigned altar with the new missal and then pull the old missal from under their vestments. Now, after getting Castrillón's written permission, they could do it openly—but only in the Hungarian Chapel beneath the main level of Saint Peter's. One experienced Roman cleric noted that the Hungarian Chapel stood immediately next to the tomb of Pope Paul VI, the pope who had banned the Tridentine rite. The priest suggested the juxtaposition could not have been accidental.

"Poor Paolo Sesto must be spinning in his grave," he said.

I phoned Bishop Fellay in Switzerland and asked what he thought of Castrillón's Tridentine Mass. "Without a doubt, it was a good thing, and so we rejoice about it." The Vatican was finally showing "progress in the direction of Tradition." The words were there, but he sounded a little dubious to me. We chatted a while longer, and soon the caveats began. He didn't like the fact that, in his sermon, Castrillón had referred to the papal order of 1988, which had announced the excommunication of SSPX leaders. And he didn't appreciate Castrillón's saying that traditionalists must also accept the revised Roman Mass; that seemed designed to downplay this moment of Tridentine glory.

When I hung up the phone, I wondered whether these two partners could ever really come to an agreement. The misgivings ran so deep.

Not only were they ideological opponents, but each side was fighting internal battles as well. The split between the hard-liners and the accommodationists in the SSPX was an open secret, and extended through the Society's estimated one million followers. As he tiptoed through these preliminary talks with the Vatican, Fellay was constantly looking over his shoulder, at a fellow bishop who could bring it all crashing down at any moment.

Bishop Richard Williamson cut a dashing figure among SSPX loyalists. Silver-haired and imposing, with a piercing gaze that he wielded like a weapon, the English bishop did not brook fools gently. His wry smile betrayed a biting sense of humor that often veered toward sarcasm. A convert from Anglicanism, he had a reputation for flair, wit, energy and incredible money-raising abilities. He mistrusted the Vatican completely and made no attempt to hide it. He was popular with conservative audiences, especially when he criticized "feel-good" culture in all its manifestations, from "the mentality of sweet compassion for homosexuals" to excessive grief for Lady Di. He once famously described *The Sound of Music* as "pornographic soul-rotting slush" that threatened parental authority. Modern feminism, he said, was tied to witchcraft. Many traditionalists thought the Society would have been better off with Williamson at the helm, instead of the "liberal" Fellay, who always seemed to be dealing with the devil. Some felt Williamson was in his heart a secret sedevacantist, one who believed the last true pope was Pope Pius XII and that the pontiffs in office after the Second Vatican Council were illegitimate.

Bishop Williamson viewed Cardinal Castrillón's Tridentine Mass in Rome as little more than good theater. In fact, in the months that followed, talks between the Vatican and the SSPX essentially came to a standstill—something that pleased the traditionalist hard-liners. Then came John Paul's death and Benedict's election. In August of 2005, after learning that Bishop Fellay was preparing to pay pilgrimage to the new pope, Williamson quickly moved into spoiler mode. He tipped off SSPX followers and the press about the meeting a week before it occurred—ironically, as Williamson saw it, on the feast of the Beheading of Saint John the Baptist. In a newsletter Williamson blasted Rome and suggested that Fellay was being naive.

"Have we not heard this same song before? 'Come into my parlor, said the spider to the fly.' The web of deceit has been spun for far too long," Williamson wrote. "In fact, a Rome-SSPX agreement seems impossible. And of course if the Society rejoined Rome, the resistance of Catholic Tradition would carry on without it, and if the pope 'converted,' then instead of the gentle war now being waged on his right by Tradition, he would be faced with a savage war being waged on his left by the cabal of neo-modernists. Either way, the war goes on between the friends and the enemies of the faith of our Lord Jesus Christ."

Fellay's meeting with Pope Benedict did nothing to allay the hard-liners' contempt, which was openly expressed on traditionalist Web sites. Fellay was denounced as "pusillanimous" for failing to meet the press; he should have used the occasion of the papal audience to broadcast the traditionalists' complaints. Fellay and Schmidberger were ridiculed for using a back entrance to and from their papal meeting. One popular site said the two had "put their tails between their legs and 'escaped' out of a side exit, perhaps through the pope's kitchen." Others said it had been a mistake for Fellay to ask that all priests be able to use the Tridentine rite—why would they want "modernist" priests trained in Vatican II celebrating their Mass? The conservative end of the Catholic spectrum had become crowded with traditionalist groups, and they all seemed to have an opinion on how the SSPX should be conducting itself.

Meanwhile, inside the Vatican walls, similar divisions were coming into the open.

Despite popular perceptions, Pope Benedict was not an ardent advocate of the Tridentine Mass, a disposition he made abundantly clear when, as cardinal, he addressed a fifteen-hundred-strong "Catholic Traditionalist Pilgrimage" at the Vatican in 1998. Ratzinger told the old Mass crowd that the Tridentine low Mass, with its whispered prayers at the altar and its silent congregation, "was not what liturgy should be, which is why it was not painful for many people" when it disappeared. He then urged the traditionalists to show respect for their bishop's decisions and do nothing that would undermine the unity of the church.

While Ratzinger was also sharply critical of what he called "exaggerations" in the new Mass—the showmanship, the focus on the congregation instead of God, the weak music, the minimizing of mystery—he always made it clear that what bothered him were the abuses, not the basic reform of the liturgy, which he considered a good thing. It made sense to celebrate Mass in the vernacular, he said. And while he preferred the customary practice of the priest's facing the same direction as the congregation, he felt it would be too confusing to turn things around again.

What concerned Ratzinger most about the new Mass was the way it had been introduced: as a wholesale and abrupt replacement of the old rite. In his view, that was using the Second Vatican Council as a sword to cleave the modern church from its traditions—as he would say as pope, the "hermeneutics of rupture."

Ratzinger therefore tended to support the idea of freeing up the Tridentine alternative, out of respect for the four-hundred-year-old rite and out of pastoral charity for its followers. In that same 1998 speech to traditionalists, he offered them a strategy for reclaiming the Tridentine option: stop opposing the new Mass. If people accepted the beauty of both liturgies, he said, "we can convince bishops that the celebration of the old rite is not divisive."

Now, as Pope Benedict, he was trying to implement that strategy. Yet his intentions were not all that easy to read. In 2006 he called meetings of the world's cardinals and the Roman Curia to solicit their advice. Not surprisingly, there was strong opposition to concessions to the Lefebvrists, and strong doubts about the wisdom of offering an "alternative" liturgy to the world's faithful.

For his part, the pope's own Masses continued to follow the post–Vatican II liturgy, though he did have some changes in mind. Benedict was planning to replace Archbishop Piero Marini, John Paul's chief liturgist, with a more traditionally minded "designer" of papal Masses. The pope brought back older vestments and rediscovered outdated liturgical paraphernalia in Vatican storerooms. Before long he would stop distributing Communion in the hand; instead, those receiving the Eucharist from the pope would kneel and receive it on the tongue, as in the old days. Benedict seemed to be embarking on a liturgical revolution, but with baby steps.

By the spring of 2007 traditionalist Catholic bloggers found themselves tossed between exultation and quiet panic. If they could believe what Vatican officials were hinting, Benedict had already decided to approve the Tridentine option. It would be a brief document issued *motu proprio*, Latin for "on his own initiative." The phrase *motu proprio* soon became so often used that when it appeared in Roman conversation or online, everyone knew what it stood for. But why didn't the pope publish the document? The traditionalists continued to worry that Benedict might lose his resolve and cave in to liberal pressures. They fretted lest he become infected with the Roman Curia's compromise mentality. They prayed for the pope to act with courage, and to act quickly, before some delegation of bishops could dissuade him. Across the Internet they buoyed one another's hopes and spread the latest optimistic rumors. Their message was: Be patient; it's coming. One of the most well-informed blogs was run by a priest who shuttled between Minnesota and Rome, Father John Zuhlsdorf. His oddly named site, *What Does the Prayer Really Say?* sifted through Roman gossip and Vatican communiqués for some nugget of certainty about the pope's intentions. On more hopeful days, Zuhlsdorf ran a photo of a chilled bottle of Veuve Clicquot and two glasses—an image that caught on among other conservative Catholic bloggers. They were ready to pop their corks.

Recycling stories is part of what journalists do, but "the *motu proprio* is coming" was growing stale by the fifth or sixth time it had been revived. Like so many issues in Benedict's two-year-old pontificate, it had been reported as a done deal for so long that when it did happen—if it ever happened—it would seem like old news. Our news service wanted an article on the old rite, but not more speculation, so I decided to hunt down a Tridentine Mass in Pope Benedict's backyard. Surely the Diocese of Rome had given permission, the famous "indult," for local Catholic traditionalists to celebrate the old Mass on a regular basis. But where?

I found it on a sunny Palm Sunday morning in 2007 on a small dead-end street near the Tiber River, less than a mile from Saint Peter's Square, where the pope was celebrating Mass with sixty thousand people. When I arrived, the pews in the tiny Church of San Gregorio dei Muratori—Saint Gregory of the Bricklayers—were quickly filling to capacity. Capacity, however, was only about forty people. Several priests were preparing the altar, the celebrant outfitted in a heavy chasuble from the 1950s and the others in lacy cassocks. I looked around the dim interior and noticed two things: The congregation was young, and many appeared to be American. This was a church for Neocaths.

I stepped outside to do some quick interviews with new arrivals. Coming down the street in a dark fedora was Gary Tarizzo, who turned out to be an airline pilot from Chicago. I asked him what the attraction was for him here and why he wasn't over in Saint Peter's Square instead. "In a word, it's reverence," he said. "There are moments of silence in this Mass, which is important. There's no sense of reverence at a papal Mass—people are eating as if it's a picnic." Tarizzo recounted an occasion when he had just landed in Rome and raced into Saint Peter's Basilica to catch the last half of Pope John Paul II's Mass. He entered as the pope was finishing his sermon and was shocked to find hundreds of people walking out. For them, he said, it was just another stop on the tourist cycle.

I chatted briefly with Eric Hewett, a thirty-two-year-old American from Philadelphia. He had grown interested in the Tridentine Mass as a student of Latin and church history, so he bought a 1962 missal online and started coming to San Gregorio. Was Latin necessary to make sense of the old Mass? I asked. Not really, Hewett said. There was always the parallel text on the right-hand page. And even if you couldn't understand the words, this Mass, he said, had a "coherence of symbols"—the vestments, candles, bells and chant.

I stepped inside, and a bell rang. In came a mini-procession of clergy. One of them lit an incense burner, swinging it skillfully back and forth, and the place filled up with aromatic smoke. As the priest intoned, "*Introibo ad altare dei,*" the smell of incense and the Latin prayers took me back to my own altar boy days in Minnesota. "*Ad Deum qui laetificat iuventutem meam.*" At the age of twelve, I had excelled at memorizing these responses, even the long ones that most altar servers mumbled through. At the time it didn't matter to me what the words signified; the Latin was for the sound, not the meaning. And the sound was beautiful. I still knew the Mass choreography

by heart: the genuflecting, the bows, the diagonal crossings, the lifting of
the priest's chasuble at the consecration, the positioning of the missal, the
handling of the cruets of water and wine. It was complicated, and small errors were not uncommon, but usually no one would notice but the priest.
The hardest thing about being an altar boy, as I remembered it, was the
slight but real risk of a catastrophic accident—tripping over the hem of a
cassock and taking a dive, for example, or dropping the paten during Communion. Of course, there were many lesser opportunities for embarrassment. Even the simple act of lighting the candles before high Mass required
a certain skill. These were the three-foot-tall candles set in high candlesticks on the altar's upper shelf, and to reach them we used a long pole
equipped with a sliding wick. If the candle was a dud and refused to light, it
was the altar boy, not the candle, that was deemed suspect by the congregation. For me, though, the greatest peril of all was laughter—the risk that
during the celebration of the Holy Mass, perhaps stricken by the absurdity
of my own unworthy presence in this liturgical theater, or perhaps looking
at the mismatched socks of my fellow server, I would burst into paroxysms
of uncontrollable laughter, laughter that would inevitably be misconstrued
as sacrilege or blasphemy, and I would be disgraced and blackballed forever
from the Knights of the Altar. Laughter was the real danger, the precipice.
On several occasions, I came very close to the edge. That memory, too, was
still vivid.

Lost in reminiscence, I looked up and realized that the priest was already about to read the Gospel. Next to me Eric Hewett was slowly turning the pages of his missal and offered to share. But I was a million miles
away. This, too, was a vaguely familiar sensation. As a youth, when I
wasn't serving at the altar, I daydreamed my way through many Masses
down in the pew. I always tried to rally around Communion time, and
sometimes listened to the sermon. But I lived for the final blessing, unen-
gaged in the liturgy, and I supposed there were many like me in the pews
of my Minnesota parish. As I looked around the Church of San Gregorio,
I wondered what made these young adults so different. Were they better
Catholics? Was it the mystique of Latin? Did they appreciate all this because it had been taken away? Was it, in part, the sense of belonging to a
minority? And if so, what would happen if Pope Benedict granted this

special permission to the entire church? If Tridentine Masses could be offered in any Catholic parish, how long would it be before this group lost its cult status?

In July 2007 the *motu proprio* finally arrived. Titled "Summorum Pontificum," it was only four pages long. In essence the pope decreed that when a group of Catholics wanted a Tridentine Mass, the local priest should make it available. In an accompanying letter, Benedict explained to bishops that he was not lessening their authority—he was simply taking the decision out of their hands. He said that he had listened to the objections and found them unconvincing. He dismissed fears that this decree would foment divisions in the church or be seen as a retreat from the Second Vatican Council. The tone he took was: This shouldn't cause such angst. The new Mass would surely continue as the normal way of worshiping, but now the old Mass would be a valid option for the minority who desired it. The alternate versions of the Mass were simply two expressions of "the one Roman rite," he wrote.

The pope's document was based on the premise that the Tridentine Mass had never really been suppressed, so it didn't require any special permission to be celebrated. That was a new interpretation of history, to say the least. As cardinal, Ratzinger had focused his complaints precisely on the fact that the old Mass had been banned—something that "had never been seen in the history of liturgy"—and that "the old structure was dismantled, and its pieces were used to construct another." But now as pope he could act as if that had never happened, at least officially, because there had never been an authoritative act of abrogation. That may have seemed legalistic to some, but it was in fact an important endorsement of the Lefebvrist position.

The pope's letter contained another unmistakable signal of sympathy with traditionalists. He wrote that he understood those who had been driven away by liturgical abuses: "I am speaking from experience, since I, too, lived through that period with all its hopes and confusion. And I have seen how arbitrary deformations of the liturgy caused deep pain to individuals totally rooted in the faith of the church." With that indictment, Benedict may not have been thinking specifically of liturgical jugglers and cheesehead Masses, but his readers at SSPX headquarters were. With those two sentences alone, they felt vindicated.

The *motu proprio* was issued only in Latin, unlike other Vatican documents, and that, too, was a signal. The Vatican press office had to make an unofficial Italian translation available to reporters.

The initial reaction from Lefebvrists was cautiously favorable. In a letter posted on the Society's Web site the same day, Bishop Fellay seized upon the key issue: The Tridentine Mass had never been suppressed, as the pope said, and therefore SSPX's fidelity to the old rite was never an act of disobedience.

But there was a problem here, and it surfaced in the second half of Fellay's letter. In contrast to Benedict's "continuity versus rupture" reading of the Second Vatican Council, the Lefebvrists did not abandon their conviction that Vatican II had indeed broken with the church's Tradition. "This denial of a rupture caused by the last council . . . shows that what is at stake in the debate between Rome and the Priestly Society of Saint Pius X is essentially doctrinal," Fellay wrote. Rather amazingly, he suggested that the pope's concession be followed by "theological discussions" to examine these wider doctrinal issues. Clearly Fellay viewed the Tridentine concession as the first step in a long process of conversion—conversion for Rome, not for the SSPX.

These reservations were not shared by most of the traditionalist blogosphere, which was enjoying the sweet taste of victory. The online exuberance was captured at Zuhlsdorf's *What Does the Prayer Really Say?* which finally popped the virtual bottle of Veuve Clicquot and ran a lyric parody of the song "Turn, Turn, Turn":

> Go to the altar (turn, turn, turn),
> look to the East now (turn, turn, turn),
> there's a time for every Mass now, if it's valid.
> The time for banjos and dancing is gone,
> dust off the censer, and toss out the bong.
> No need for hugging, we all get along,
> let's keep our focus together, on Jesus.

◆ ◆ ◆

By the fall of 2008, a year after "Summorum Pontificum," Bishop Bernard Fellay was discovering just how little had changed for the Society of Saint Pius X. Although the papal letter had been widely seen as a concession to the SSPX, in fact, by making the Tridentine rite available—theoretically—in every local parish, the pope's new policy had weakened the Society. The SSPX was no longer the exclusive provider of a liturgical alternative.

Meanwhile, its talks with the Vatican were going nowhere, and the world seemed to be paying less attention. While the SSPX continued to have deep concerns that went beyond the liturgy—ecumenism, interreligious dialogue, the role of laypeople and the more "modern" behavior of priests and nuns, all of which were seen as the dark legacy of the Second Vatican Council—as Fellay himself realized, even most conservative Catholics didn't see a rollback of Vatican II as a practical possibility. However much they loved the Tridentine Mass, the younger traddies, in particular, had little appetite for a war on modernism. They might not even know what modernism *was*. In short, the SSPX's list of grievances now lacked a headliner and was of interest to few people outside the Society.

Bishop Fellay calculated some other factors. He knew that his Vatican contact, Cardinal Castrillón, was approaching his eightieth birthday and mandatory retirement. No one at the Vatican would carry water for the SSPX as Cardinal Castrillón had. And Castrillón, Fellay reasoned, would like nothing more than to go out on a triumphant note: After years of failed talks, an agreement with the Lefebvrists would be the finest prize. The SSPX could exploit Castrillón's eagerness to achieve that, but Fellay had to be careful: If he took part in serious talks with the Vatican about reintegration with no preconditions, he would be seen by militants like Bishop Williamson as selling out. The important thing was to make it look as if the SSPX was setting the agenda and forcing the Vatican's hand. And Fellay had a plan to that end. He let Castrillón know that the SSPX had a nonnegotiable demand: Pope Benedict must lift the excommunications incurred by himself and the three other bishops illicitly ordained by Archbishop Lefebvre in 1988.

Fellay knew there would be opposition in the Vatican to such a move; it would be seen not merely as a gesture of reconciliation, but as a symbolic betrayal of Pope John Paul II. But Pope Benedict might agree to it, if he could be convinced a settlement was in sight. To sweeten the deal for the Vatican, Fellay was prepared to open a new chapter of negotiations: serious, regular talks aimed at regularizing the order. To his own people, Fellay would present these discussions not as surrender to Rome, but rather as a chance to finally put the Second Vatican Council on trial. The subject of the talks would be the SSPX's objections to the doctrinal errors of Vatican II. Instead of harping from the sidelines, the SSPX would be engaging in battle within the Vatican itself. They would be taking the traditionalists' struggle to another level.

Not surprisingly, Castrillón supported the plan enthusiastically and by the end of 2008 had Benedict himself on board. Castrillón went to the pope with a formal letter from Fellay dated December 15, in which the SSPX leader requested the lifting of excommunications as a first step toward sincere dialogue. Castrillón pointed to the line where Fellay pledged that the Society would accept the pope's teaching "with filial spirit." Fellay had also padded the letter with the kind of rhetoric that would make it easier for his own followers to accept: "We are ready to write the Creed with our own blood, to sign the anti-modernist oath, the profession of faith of Pius IV, we accept and make our own all the councils up to the Second Vatican Council, about which we express some reservations."

On January 21, 2009, Pope Benedict approved a one-page decree that lifted the excommunications of Bishop Fellay, Bishop Williamson, French Bishop Bernard Tissier de Mallerais and Argentine Bishop Alfonso de Galarreta. The decree emphasized that the excommunications were being revoked in order to "arrive quickly at a full and satisfactory solution of the problem" with the SSPX. The Vatican would make the decision public three days later—on January 24, a Saturday, which would lessen the media echo. It also happened to be the eve of the fiftieth anniversary of Pope John XXIII's announcement of the Second Vatican Council, a detail that delighted Fellay.

Pope Benedict braced himself for what he assumed would be a brief storm of objection by some in the church. In his view, lifting the excommunications was a necessary step to get the SSPX to the bargaining table. Those talks would indeed focus on the Second Vatican Council, but the pope's agenda went far beyond the complaints of the Lefebvrists. The negotiations would offer Benedict a chance to recast Vatican II teachings in his "hermeneutic of continuity" mode—not a rollback exactly, but a more conservative trajectory that, in the long run, would be much better than a rollback. He was convinced that ten or twenty years in the future, this course correction would take the church back to its traditional identity. *Ad extra*, some things could not be completely undone, like dialogue with other churches and other religions. But Benedict's goal was to restore evangelization as the priority in dialogue and curb the church's participation in worldly enterprises that did not explicitly spread the Gospel. *Ad intra*, the pope had much more leeway: restoring a more traditional liturgy, retooling religious orders as frontline missionary forces and above all instilling among lay Catholics the sense that they belonged to the Body of Christ and not just to a vaguely religious philanthropic organization. And in this project, the SSPX would be eminently useful. It was classic triangulation: Benedict would play Fellay against the liberal wing of the church, thus creating a new "middle" ground over which the pope, as the protector of unity, would reign. This was Benedict's grand design. He had little trust in Fellay and his ilk, but recognized that they would serve as the perfect foil.

So, yes, Benedict knew there would be conflict, but like all in-house church issues, it would be manageable. The wider secular world, including hostile media and political critics, didn't really care about how Catholics worshiped or whether nuns wore habits or how many theologians were brought to heel.

What the pope never envisioned, however, was a development that would quickly move this internal controversy onto the global stage. He never saw it coming because none of his closest aides had informed him of it—until it was too late.

Father Federico Lombardi looked as if he had swallowed a toad. I stood next to him in the Vatican press room and felt the crush of thirty other reporters who strained to hear what he was saying. Lombardi was making an appearance to announce the lifting of excommunications against the SSPX bishops. He had his talking points ready: The pope had taken this step in order to promote "the unity in charity of the universal church and [to] succeed in removing the scandal of division." No, it didn't mean Vatican II was being forsaken. Nor did it mean that the four bishops were being fully reintegrated in the church; that would come after an agreement was nailed down in talks with the SSPX.

But by now no journalist particularly cared about the finer points of future negotiations with the Lefebvrists. They wanted to know one thing: How could the pope rehabilitate an anti-Semitic Holocaust denier?

Three days earlier, as the pope was signing his decree, a Swedish TV network aired an interview with Bishop Richard Williamson, a man who never stopped looking for a way to sabotage the reconciliation talks. In the interview Williamson stated that, based on "historical evidence," he believed that not a single Jew had died in Nazi gas chambers. Citing revisionists from memory, he allowed that perhaps two hundred thousand to three hundred thousand Jews had died in the "quote-unquote Holocaust," but not six million. Williamson was soon volunteering details about the properties of cyanide and explaining why it wouldn't have been possible to use the Auschwitz buildings as gas chambers. He then proceeded to discuss the Jews' "huge exploitation" of Europe's guilty conscience.

For three days this interview had been circulating in the world's media and on YouTube. As the criticism grew louder, those of us who covered the Vatican full-time presumed there was no way the pope would welcome Williamson back into the church under these circumstances. He would at least delay the announcement until the interview had faded from the front pages, and perhaps do some advance bridge building with Jewish organizations. We imagined that the high officials of the Vatican's Secretariat of State were working overtime to avoid an embarrassing moment for the German pontiff. What we could never have guessed was that even as Father Lombardi came out to meet the press, the pope, unlike the rest of the world, remained ignorant of Williamson's comments. No one had bothered to tell him.

"Doesn't the pope know what damage this will cause to the church's relations with Jews?" Phil Pullella asked of Lombardi, whose expression was growing more sour by the minute. "Saying a person is not excommunicated is not the same as saying one shares all his ideas or statements," the spokesman said without enthusiasm.

Even before we could finish writing our stories, negative reactions began erupting—and not just from Jewish groups. Media reports quickly un-earthed a whole string of previous similar statements from Williamson that were available, as critics of the Vatican pointed out, to anyone who knew how to use Google. Even his own colleagues confirmed that William-son's anti-Semitism was widely known. Father John Rizzo, a former SSPX seminarian, told the *Boston Globe* that Williamson had once commented on his sizable nose by saying, "Rizzo, are you baptized, or are you a Jew?" Rizzo recalled that there was another seminarian named Oppenheimer, and Williamson would say, "Oppenheimer, I don't like your name. If you keep it up, there's a gas chamber waiting for you at the boathouse."

The Vatican officials in the Secretariat of State waited for the storm to pass, but the situation only grew worse. Israel's chief rabbinate suspended ties with the Vatican. Rabbi David Rosen, head of the American Jewish Committee, said that Benedict's action had made a mockery of Pope John Paul II's condemnation of anti-Semitism. Nowhere was the criticism as pointed as in the pope's native land. Germany's Central Council of Jews broke off contact with the Vatican, and its vice president, Salomon Korn, blasted the pope: "A German pope of all people—and this is how the world will see it—has pardoned a Holocaust denier, and that just before Holo-caust Memorial Day. I thought I was dealing with a considerate and far-sighted man. Obviously I was wrong." Chancellor Angela Merkel charged that the pontiff had given the impression that Holocaust denial was per-missible, and called on him to undo the damage. The popular magazine *Der Spiegel* ran a cover story on Benedict titled "A German Pope Disgraces the Catholic Church."

It was, for Benedict, a low point in his pontificate. What stung him most was the criticism from within: Catholics, including bishops, were openly questioning not only his judgment but his commitment to the path of dialogue with Jews. He asked his Vatican aides to quietly repair the damage with Jewish groups and bring Williamson to heel. The Vatican in-sisted that Williamson unequivocally disavow his statements on the Holo-caust—a demand Williamson proceeded to ignore, leaving them at a stalemate. At this point Bishop Fellay began to worry that the Williamson debacle might actually unravel his agreement with the Vatican. Fellay per-sonally apologized to the pope and put a gag order on Williamson, warning

him that he'd be expelled from the SSPX if he broached the topic of the
Holocaust again. Most people viewed that as an empty threat; for better or
for worse, the SSPX and Bishop Williamson seemed stuck with each other.
As Bishop Fellay himself told *Der Spiegel*, Williamson was like uranium:
"It's dangerous when you have it," he said, "but you can't simply leave it by
the side of the road." For die-hard traddies, however, Williamson was fast
becoming a martyr. In Argentina, where Williamson had been serving as
rector of a traditionalist seminary, the government banished him from the
country, accusing him of having offended all humanity with his statements.
Williamson flew to London for what he sarcastically referred to as his "ex-
ile." TV news broadcasts showed the bishop, in sunglasses and a baseball
cap, shaking his fist at a reporter as he left Buenos Aires.

Back at the Vatican, Pope Benedict was distressed and his top aides
were furious. It had become clear by now that the whole affair had stemmed
from a failure to keep the pope and others informed about the potential
hazards in dealing with the SSPX. Their wrath soon fell on Cardinal Castrillón Hoyos, the architect of the reconciliation. Cardinal Walter Kasper,
who coordinated Vatican dialogue with Jews, told Vatican Radio that the
controversy was the result of "management errors in the Curia" and might
have been avoided had his office been consulted. Father Lombardi, the Vatican spokesman, made clear that Pope Benedict had not known in advance
about Bishop Williamson's views on the Holocaust.

"If someone should have known, it was Cardinal Castrillón Hoyos,"
Lombardi said. Such accusations were the equivalent of civil war in the Roman Curia. Castrillón fought back, but his days were numbered. A few
months later he was quietly retired as the head of the Ecclesia Dei commission, which was now placed under the authority of the Congregation for the
Doctrine of the Faith.

The Williamson episode did no lasting damage to Catholic-Jewish relations, and the pope actually thanked many of the church's Jewish dialogue
partners for coming to his defense at a time when the whole world seemed to
be against him. Weeks later he issued a remarkable letter that revealed how
deeply he had been stung by the storm of criticism. "I was saddened by the
fact that even Catholics, who, after all, might have had a better knowledge of
the situation, thought they had to attack me with open hostility," he wrote.

The letter also contained the first papal mea culpa for failing to use Google: "I have been told that consulting the information available on the Internet would have made it possible to perceive the problem early on. I have learned the lesson that in the future in the Holy See we will have to pay greater attention to that source of news."

In late 2009 Pope Benedict and Bishop Fellay took the next step in their long and fitful pas de deux when the Vatican announced that it was opening formal talks with the Society of Saint Pius X, aimed at reaching a full reconciliation. Once again progressive Catholics feared that the pope intended to create a traditionalist enclave inside the church. That may have been true, but Benedict had no illusions about Bishop Fellay and his brethren. The remaining differences with the SSPX were matters of doctrine and obedience, and Benedict told the Vatican delegates to give no ground on them. He named a lineup of doctrinal heavyweights to sit at the negotiating table. Cardinal Castrillón Hoyos was not among them; he continued to walk the Roman sidewalks around the Vatican carrying a briefcase but with no place to go. For his part, Fellay announced that the purpose of the dialogue was to "dispel the errors" in the church, and opined that it might take a century to complete the church's restoration.

By the spring of 2011, the talks between the Vatican and the SSPX appeared in jeopardy. Fellay had publicly castigated the Vatican for stubbornly defending the "spirit of Vatican II." Not only that, he said, but Pope Benedict was going further down the wrong road with his insistence on dialogue with other religions. The SSPX leadership was incensed that Benedict had recently announced an interreligious prayer meeting in Assisi for October of 2011, to commemorate the first "prayer for peace" encounter convened by Pope John Paul II twenty-five years earlier. For the Lefebvrists, Assisi had been one of John Paul's capital sins against Tradition, and Benedict's memorializing it was simply too much to take. Fellay could not hold his tongue and added that the planned beatification of Pope John Paul also created a "serious problem." An editorial published on the SSPX Web site cataloged the supposed errors of the Polish pope: "This beatification raises the question about a pontificate that publicly took the Second Vatican Council as its compass: the interreligious meetings in Assisi, kissing the

Koran, the invocation 'May Saint John the Baptist protect Islam,' participating in pagan worship in a 'sacred forest' in Togo, bestowing the pectoral
cross on two Anglican 'bishops'—is all that in line with the direction set by
Vatican II? And if so, where is the continuity between that Council and all
the ones that preceded it?"

That did not go down well inside the Vatican. Criticizing Assisi was one
thing, but disparagement aimed at "Blessed" John Paul went over the line.

Their discussion exhausted, in 2012 the Vatican offered to recognize
the SSPX as a personal prelature, as long as Fellay would sign a "doctrinal preamble" adhering to essential church teachings. Fellay balked,
then convened a chapter meeting of SSPX leaders, who raised a host of
objections. Notably missing from that meeting was Bishop Williamson,
who continued to warn against any deal with Rome; Fellay had declared
him persona non grata and a few months later would expel him for encouraging "rebellion."

From my point of view, it looked as if Fellay and the SSPX had been
outmaneuvered on the chessboard of ecclesial politics, having locked themselves into a dialogue they could not win. If they accepted a Vatican offer
and came back into the fold, they'd have to compromise their extreme positions and tone down the associated rhetoric. What they considered to be
their prophetic role would consequently disappear: As an officially sanc-
tioned minority, they would be the keepers of a traditionalist ghetto, not
the leaders of a churchwide restoration. Meanwhile, their base was eroding.
Benedict had skillfully reached out to younger conservative Catholics, traditionalists who were content simply with being able to attend Mass in
Latin.

I made a phone call to my liturgical expert, the Warbler, who did not
disagree with my analysis.

"Of course, the pope knew what he was doing. These people are fanatics,
but they can't resist flattery, especially when it's such noble flattery.
Imagine—the Vatican talking about their 'spiritual distress' and rolling out
the red carpet like they did.

"When they sat down at the table, though, it was the same old story.
This dialogue has been like theater with no audience, just the actors reciting the same lines. So it goes nowhere. Benedict is very patient, and he fig-

ured he could wait them out. The problem is, the SSPX is just as patient. They know this pope is eighty-four years old, that a new pope can go in a new direction—and now they have a toehold in the Vatican. They may have lost this battle, but don't count them out. They see themselves as the keepers of the flame."

CHAPTER SIX

LATINIST

THE SWISS GUARD paced back and forth along a section of the covered loggia, down the hall from the pope's apartment. His heels ticked against *cipollino* marble, buffed to a lustrous milky green. In the ceiling vaults above him, biblical scenes unfolded in splendid Renaissance frescoes. His cell phone lay on the travertine balustrade; superiors didn't like that, but what was he supposed to do? His striped uniform had no pockets. The guard snapped to attention when the elevator door opened and two monsignors scurried past, heads bent, whispering their way toward the secretary of state's foreign affairs offices. Then he heard the booming voice.

"*Mundus vult decipi, ergo decipiatur*—The world wants to be deceived! *Mundus Vaticanus vult decepi!* That's it, friends. Look around you! All this stuff, all these offices, making more documents, more of the same drivel. Do you think Jesus would recognize this place? O Lord, deliver us! Believe me, if Jesus came back here today, they wouldn't even let him in!"

The Swiss Guard relaxed. It was only Foster.

Ambling slowly, flanked by two dazed visitors, Father Reginald Foster was giving one of his unauthorized tours of the Vatican's inner sanctum. Dressed in a frayed blue workman's uniform from JC Penney, he looked more like a washing machine repairman than a Catholic priest. His round head was bald except for some silver trim, and it glowed red when he got worked up, which was often. His smile was mischievous, and his guests seemed to be having trouble figuring him out. Every now and then he paused, heaved his shoulders in an exaggerated shrug and laughed to himself. "Hee, hee, hee!"

Foster cocked his head and gestured to the Swiss Guard. "Our friend!" And soon he was telling his visitors the story about the guard's hometown on the other side of the Alps. The Swiss Guards on the whole liked Foster:

He talked to them and actually seemed interested in their lives. Technically, the guard should have reminded Foster that he wasn't supposed to be leading visitors through here anymore. The rule had come down years earlier. But Foster was an exception, it seemed, to every rule at the Vatican.

"That's where the pope *lives*, people, get it?" Foster pointed to the closed doors at the end of the hallway, only a stone's throw from his own office, where he and four other Latinists translated papal letters and documents into the church's official language. The pope, however, never strayed casually into their workplace. When he did pay a visit—once in a pontificate, usually—it was an official one, accompanied by much pomp. That was the kind of thing Foster couldn't stand.

"They've got the pope closed up here, writing encyclicals that *no one ever reads*!" He roared out the words, and his visitors quaked, glancing around nervously, as if afraid someone important would hear him. "The pope should go down to the sidewalks and listen to what people are talking about! He should go ride the Sixty-four bus for a day! Then he'd learn something!"

In late 1978 the election of a foreign pope was just beginning to have an effect in the network of Rome's pontifical universities. The student body was changing: No longer were these institutions the exclusive academic realm of priests and seminarians, but laypeople from all over the world were now signing up for courses. Every Tuesday and Thursday afternoon I would follow a crowd of mostly young people up the marble steps of the Pontifical Gregorian University at the very center of the city. We made our way down a maze of halls to a large classroom where Father Reginald Foster presided over what he called his five Latin "experiences." Signing up for a Foster class was like declaring a vocation. He demanded loyalty and enthusiasm, and those unprepared to pledge them shouldn't be taking up valuable space in the classroom. If you were there only for the course credit, he announced on the first day of class, you were free to stay home, and he'd give you a passing grade. This cavalier attitude toward academic bookkeeping, plus the fact that at least half his students never bothered to register or pay for the course, caused him no end of trouble with the university's authorities.

Foster's classroom methods were iconoclastic. He was convinced that the mainstream academic approach to Latin was all wrong. He believed in meeting Latin literature head-on, instead of pussyfooting around with grammatical paradigms. He also took a personal interest in each of his students. There must have been sixty people in the class, and by the second week Foster knew us all by name.

Like many in the room, I had ended up in Rome accidentally. I had come to Italy on an archaeological dig and stayed on, having fallen in love with just about every facet of Italian life. My journalistic career began the day Aldo Moro was kidnapped by the Red Brigades; I walked into the offices of the *Rome Daily American* and was hired as a headline writer. In my spare time I began doing *ludi domestici*—Foster's hand-typed and mimeographed homework sheets.

Foster's own path to Rome had begun in Milwaukee. The son of a plumber, he'd entered the Saint Francis Minor Seminary at the age of thirteen and, in standard seminary practice, began studying Latin. He fell in love with the language and recalls spending hours in the library, just reading entries in the ten-pound Lewis and Short dictionary, the Latinists' Bible.

After joining the Carmelites, Foster came to Rome to study in the 1960s, seeking a degree in Latin. He never got the degree, though, because in his first year of studies Pope Paul VI's chief Latinist became quite ill. Word of Foster's academic achievements had already spread and, to his amazement and delight, he was invited to work in the Vatican's Latin letters section. This squad of Latin scribes was one of the Holy See's oldest institutions. Once known as Secretary for Briefs to Princes, it had recently been renamed more prosaically as the Latin Language Department of the First Section of the Secretariat of State. No longer headed by a cardinal, it had lost some of its luster, but it remained the real communications hub at the Vatican. Father Foster's job was to help translate virtually every missive and document that went out under the pope's name, from congratulatory letters to papal encyclicals. To the young man from Milwaukee, it all seemed very serendipitous—he was twenty-nine years old and living his dream.

Eventually, Foster became the team's cleanup hitter, stepping up to the plate when one hundred pages of text were dropped off with a note: "Need in two weeks." Because he essentially lived and breathed Latin, churning out pages of a lengthy document was more like a game than labor. He worked in a labyrinthine wing of the building, where he was a unique and familiar figure. His Vatican office looked like a monastic cell: small and unfurnished, except for a chair and a table on which a few books were stacked. A telephone sat on the floor. He would sometimes lead visitors on personalized tours of the Vatican, explicating inscriptions, evoking history and broadcasting his candid opinions about the latest church developments.

The teaching began in 1973, when Foster was given a class at the Jesuit-run Gregorian, the "university of the popes." It was the post–Vatican II era, and seminarians enrolled there were increasingly wondering why they had to study Latin at all. Foster had answers. Without Latin, he told them, they would never understand the church's history, the arguments of church fathers or the beautiful expressions of faith penned by writers through the centuries. As he summed it up famously during one introductory class: "If you have this thing, you have something, friends. If you don't have Latin, you're just sitting there looking *stupid!*"

He would read from a sermon of Saint Bernard of Clairvaux and make his students weep.

"That's it, friends. *Glorious!*"

As the years went by, Foster's eccentricities became more pronounced. He shed his Carmelite habit—the flowing brown robes collected too much chalk dust from the blackboard—and adopted the distinctive polyester blue work suit. He avoided sit-down meals and appeared to nourish himself on sugar wafers and beer, which he consumed while walking from his Vatican job to his classroom. Most of all he tossed out the old ways of teaching, convinced that too much instructional garbage was standing in the way of the language.

"Latin is not difficult, friends. It's not reserved for experts. My God, every prostitute in ancient Rome spoke Latin," he reminded anyone within earshot.

Foster's approach was to throw students into the language and let them swim, giving them just enough grammar to stay afloat. On the first day of class he had them reading Cicero; before learning declension models they were marveling at the comic scenes of Plautus, pulling the lines apart and working with the words. The grammar came organically, over the course of four years. Foster's method was not exactly easy, but it was entertaining, and it worked.

By the 1980s Foster had developed a cult following among Latinists around the world. Notes from his classes were copied and passed around like a cabalistic treasure. Latin scholars would take their sabbatical year in Rome just to sit in on his classes. He added an intensive summer program that drew the best Latin teachers from around the world; its classes—free, of course—were held *sub arboribus*, under the trees next to his Carmelite monastery on the Janiculum hill. Meanwhile, his regular classes at the Gregorian grew huge, drawing 150 new students each year. He infected many of them with his enthusiasm and love for the language; he was turning out Latin missionaries.

For all his teaching success, however, Father Foster never felt at home in academia. And in Rome university circles, he was not really presentable. Here was a professor who during his classroom lectures would reach into his metal briefcase, pull out a *quartino* bottle of wine and take a long and satisfying swig, without missing a beat. His eyeglasses dug into the back of his ears, so he would wrap the ends of the frames in rubber bands. He refused to ingratiate himself with the university elite, and when summoned before authorities of any kind he could be relied upon to blurt out things that others might think but would never dare to say. The writer Alexander Stille, in a memorable article written for the *American Spectator*, described how Foster was invited to address a conference of Latin professors at the American Academy in Rome. Foster showed up reluctantly and listened to a long and boring discussion about teaching methods. When he took the podium, he proceeded to lambaste their academic approach to Latin, complaining that they were teaching Latin as merely a preparation for an exam and not as a living language. He likewise ridiculed the idea of teaching Latin so students would know English better. "It's like the people who play the piano to help them with their arthritis. You don't study Mozart because of arthritis, and you don't study Latin because your school is a disaster!" he barked. He questioned the teachers' "obsession" with poetry, saying it was keeping students from the real-life, ordinary language as spoken by Romans. "After what I've heard today, I'm surprised anyone is taking Latin!"

he said. The teachers were stunned, and one of the participants remarked afterward, "I came expecting to meet Mr. Chips and I got the Terminator."

Foster had been passed over many times for promotion. He was not the boss, just the oldest in his office, he made a point of telling visitors. In many ways he was the Vatican's official black sheep. In the summer of 1998 he unwittingly—he claimed—gave an interview to a student who was also a journalist. It was classic Foster: The church was "obsessed with sex" and abortion, he said, while it ought to be more worried that its own faithful didn't know who the pope is, where the Bible came from or how many sacraments there were. As a kicker, he disclosed: "I'm a naturalist, I'm a nudist. I like to say Mass in the nude, too. If God doesn't like that, sorry." The story ran on the front page of the *Minneapolis Star-Tribune*.

When he returned to Rome from his summer vacation in Milwaukee, Foster found the newspaper sitting on his desk. He was called into the Secretariat of State to explain. It was the one time he thought he might be in serious trouble. The problem was not so much his Vatican minders; it seems some U.S. bishops had complained.

Within most church circles, however, Foster somehow managed to become popular on both sides of the liberal-conservative Catholic divide. The traditionalists loved him because, of course, he was leading people to the depth and beauty of the church's rich store of Latin literature and liturgy. The liberals loved him because he was so outspokenly critical about what went on at the Vatican.

"They're spending *milioni e milioni* fixing up these buildings at the Vatican! I tell them: Good Lord, people, what do we need all this for? Jesus was born in a barn! But no, they love to spend the money!"

Foster's acid tongue would occasionally shock. A few years ago a young American Catholic woman was trying to organize a session of Theology on Tap in Rome, an informal encounter designed to attract young people for a beer and conversation about religion with a known church figure. Someone recommended Foster, and she arranged to meet him in a coffee bar one morning. She found him at nine a.m., tossing back red wine and ranting about what was wrong with the church, denouncing some of the Vatican's better-known prelates. She quickly dropped him from the program.

A Catholic journalist friend of mine, having heard about the legendary

Foster, spied him sitting on the steps of the Gregorian University one after-noon before class. He was basking in the sun, sipping on a cold *birra grande*. The reporter explained who he was and talked a little about covering the pope for a Catholic publication. Foster took a long draw on his beer, squinted and asked, "Do your bosses let you write that the pope is full of *crap?*"

My CNS colleague Cindy Wooden, shortly after arriving in Rome, wrote a news story about a document Pope John Paul II had issued on the figure of Saint Joseph. That afternoon, while ordering coffee at the Grego-rian University bar, she heard a voice booming from across the room: "My God, the pope thinks Mary and Joseph *never had sex*! They could have had their marriage annulled!"

Those treated to a dose of Foster frequently come away with one ques-tion: "How does that guy survive at the Vatican?"

The morning after he was elected, Pope Benedict XVI celebrated Mass in the Sistine Chapel to officially end the conclave. It was the world's first look at the new pontiff, and at the end of the long liturgy he took his seat on a beige throne and delivered a five-page sermon.

In the Vatican press office reporters looked at each other in disbelief: The pope was speaking in Latin instead of the usual Italian. Surely this was a sign of . . . something.

As we scrutinized the Italian translation that was handed out at the press office, murmurs filled the room at the surprising content. Pope Bene-dict was announcing that the Second Vatican Council would remain the "compass" for the church under his pontificate. His goal, he said, would be to build an "open and sincere dialogue" with everyone. He stressed his com-mitment to ecumenism and bridge building with other religions, as well as to the church's efforts to promote justice and peace in the world.

Pope Benedict, the church's doctrinal watchdog and conservative theo-logian par excellence, was taking a liberal stance in his first major address as pope. It made for a good story line, and we all wrote articles suggesting that, right at the outset, Benedict had signaled that his papacy would not be boxed in by the expectations of traditionalists. Indeed, by outlining such a progressive agenda *in Latin*, perhaps the new pope was sending a subtle message to the church's most conservative wing: I speak your language, but don't share your mind-set.

Some time later, when I mentioned to Foster the importance of the pope's inaugural sermon, he guffawed. "Are you kidding? That was just a canned thing. We wrote it a week before the conclave!" he said. What do you mean? I asked. "They needed something to hand the new pope, something all-purpose, got it? We had him say something about everything. It was generic: Vatican II was great, a bit about war and peace, something nice about young people, ecumenism, the whole bag." He paused, then snorted. "Don't tell me you people thought this man was elected pope one evening and pulls out a five-page homily in Latin *the next morning*! Come on!" I went back and reread the sermon. Sure enough, except for a few introductory lines, it was Vatican boilerplate—surprisingly well-assembled boilerplate, though.

As for the significance of the pope's delivering his first sermon in Latin, Foster pointed out that it had always been done that way. He was right about that, too, of course. It had been a long time between popes, and reporters had simply forgotten.

The 2005 conclave was covered worldwide, and the climax came when an elderly cardinal announced the name of the new pontiff with the Latin phrase "*Annuntio vobis gaudium magnum*." Foster scorned the idea that people watching on TV would need a translation: "Everyone understands that kind of Latin . . . a *dog* could understand that!" In his heart, though, he must have known that most of the seminarians standing in Saint Peter's Square that day would likely not have accurately translated the cardinal deacon's twenty-three-word announcement, save for the words "Iosephum Ratzinger."

When Pope Benedict made it easier to celebrate the pre–Vatican II Tridentine rite, everyone saw it as a boon for Latin. But Foster was no fan of using the old liturgy as a vehicle for the ancient language. "The pope should stand up at his window and read Latin for a couple of hours *every day*! Now *that* would get people's attention!"

Foster knew Pope Benedict had a genuine love for Latin and an appreciation for the church's best writers. But Foster was also well aware that trying to bring Latin back as the church's common language was an effort in futility. That could be accomplished only if seminaries and Catholic universities made Latin obligatory again—and that wasn't on the horizon.

In the 1980s, to boost the dying language, the Vatican brought out a new Latin lexicon with modern terms like *fluxio interclusio* (traffic jam) and *sphaeriludium electricum nomismate actum* (an "electric game with a ball put into motion by a coin," i.e., a pinball machine). It was an expensive, nine-hundred-page, two-volume set, and practically no one bought it.

The truth was, the people who counted no longer communicated in Latin. Although the Second Vatican Council had been conducted almost entirely in Latin, at modern synods of bishops fewer and fewer prelates were signing up for the Latin-language discussion groups, and they were finally dropped.

For years Pope John Paul II prayed the Our Father in Latin at the end of his Wednesday general audiences, until one day his aides switched to Italian—without bothering to notify the stunned pope ahead of time. Papal documents, too, were no longer initially written in Latin. They went from Polish to Italian to other languages; Latin was an afterthought.

When the Vatican launched its Web site, it was available in five contemporary languages but not Latin. Eventually a sampling of Latin documents was added to placate the traditionalists, but by now more effort was being expended in translating Vatican materials into Chinese and Arabic than into the language of the church fathers.

In 2002, a group of Latin enthusiasts and scholars gathered at a pontifical university in Rome. The assembled monsignors were indignant that efforts to revive Latin had made no ground and were heartened when their conference received a letter of support from Pope John Paul. But when the pope's Latin-language missive was read aloud in the auditorium, so few of the participants could understand it that they had to find an Italian translation.

When Father Foster would walk down the halls of the Apostolic Palace and toss out Latin greetings to his Roman Curia brethren, more and more often he'd receive blank stares. He took it all in stride. He had no illusions about a Latin comeback in the church.

"It's not going to happen. We've lost too much in the last thirty years. It would take a total church revolution to bring Latin back at that level," he said.

But Foster still had plenty of work translating documents into Latin, which the Vatican considered the language of its official record. Foster would review the texts as he translated. When Pope Benedict wrote an apostolic exhortation on the Eucharist in 2007, Foster let everyone within hearing range know exactly what he thought.

"*Scrutaria*. You know what *scrutaria* is, right? Garbage. I told Sardi [one of the top officials of the Secretariat of State] *no one* is going to bother to read this thing. The *verbosity*! It's just a diarrhea of blah, blah, blah, the Eucharist and this, the Eucharist and that. I said, why don't you write a chapter about 'The Eucharist and Eurostar' or 'The Eucharist and Google'? O Lord, deliver us! One hundred and twenty *pages* of this stuff! I said, who in the world accepted this thing? 'Oh,' he said, 'the pope liked it.' I said, okay, good luck, Jack!"

His superiors would grin and bear it with a gently remonstrating, "Now, Foster, be good." And that's as far as it ever went. Anyone else would have been shown the door. But Foster was simply too good a Latinist to let go.

Among the things Foster got away with was a Vatican Radio show called *The Latin Lover*. Veronica Scarisbrick would interview Foster about almost anything that had to do with Latin past or present. Asked about Pope Benedict's first encyclical, *Deus Caritas Est* (God Is Love), which he translated, Foster growled and groaned. He'd found it lacking.

"He spends about forty pages on the difference between *eros*—you know, like passionate love—and *agape*—spiritual love—and charity and *dilectio*. He goes through all the words, on and on. What's hardest is this jargon. Like love turns someone into a 'we,' you know, a love of our friend turns our friend into a certain 'we.' Unnhh! And you go on and on like this—well, it's just impossible to translate this stuff. The Romans never thought that way: 'I'm going to miss a little of my own ego.' Everyone's talking this way today, and it's horrible. We went around and around, we were almost going crazy with this thing."

Veronica dared to ask about the quality of Pope Benedict's Latin. Foster labeled it "square and chunky," adding for good measure, "That's his language and his nature and everything else."

One day in late 2007 I met Foster at our usual rendezvous place—the obelisk in Saint Peter's Square—and walked with him toward Saint Anne's

Gate, the "business" entrance to Vatican City. He had agreed to give one of his unique and unauthorized tours through the Vatican to a visiting Midwestern couple, and I asked to tag along. I was alarmed at how slowly he was moving; although a robust man, his legs were bad, and it took us ten minutes to walk the short distance to the entrance. Of course Foster was in no hurry. He paused, scanning the horizon of tourists, chuckled at something and pointed to the pope's window above the square. The Midwestern couple volunteered that they had seen the pope the day before, giving his blessing to the crowd. Foster groaned like someone being tortured. "I know, I know. He was at his window talking about sex! Oh, I just about give up!" The couple, clearly unprepared for this experience, blanched in unison.

Foster, tapping the metal briefcase that he lugged everywhere, said, "I've got his latest encyclical in here." The pope's third encyclical, *Spe Salvi* (Saved by Hope), was due out in a few weeks, and Foster was halfway through the translation. I asked what he thought of it, prompting another moan. "It's this nice meditation, which is okay. But a papal meditation shouldn't be foisted on the whole church as an encyclical! And it goes on and on—this thing is a hundred pages long! It's supposed to be about Christian hope, but by the time you finish it you'll be in total despair!"

When we reached Saint Anne's Gate, the Swiss Guards greeted Foster warmly and waved us in without a pass. As we inched our way toward the Belvedere Courtyard, Foster gave his guests a fifteen-minute course in church history, dwelling at length on the eccentricities of popes through the ages. Four hundred years ago, he told them, Pope Leo X had a pet elephant, a gift of the king of Portugal. "Oh, he loved this elephant. But after a couple of years it died. And right over *there*"—he gestured to the middle of a large parking lot—"they were digging in 1985 to put in some plumbing, and they found the *elephant's bones!*"

Across the Belvedere Courtyard he pointed to a barely visible hole in a wall of a tower. "Right there, about a foot and a half from the top of the drainpipe—that's the birthplace of the Gregorian calendar!" he exclaimed. In the late 1500s Pope Gregory XIII's astronomers used the hole to track the sun's movements across the floor and discovered that the existing calendar was eleven minutes off per year, which by 1582 had accumulated to a ten-day discrepancy. Pope Gregory decreed the new calendar in a papal bull that began, *"Inter gravissimas pastoralis officii nostri curas"*—"among the most serious duties of our pastoral office." "Why, certainly! This was important *stuff*! *Get it?*" Foster roared. "That's our modern calendar! And *that's* where it happened!"

Foster turned a corner and walked into the Vatican firehouse, chatting briefly with the firemen, who all seemed to know him. "They're all excited—they've got a new fire truck. There it is!" A new Mercedes fire engine gleamed in the sunlight. "These German companies *give* these things to the pope, of course. They're standing in line to give things to the pope."

Facing the rooms of the original Apostolic Palace, he pointed to a row of windows. "See that room?" The Midwesterners squinted. "The Room of the Signatura. That's where every important papal document was signed for centuries. *Our world* was decided in *that room*! Remember after the discovery of the New World, and the pope divided up mission territory between the Spanish and the Portuguese? *Right there!* This is where *history* was made, people!"

Foster moved inside toward an elevator, greeting the uniformed operator with a sardonic aside about the VIPs who were scheduled to arrive soon in the ceremonial courtyard above. The elevator whirred quietly to the top floor of the Apostolic Palace, and Foster led us through a warren of stuffy rooms, pausing in a hallway before an ATM machine operated by the Vatican bank. "I wrote this," he said. "Hee, hee, hee." The instructions on the screen were in Latin: *"Inserito scidulam quaeso ut faciundum cognoscas rationem."* He translated: "'Insert your card—*scidulam*—so you can access the operations allowed.' It's baby talk, really." The husband looked at his wife and said something in pig Latin; I was hoping Foster hadn't heard it.

We squeezed down a narrow hallway and entered Foster's office. On one wall was a crucifix and a portrait of Pope Benedict, the latter having been a bone of contention. For years Foster's superiors had told him to allow workmen to hang a photo of the reigning pontiff. Foster said he didn't want it; they insisted, and he resisted. "Isn't that enough?" he would say, nodding toward the crucifix. One morning he arrived to find Benedict's portrait firmly affixed to his wall.

With no place for visitors to sit in Foster's office, the Midwestern couple stood uncomfortably. Foster was explaining to them what he did, how the documents were brought down in sections for the Latinists to work on. When there were no long documents, he worked on a stack of congratulatory letters that were still sent out in Latin—for bishops' appointments, major local church events or ecclesial anniversaries. "We now have bishops who send these things back asking for a *translation*! We might as well be writing in Mandarin," he said. He held up a letter and pointed to the first line. "'*Te laudamus ut semper opera magna facias*.' Now see, this is all very calculated. I was told to give this bishop the subjunctive treatment." He pointed to the text. "See, if you write in Latin, 'We praise you because you've done a good job,' and you put it in the indicative, it's good, like stating it as *fact*. If you put it in the subjunctive, it means, 'You've done a good job *as some people say*.' We do that all the time—you quote someone else, you deflect responsibility and take it down a notch." Chortling, he reached into his briefcase and pulled out a small bottle of white wine, unscrewed the cap and took a long drink. He set the bottle on the bare table. It was ten thirty in the morning. The couple looked aghast.

In 2008 the Secretariat of State again warned Foster that he couldn't just show up with people and walk them through the Vatican unannounced. After all, he worked a few steps from the papal apartment, and his guests were completely unregistered. He had to put in a request and get a pass like everyone else. Foster ignored the order. One week he'd show up with a few nuns from Sheboygan, and the next with the in-laws of a former student. Garrison Keillor got a tour, pronounced it wonderful and then managed to work Foster into his Lake Wobegon monologue the following week.

One day Foster mentioned that he'd just taken Bill Maher through the Apostolic Palace. "Bill Maher? The comedian?" I asked. Yes, *that* Bill Maher, Foster replied. "Asking all these questions about *religion*! Then I took him up to the office. I think he had a wire." In fact, Maher was working on *Religulous*, his mocking pseudo-documentary on religion, and Foster had let the enemy inside the gate. Maher and his crew also talked Foster into being interviewed in front of Saint Peter's Square. They had undoubtedly heard about the free-speaking priest from Wisconsin and figured he'd be the perfect subject. This news set off alarm bells among those of us who had known Foster for many years. He'd always gotten away with his eccentric behavior, but under the new regime in the Vatican, it wouldn't take much to tip the scales in the other direction.

A year and a half earlier, in fact, Foster had found how quickly his world could change: He'd been "fired" from the Pontifical Gregorian University. Actually, university administrators couldn't fire him, so they simply canceled his classes, thus ending their Latin program. One weekend they sent him an e-mail and told him to clear out. Foster's classes were among the most popular at the Jesuit institution, but the university had lost patience with his free-school approach. Overnight, students and benefactors rallied around their professor. They found him a new classroom near the Pantheon, and within days Foster announced "*festive ac jucunde*" (joyously and delightfully) the opening of a new "*Academia Romae Latinitatis.*" Classes were free. The episode reminded everyone, however, that not even as popular a figure as Reginald Foster was untouchable in the world of Roman church politics.

When *Religulous* was finally released, Foster was indeed a featured character, there on the big screen, telling Bill Maher and the world that several traditional church beliefs were nonsense. But what came through even more clearly was that Foster had no time for Maher's puerile questions about biblical literalism. (How do we know the real date of Christmas? How could Jonah really live inside the whale?) Maher aimed in his documentary to try to discredit religious belief with such objections, but to Foster all this was trivial—and he let his judgment show. As a result his appearance in *Religulous* actually won some fans. Compared to the evangelicals interviewed in the film, the Catholics sounded sane.

Maher never asked Foster about the deeper questions of faith, the writings of Scripture or the beauty of Latin, which was too bad, because Foster's opinions might have been enlightening to millions of people.

In the summer of 2008 Foster fell and broke his thighbone. As often happens in Rome, one seemingly manageable health problem mushroomed into others. He lived in a half-empty Carmelite monastery on the Janiculum hill, which had no nursing facilities, so recovery from his operation consisted mainly of lying in bed. He was in no condition to teach the fall semester, and could not get to his Vatican office, either. Depressing weeks went by, and his condition seemed to grow worse. In early 2009 two long-time students became alarmed after visiting him and tried to get him some physical therapy. A few days later, an infection set in, and he was admitted to the Fatebenefratelli Hospital on Tiber Island.

Those of us who went to visit Foster found him in the intensive care unit, among the very sick and dying. He was barely able to speak. We could never get a straight answer from his doctors; in fact, it was not precisely clear who his doctors *were*. We were told his spleen had ruptured. But if that was true, why weren't they doing surgery to remove it? He lay on a bed, a half-drawn curtain offering the merest veil of privacy, attached to a drip bag and some machines that monitored his vital signs. There was no lack of visitors, at least initially. But given Foster's condition, the best we could do was say a few words and leave quickly. Foster did not want people keeping a vigil at his bedside, a fact that was painfully clear from the few phrases he did manage to scratch out on a sheet of paper for his callers: "I am sorry, I am tired." "Can't talk." "Come another day." "Not today, so tired." It was shocking, and sad, to see someone of such volcanic energy and expression reduced to dormancy. I would arrive, don the disposable (except here they were reused) hospital gown, bonnet and shoe covers, and walk slowly through the crowded ward. Occasionally a bed would go empty for a few hours, but was soon filled by a new arrival. I got the picture: Most people left here in a hearse.

One Saturday night in January the ward was practically empty of visitors. When I approached his bed, Foster opened his eyes but couldn't speak. I tried to remind him where he was, and of the view of the river out the window of the room. I recalled that Tiber Island was dedicated to Aesculapius, the Greek god of medicine. In fact, a temple to Aesculapius had been built here in the third century BC, and the island had been a center of healing ever since. As I spoke, it occurred to me that I had probably learned this information from Foster, on one of his many walking tours of Rome.

Suddenly a team of doctors and nurses came over and looked with concern at the flashing numbers on the monitoring equipment next to Foster's bed. They shooed me away and drew the curtain closed. Five minutes later they emerged, scattering to various points in the ward. I followed the guy who looked like the chief doctor, who was now standing at the main desk holding a telephone, and asked what was going on. "His heart is failing. He needs to have surgery, urgently. I can't reach his superior. Are you a relative?" No, I said, but I had his superior's cell phone number. I asked when they planned to operate. "Tonight. But not here. We have a specialist at the European Hospital. He's very good." A few minutes later an ambulance came and Foster was wheeled away. A nurse put his few possessions into a plastic bag and handed them to me: six get-well cards, a Bic pen, four sheets of paper with little phrases written down, and his glasses, with a yellow rubber band wrapped around each earpiece.

I went home and wrote Foster's obituary and waited for news.

Amazingly, the news was good. The operation had been a success, the Carmelite superior told me the following day. Foster had two valves replaced, and from a technical point of view his heart was fine. Now the question was whether he could fight off the lingering infection.

The European Hospital was on the outskirts of Rome, and as Foster's visitors were limited, I had to rely on the Carmelites for information. As the days went by, the news got better. Foster was gaining strength.

In April, when he returned to Fatebenefratelli Hospital, I went to see him—back in the same intensive care ward as before. When I walked into the room I was shocked: He was sitting up in bed, smiling and talking. I asked him about the surgery and his recovery.

"I didn't even *know* I had heart surgery until a few *days* ago! The doctors are telling me, 'They brought you back from the *dead*, friend!' I feel pretty good. Still tired. They say I need therapy, so I'm doing these exercises. Fine. I know, I know—it will take time. But I've *got* to get out of this place!" he said, looking around with a shudder.

The change from the last time I had seen him left me speechless. Foster was as quick-witted and sharp-tongued as ever. Although he still couldn't get out of bed, he was free of tubes, and his spirits were remarkably good.

Two days later I got a note from a Latinist friend in the Vatican: Foster was on a plane for Milwaukee. The doctors and the Carmelites had decided that, for a full recovery, he needed intensive physical therapy, and the United States had the best facilities.

After nearly fifty years in Rome, Father Foster was going home. There were no long good-byes, no Latin commendations, no send-off from Vatican officials—just a plane ticket and a taxi to the airport. That's how Foster wanted it. As he told me later from Milwaukee, where he was teaching again, he didn't miss his job at the Vatican: "Listen, friend, I'm just so happy I'm far away from all that. I got out while the getting was good."

CHAPTER SEVEN

THE POPE WHO
WOULD BE SAINT

MONSIGNOR PIETRO PAROLIN watched the rain fall as his limousine slid through the heavy Roman traffic. The driver was doing his best to get them to the Pontifical Lateran University on time, but it was stop-and-go around the Baths of Caracalla. In ten minutes, the doors would close in the Lateran auditorium, and Parolin did not want to make a late entrance. His assignment today was to smooth the waters, not create an incident.

Parolin was a consummate diplomat. He carried a long and awkward job title—Undersecretary for Relations with States, Secretariat of State—which translated to a simple reality: He was number three among Vatican foreign policy officials. A native of Vicenza in northern Italy, at fifty-one he was ahead of the Vatican curve career-wise, and no one doubted that greater things lay ahead. Journalists found Parolin an amiable conversation partner at cocktail parties. He had a strong handshake and wore a disarmingly naive expression on his big oval face, along with a smile. Yet he was no innocent. He had been well trained at the Vatican's diplomatic academy, spoke four languages fluently and seemed to have a mental file of policy positions for any country on earth. He had done time in Vatican nunciatures in Nigeria and Mexico, and now, back at central headquarters, his charge was the world. Yet, except for annual trips to Vietnam and occasional appearances at international conferences, he rarely left the Vatican.

As his car pulled into the Lateran University gates, Parolin glanced at his watch and saw that he would make the opening bell, after all. He breathed more easily, unaware of the trap that awaited him.

The Lateran auditorium felt like a steam room, and I found a seat high in the back of the lecture theater, stowing my wet rain gear beneath the writing table that folded out in front of me. Riding a *motorino* in Rome has its advantages, but not in a thunderstorm.

It was April of 2006, and I didn't really want to spend the next two and a half hours at what promised to be an endless series of speeches. Attending these Rome academic conferences was like fishing on a slow day—you waited a lot and hoped something would bite. This one, at least, had marketable subject matter: Pope Pius XII and his legacy of saintliness. Every reporter in Rome knew that Pius XII could always earn them a byline, even though the content was usually a recycled mix of accusations and justifications on the single question: Had Pius done enough to help Jews during World War II?

The lineup of speakers at the Lateran included the priest doing the legwork on his sainthood cause, Jesuit Father Peter Gumpel, an outspoken critic of Pius's critics and a man who frequently confided to reporters his suspicions that the late pope was the victim of a campaign orchestrated by "certain Jewish organizations." Also on the dais was a U.S. rabbi, David Dalin, whose book defended the wartime pope against what he called a "smear campaign." An American nun, Sister Margherita Marchione, who had researched the Vatican's aid to Jews during the war, was a featured speaker. There were cardinals and Roman political leaders. Even Giulio Andreotti, a five-time premier and the walking ghost of the Italian Christian Democrat Party, showed up to wave the flag for Pius.

The monolithic praise of Pius XII and the lack of any real news coming from the speaker's platform soon made my eyes heavy, but when Monsignor Parolin took the stage, there was a detectable shift in tone. Parolin was there to represent the Vatican and, in a sense, Pope Benedict XVI. The new pope had yet to publicly reveal his sentiments about declaring Pius a saint, so Parolin's words would be carefully parsed. As he began his salutation, however, instead of a rousing call for canonization, Parolin delivered a cautious endorsement, saying the Vatican was happy to see due attention given to the late pope's efforts to "prevent the war, ease its pain and hasten its end." Nothing was said about sainthood, which was the whole point of this encounter. Parolin was far too generic for this crowd, as their muted reaction made clear.

With the exception of some students, the average age of those in attendance was probably close to seventy. These were church figures, many from the Rome diocese, who had lived through the war and who saw Pius XII as one of their own—someone born and raised in a central Roman neighborhood, the last pontiff who was truly a *romano di Roma*. In two years the church would mark the fiftieth anniversary of Pius's death, a perfect opportunity for his beatification, the first major step toward sainthood. There was a sense of urgency in the room precisely because unless things got rolling, that anniversary would pass without action. With each year Pius's staunchest supporters, the ones who lived and worked with him, were dwindling in number.

A year earlier, these same people had witnessed the passing of Pope John Paul II, a foreigner, and heard the calls of "*Santo subito!*"—Sainthood now!—that sprang from the crowds and that seemed to be taken seriously by the Vatican's own saintmakers. Pope Benedict, after all, had waived the five-year waiting period for the initiation of John Paul's cause, which had given the campaign momentum. No one in the room would have argued against the canonization of John Paul II, but it didn't seem fair that the cause of Pius XII continued to linger. The holdup was at the Vatican, where political ramifications weighed as much as holiness when it came to declaring someone a saint. A figure who might create diplomatic problems, like Pius XII, could wait another century for his day on the altar. To this audience, diplomats like Parolin were the reason for that.

The man now being ushered to the podium was no diplomat, but a partisan supporter. Cardinal Fiorenzo Angelini was, in a sense, the living vestige of Rome's former influence in the church's upper echelons; remarkably, in fact, he was at present the only native Roman in the College of Cardinals. Angelini was a big man who gave the impression of having never turned down a second serving of *spaghetti all'amatriciana* in his life. He was a prominent Roma soccer fan, and the local media loved him for that. A personal friend of Pius XII, who had ordained him a bishop, Angelini was now a champion of Pius's sainthood cause. At eighty-nine, he moved slowly these days, but he kept a feisty demeanor and a sharp tongue, as Monsignor Parolin was about to discover.

Angelini's oratorical style featured long pauses and high volume, and the audience at the Lateran quickly warmed to his remarks. Blasting the international media for viewing Pius strictly in the context of World War II, he described the pontiff as prophetic in his teachings about materialism and communism, and argued that he had set in motion the events leading to the Second Vatican Council. Often overlooked, Angelini continued, were Pius's groundbreaking statements about modern medicine. To a wave of applause, Angelini declared: "He was a man of God and a man of prayer, an ascetic and a great pastor. The holiness of Pius XII doesn't need to be defended. It needs to be better known."

Then, in a few quick strokes, Angelini dispensed with Parolin. To the delight of the crowd, he asked the monsignor to take a message back to his superiors: "Pius XII must be declared a saint! Admiration isn't enough—people need to get moving!" An ovation erupted. "Too much time has already passed!" More applause, as Angelini fixed his eyes on the Vatican representative and let the words sink in. Parolin endured it gracefully, but he got the message.

Over the years I had observed a fault line running through the Vatican that now and then would surface. On one side of this line were officials who swore by the prudent, protective methods of "Mother Church," who never provoked an unnecessary fight, who favored dialogue and patience with adversaries in the confidence that, in the end, the church's mission would prevail. On the other side were those who felt Catholic institutions and leaders needed to be bolder on the public stage; they would choose confrontation over diplomacy any day. During his lifetime Pius XII himself had undoubtedly been among the practitioners of prudence, so it was more than a little ironic that the Vatican diplomats were the ones advising caution regarding his sainthood, while the risk takers thought postponement showed weakness.

The question was: Where did Pope Benedict stand?

The election of Pope Benedict in 2005 had thrown Pius's supporters into a state of agitation. First, the pope was German and had himself served (albeit reluctantly) in a Nazi antiaircraft unit, which meant that he could not beatify Pius without stirring up the entire cauldron of World War II issues. Second, Benedict seemed to have a particular affection for the Jews. He had written eloquently about the Jews' special place in salvation history and their special relationship with the Catholic Church, declaring, "Judaism is not just one of many religions but is the foundation, the root of our faith." Third, the new pope was not in a hurry to add more saints to the church's roster, and he was no fan of Pope John Paul II's record-breaking pace of beatifications and canonizations.

Even as John Paul lay dying, Pius's promoters had attempted to force the hand of whoever would succeed the Polish pope. It was a typical end-of-pontificate maneuver, in which unfinished agendas are sometimes desperately advanced as a pope's "dying wish" by lower-level Vatican officials. In this case, as John Paul was in and out of the hospital in his final days, the U.S. Catholic magazine *Inside the Vatican* cited an unidentified source who said the ailing pontiff had recently affirmed, "I will not die before I canonize Pope Pius XII." The tactic was so transparently calculated that virtually no one took it seriously.

During his first year or two in office, Benedict was frequently claimed as an ally by hard-liner Catholics, who believed the German pope would carry a big stick—and use it. It was soon apparent, however, that Benedict never saw himself or his mission in such a light. While he could be firm on points of doctrine and tradition, in a few telltale decisions he revealed himself as a man of great patience and caution. One of these decisions, in particular, worried the supporters of Pope Pius XII.

In mid-2005, just two months after his election, Pope Benedict was handed a dossier on a proposed saint, French Father Léon Dehon. In the late nineteenth century, Dehon had founded the Sacred Heart of Jesus, one of the world's most influential religious orders. He had been scheduled for beatification in April, but with John Paul II's death the ceremony was postponed. Rescheduling should have been a simple matter, but when he opened the dossier, Pope Benedict was disturbed by what he read.

Father Dehon, like many European Catholics of his time, apparently had an anti-Semitic streak, a tendency that was evident in seven texts that had been unearthed by the French historian Jean-Dominique Durand and printed in the French Catholic newspaper *La Croix*. Dehon had written in 1898 that the Jews were "thirsty for gold" and "united in their hatred of Christ." He said the Talmud, the Jewish holy book, was a "manual for the bandit, the corrupter, the social destroyer." He supported the idea that Jews should be marked by special clothing, isolated in ghettos and excluded from certain professions like teaching.

When the writings had begun circulating earlier that year, the French government quietly informed the Vatican that it would not be sending a representative to the beatification, and French bishops sent their own protest to the Vatican.

It was not an easy judgment for Benedict. If he canceled the beatification, he would be seen as delegitimizing an action of his beloved predecessor, who had, after all, paved the way for beatification by declaring that Dehon had lived a life of "heroic Christian virtues." But if he went ahead with the ceremony, he would be seen as beginning his pontificate with an egregious insult to the Jews.

Benedict accordingly did the cautious and prudent thing: He appointed a commission to study the question. That sent rumblings through the Roman Curia, whose members knew that "appointing a commission" meant that a question could remain "under study" for decades. The commission's membership was secret, as were its deliberations. The Dehonian order was informed that there would be no beatification for the imminent future.

When I learned of the pope's decision, I called Father Peter Gumpel, the Jesuit in Rome who was well informed on sainthood causes and happened to be the relator, or investigating judge, for the cause of Pius XII. Gumpel was clearly upset that Dehon's cause had been delayed and pointed out that the Vatican's Congregation for the Causes of Saints had already researched Dehon's life, found him worthy and even credited him with a miraculous healing—all of which had been approved by Pope John Paul II. To call off the beatification now, Gumpel said in his thick German accent, would cause "a certain amount of bewilderment" among the faithful.

"This could create a very serious precedent. There is a miracle, so it seems God is in favor of it, and yet there are problems?" Gumpel said. As always, he was especially worried that the Vatican might give the impression of bowing to outside pressure when it came to declaring its own saints—pressure from "certain very powerful organizations of the Jewish persuasion; I don't think I need to tell you who they are."

There was one other reason for Father Gumpel's anxiety, which he didn't mention: He had recently finished assembling the final report for the beatification of Pope Pius XII. If Benedict could call a halt to the case of Father Dehon, what would he do with the most divisive sainthood cause in modern history?

Accusations that Pope Pius XII had done little or nothing to oppose Nazi persecution of Jews had been routinely made for decades, but they became an industry in the late twentieth century. My bookshelf had gradually filled up with volumes documenting Pius's alleged failures to act and even his indifference to the fate of Jewish victims. More recently publishers were releasing an almost equal number of books defending the wartime pope. It was becoming a full-scale propaganda war, in which historians and scholars and religious leaders were not allowed to remain neutral: Pius was either the quiet hero or the ultimate bystander.

Most experts agreed that Pius emerged from the war with an apparently undamaged reputation. Vatican officials were fond of pointing to a series of early tributes from Jewish sources that, in their view, represented a firewall against subsequent criticism:

+ A personal message of thanks sent to the pontiff by Isaac Herzog, the chief rabbi of Jerusalem, in February 1944, who wrote: "The people of Israel will never forget what His Holiness and his illustrious delegates, inspired by the eternal principles of religion which form the very foundations of true civilization, are doing for us unfortunate brothers and sisters in the most tragic hour of our history, which is living proof of Divine Providence in this world."

+ Public appreciation from the World Jewish Congress in 1944, expressing gratitude for the Holy See's protection of Jews, especially in Hungary. A year later, the WJC made a donation to the Vatican in recognition of Pius's work to save the Jews.

+ A eulogy when Pius died in 1958, delivered at the United Nations by Golda Meir, then Israel's minister of foreign affairs: "We share the grief of the world over the death of His Holiness Pius XII. During a generation of wars and dissensions, he affirmed the high ideals of peace and compassion. During the ten years of Nazi terror, when our people went through the horrors of martyrdom, the pope raised his voice to condemn the persecutors and to commiserate with their victims. The life of our time has been enriched by a voice which expressed the great moral truths above the tumults of daily conflicts. We grieve over the loss of a great defender of peace."

• The 1967 book by Israeli consul Pinchas Lapide, which examined Pius's actions and concluded: "The Catholic Church, under the pontificate of Pius XII, was instrumental in saving the lives of as many as 860,000 Jews from certain death at Nazi hands." That figure, he said, was far higher than those saved by all other churches and rescue organizations combined. He added: "No Pope in history has been thanked more heartily by Jews."

As for Pius's alleged "silence" regarding Jewish suffering, Vatican officials pointed to an editorial published by none other than the *New York Times* in response to the pope's 1941 Christmas message condemning the Nazis' racial hatred: "The voice of Pius XII is a lonely voice in the silence and darkness enveloping Europe this Christmas. . . . He is about the only ruler left on the Continent of Europe who dares to raise his voice at all. . . . The pope put himself squarely against Hitlerism . . . he left no doubt that the Nazi aims are also irreconcilable with his own conception of a Christian peace."

Finally, a clinching argument for the Vatican, albeit a sensitive one that had to be used with caution, was the fact that the chief rabbi of Rome, Israel Zolli, had converted to Christianity after the war ended and had taken the name Eugenio—out of admiration for Eugenio Pacelli, Pope Pius XII.

The criticism of Pius began to take shape after a little-known German playwright, Rolf Hochhuth, published a work in 1963 titled *The Deputy: A Christian Tragedy*. The play was strongly critical of Pius's wartime role, accusing him of failing above all to save the Jews of Rome, who were loaded onto trucks for deportation practically in front of the Vatican. One of the fictional protagonists of the drama, a young Jesuit priest, declares: "A Vicar of Christ who sees these things before his eyes and still remains silent because of state policies, who delays even one day . . . such a pope is a criminal."

The play opened in Berlin that year, was performed by the Royal Shakespeare Company in London and the following year opened on Broadway.

There were protests over its clearly anti-Catholic theme, which only helped fuel the publicity. Eventually it was translated into twenty languages, and has enjoyed a number of revivals; it was even used as the basis for the 2002 Costa-Gavras film *Amen*. More important, it prompted a series of books and articles about the "sins of silence" committed by Pius XII.

Church figures observed that Hochhuth was himself a member of Hitler Youth and that later in life he had defended Holocaust denier David Irving. In 2007 it was even alleged by a former Romanian spy, Ion Mihai Pacepa, that *The Deputy* was part of a KGB effort to smear Pius XII and the Vatican. But by then the damage had been done. The idea that Pius stood by and did nothing to help the Jews had become the common wisdom, not only among Jews but among many Christians and even Catholics.

The brief against Pius XII usually went something like this: that as Vatican secretary of state in the 1930s he turned a blind eye to Hitler, arranging a church-state concordat in Germany that helped legitimize the Nazi regime; that once elected as pope in 1939 he shelved the "hidden encyclical" against racism and anti-Semitism that his predecessor, Pius XI, had drafted before his death; that during the war he continued to maintain relations with the Nazi occupiers of Rome; that in general he placed the church's own interests first, and from that perspective feared Soviet Bolshevism more than Hitler.

Perhaps the most specific accusation against Pius was that when the Nazis conducted a roundup of Jews in Rome in October 1943, the pope made no public protest. Here the historical record could not be denied, Pius's critics maintained: He was silent as Jews were seized in Rome's old Jewish ghetto neighborhood just across the Tiber River and deported to death camps, a roundup that occurred "under his very window."

That phrase became the title of a 2001 book by historian Susan Zuccotti, who maintained that a search of diocesan and parish records in Rome and elsewhere turned up no evidence that Pope Pius XII or his officials at the Vatican had ever taken steps to protect Jews, harbor them or protest to Nazi occupiers about their treatment. While individual Catholics and communities sheltered Jews, she wrote, "the pope did not welcome Jews in the Vatican."

Zuccotti's book, like others, relied heavily on the fact that no paper trail had been found showing that Pius had initiated or approved church efforts to help the Jews. If any such evidence existed, the critics contended, the Vatican would surely have produced it. Meanwhile, historians could not study the best and most abundant documentation of Pius's actions during the war because it was locked inside the Vatican Secret Archives. That, too, was increasingly used as an argument against Pius and his sainthood cause. As the Vatican rejected every appeal for an early opening of the archival material, the question became: What were they hiding?

In 1992 I was allowed to visit the Vatican Secret Archives, on a walking tour arranged by the German prefect at the time, Father Josef Metzler. It was eye-opening, but not in the way I had expected. I was shown the archives' new wing, an underground bunker that had doubled the facility's storage space. Built of poured concrete, it had all the charm of a parking ramp. But it was fireproof, climate controlled and could even withstand nuclear attack—or so I was told. The bunker held some sixty miles of shelf space, and as we walked past the contents, I couldn't help but notice that most of these "treasures of the archives," as journalists routinely described them, were in fact cartons of loosely bound piles of papers. It all seemed so ordinary. The outside world knows the archives by its showcase items: the papal bull by which Martin Luther was excommunicated, love letters penned by Henry VIII to Anne Boleyn or the intricate gold seals by which popes, kings and princes marked their edicts. But all I saw were endless rows of cardboard boxes.

Metzler, perhaps sensing my disappointment, tried to explain why all this was of vital historical importance. For the seventy or so scholars who filed into the archives' reading room every day, he said, this was indeed the treasure trove, where intriguing scraps of history (and maybe the theme of a new scholarly book) were waiting to be discovered. Among these approximately thirty million documents were minutes of curial meetings, confidential correspondence and heaps of Vatican contracts, inventories and diplomatic reports. Many of them had never been fully cataloged; the Vatican employed fewer than ten full-time archivists on its staff, and they were simply overwhelmed with the mountain of still accumulating history. In fact, the archives' contents were growing at a record pace, adding nearly one million pieces of paper each year. The work was lagging so far behind, Metzler said, that some of the worn volumes were now being sent to an order of cloistered nuns in Rome for repair.

"We have only thirty-four people working here. Any other archive of this magnitude would have a staff of three hundred. We're always asking for more help, but Vatican resources are limited," the priest said.

The term "secret archives," although etched indelibly on the marble doorway, was really a misnomer in the modern understanding of the word, Father Metzler explained. What it meant was that the archives were "private" as opposed to "public." Since the 1880s, when Pope Leo XIII opened the unique collection to scholars, the reading rooms had been full, and Vatican clerks had been busy retrieving volumes and papers from the stacks for consultation. But the Vatican—like many national archives—did allow the historical record to settle before opening it up to experts. There was no hard-and-fast rule, but the archival material of most pontificates had remained off-limits for about a hundred years. More recently the waiting period had grown shorter. Pope John Paul II was particularly generous, in the Vatican's view, in opening the documents of three papacies up to the year 1922.

As I surveyed the gloomy depository, I tried to put myself in the mind of a scholar and found myself wondering: Where's the good stuff? And how would anyone ever know where to begin to look?

Father Metzler offered a tip: correspondence. Official Vatican papers were typically carefully worded and vetted, and finding surprises would be difficult. But many nuggets of information had been mined from letters, he said. In older times these often took the form of "papal supplications"— petitions for special permits, indulgences and pardons that provided a wealth of detail about the leading families of the time.

I suspected that Metzler's excitement about such details was a bit exaggerated. Historians might be entertained, but I couldn't imagine any headlines emerging from these yellowed sheaves. Three years later, though, I was proven wrong, in one of the more embarrassing episodes to involve the archives in many years.

Father Filippo Tamburini, a seventy-four-year-old priest who had worked with Vatican archive material for twenty-five years before retiring, had the novel idea of publishing one hundred of those "supplications," unsought and unnoticed in the secret archives. These were no ordinary supplications, however, but those of fifteenth- and sixteenth-century penitents seeking papal absolution for their sins. The volume was unveiled at a low-key Vatican presentation ceremony in 1995, and as I paged through a copy my interest grew. Its record of true confessions offered a Renaissance sampler of depravity: murder, incest, bestiality, blasphemy and adultery, to name a few of the more common failings. A group of nuns was remorseful over trying to poison their abbess; a woman repented of dabbling in witchcraft; a cardinal regretted killing two men on his way to a conclave; a husband was contrite after castrating his wife's lover.

The book's title was *Saints and Sinners*, but the latter far outnumbered the saints. Even more shocking, many of the supplicants were priests or nuns seeking reinstatement to their ministry or religious order. As Father Tamburini put it, their accounts illustrated how deeply moral decadence had penetrated monastic and parish life in the 1500s and helped explain the reform movement that was soon to spread inside and outside the church.

I learned that the supplications had long been considered potentially embarrassing material, and in 1816 one cardinal suggested burning them. Other church experts had warned that the content was too strong to be made accessible to lay historians. Yet here, suddenly and astonishingly, was a Vatican-sanctioned book telling all.

Then, a week later, the reaction came down—hard. As it turned out, the Vatican had been blindsided by the book. The Vatican press office issued a terse statement stating that Father Tamburini had had no permission to publish the material and that its publication constituted an "abuse that can only be strongly deplored." The Vatican's argument was that these were penitential petitions and therefore deserved confidentiality. Father Tamburini countered that no special permission was necessary, but soon found himself persona non grata. His book, meanwhile, was pulled from Vatican bookstores, though most copies had already been sold. Today the volume is no longer available, but is nonetheless frequently cited by historians. Tamburini died in ignominy in 1999.

The episode illustrated that it was indeed possible for the Vatican Secret Archives to be the source of secrets and tantalizing tidbits of historical information, some of which Vatican officials would rather have kept hidden. It was that point that was made by those clamoring for the Vatican to open the archives on the pontificate of Pius XII, so that experts could assess the complete historical record of his wartime actions or inactions. Even some of Pius's defenders, like Sir Martin Gilbert, one of Britain's leading historians, pressed for a release of the material, stating that only then could a final judgment be made.

The Vatican often emphasized that it had already taken the unusual step of publishing eleven volumes of World War II–related documents from the pontificate of Pius XII, a project begun in 1965—shortly after Pius's beatification cause was introduced—and completed in 1981. A handsome set, it was filled with diplomatic correspondence and was dry reading. Jewish groups always dismissed this effort as the Vatican's sanitized version of history, handpicked documents that gave a partial picture at best. Of course there was no smoking gun to be found in its pages, they said—did anyone expect the Vatican's own experts to make the case against Pius?

In 1999 the Pius wars came to a head with the publication of the book *Hitler's Pope: The Secret History of Pius XII*, by English journalist John Cornwell. Several years earlier Cornwell had been given full Vatican cooperation for his book *A Thief in the Night: Life and Death in the Vatican*, which was intended to counter allegations that Pope John Paul I had been murdered in an inside job in 1978. The book did indeed debunk the murder premise, but in the process it portrayed the Vatican as a petty, gossipy world of unparalleled incompetence, where a sick pope was allowed to die, basically, of neglect. Clearly Cornwell had used his Vatican access well, but not to write an apology for his sponsors. He undoubtedly had something similar in mind regarding Pius XII and went into the project with the idea of exonerating the late pope. Again he was promised access and cooperation, but along the way, he explained, he became convinced by the evidence that Pius was in fact an anti-Semite who played into Hitler's hands and failed to condemn the Nazi persecution of Jews. Those were the conclusions of his book, which caused an uproar.

The Vatican felt betrayed, and counterattacked less than a month after Cornwell's book appeared. Facing a packed press room, the unlikely protagonist for the official debunking was a balding octogenarian, French Jesuit Father Pierre Blet, the sole survivor of the four-member team of experts who, more than twenty years earlier, had assembled the Vatican's eleven volumes of World War II documents. Blet had now produced an edited "greatest hits" synthesis of the eleven volumes, *Pius XII and the Second World War*, which weighed in at a mere 392 pages. It cited dozens of meetings, letters and internal communications that revealed that while Pius XII kept a public silence, he was secretly working through nunciatures and episcopates to stop Nazi deportations. Other evidence documented Pius's real fear, based on previous Nazi reprisals, that any public pronouncement by him would only have harmed the Jews. The pope did not want others to pay in blood for his words, Blet explained.

"Of course, you can imagine anything you want," Blet told reporters at the press conference. "You can imagine that if the pope excommunicated Hitler, Hitler would have come to Rome as a penitent, resigned and lived as a Trappist monk." That got laughs; the Jesuit could sense a mood of approval among Vatican journalists.

Blet responded to two specific issues raised in the Cornwell book. The first was the legendary "lost encyclical" against anti-Semitism, drafted by Pope Pius XI and, in Cornwell's account, quietly buried by Pius XII because it would have inflamed the Nazis. Blet insisted that it had been a wise decision to shelve the encyclical, which, for all its good intentions, was deeply flawed: While defending some Jewish rights, the draft had also legitimized the right of states to take certain measures against the Jews, as a form of self-defense.

Father Blet then turned his attention to a second major accusation made by Cornwell, that Pius XII was himself an anti-Semite. This was something of a new claim in the annals of anti-Pius literature. Cornwell based his judgment on a letter he had unearthed, signed by Pius when he was a young nuncio in 1919, reporting on an encounter between one of his diplomatic assistants and a group of Jewish Bolsheviks in Munich. The letter described the Bolsheviks' headquarters as a filthy place with a "gang of young women, of dubious appearance, Jews like all the rest of them, hanging around in all the offices with lecherous demeanor and suggestive smiles." It characterized the leader of the group, Max Levien, as "a Russian and a

Jew . . . pale, dirty, with drugged eyes, hoarse voice, vulgar, repulsive, with a face that is both intelligent and sly." For Cornwell, this "repugnant and ominous" letter was the smoking gun, the key to understanding all of Pius's subsequent actions, revealing a deep-seated anti-Semitic contempt.

Asked about the letter at the press conference, Father Blet was clearly on the defensive. He noted, first of all, that the letter, which Cornwell claimed had lain in the Vatican archive "like a time bomb" until he found it, had in fact not only been known but had been published in a 1992 study of Vatican-German diplomacy. Second, Blet said, look carefully at the words: The derogatory references were not religious but political, written by someone who obviously was unsympathetic to the Bolshevik revolution, not someone who hated all Jews. Finally, Blet's strongest argument was that Pius himself was probably not the author of the letter. Such reports, he said, were typically produced by a nuncio's staff—presumably by the staff member who had actually met with the Bolsheviks.

Father Blet went on to address the arguments of Pius's detractors, asking in a tone of scholarly ridicule whether critics thought the pope could have "stopped the armored tanks of the Wehrmacht with the halberds of the Swiss Guards or the threat of excommunication." The French Jesuit had mastered the art of the sound bite.

He then turned to a perennial accusation that always made headlines: that the Vatican was still holding Nazi gold taken from Jews. Quite the contrary, Blet said, and he proceeded to tell a fascinating story that was recorded in archive documents. In 1943 the Nazi occupation forces threatened to take the lives of two hundred Roman Jews unless the Jewish community delivered 50 kilograms (about 110 pounds) of gold. When they found that they were 33 pounds short of the demanded amount, the chief rabbi of the city rushed to the Vatican for help, and Pope Pius immediately ordered his aides to fill the gap. Here was a pope willing to melt down the church's own golden artifacts in order to save Jewish lives. The journalists around me were writing furiously and nodding in agreement. The ancient Father Blet had won them over.

As I paged through *Pius XII and the Second World War*, I came across something Father Blet had chosen not to highlight: a letter from Pius to German bishops in 1944 that hinted at inner doubts about his wartime policy. He wrote that it was "painfully difficult to decide whether a reserve and a prudent silence is to be followed, or a decisive word and energetic action." Here, it seemed, was a more conflicted Pius: a pope who had chosen precaution over prophetic action, and who perhaps sensed late in the war that history's judgment might not be favorable.

Blet's book became a best seller, by Vatican standards, and, more important, it demonstrated to church officials that when it came to Pius XII, the best defense was a good offense. Over the next decade the Vatican would cooperate with a number of other scholars and journalists on book projects, steering them toward archival evidence in support of a burgeoning campaign to promote the pope's sainthood. These were no longer just in-house productions, but involved experts outside the Vatican and even outside the church. The campaign hit its stride in 2005 with publication of two books: *The Myth of Hitler's Pope: How Pope Pius XII Rescued Jews from the Nazis*, by David Dalin, and *Righteous Gentiles: How Pius XII and the Catholic Church Saved Half a Million Jews from the Nazis*, by Ronald J. Rychlak. The two volumes argued that, far from being blameworthy, Pius ought to be recognized as a hidden hero of his times. Dalin, a rabbi, framed the dispute not in Catholic-Jewish terms, but as a battle in the modern culture wars: For the secular media, he argued, attacking Pius was a way to discredit not just Catholicism but religious faith in general. And noting that several of Pius's harshest critics were "lapsed or angry liberal Catholics," Dalin accused them of exploiting the Jewish tragedy "to foster their own political agenda of forcing changes on the Catholic Church today."

The Vatican, at last, had a respectable roster of allies willing to speak publicly on behalf of Pius XII, including academics, Jewish experts and journalists. Among them was one person without a significant reputation or credentials as a Holocaust expert, yet who was a favorite among the pro-Pius contingent in Rome. She called herself "the fighting nun."

The voice at the other end of the phone was gravelly, with a thick New Jersey accent. She was selling a story, something about a book she'd written on Pius XII. I'd never met her, but she was about to correct that. "You better come see me, dear. This is going to be big."

It was 2003, and with the debate over Pius and the Holocaust reaching a crescendo, it seemed like a good story. I went to see her at the convent near the Vatican where she was staying, a house of the Religious Teachers Filippini, an order founded more than three hundred years ago. Sister Margherita Marchione, eighty-two years old but you'd never guess it, came into the foyer not with one book but with a stack of various volumes and slapped them down on the table. "There you go, darling. You've got plenty to write about now." She stood about five feet tall and wore the dark habit of her order, a black shawl-like affair that she tugged at as she sat down in front of me. Her graying hair was visible under a soft black bonnet, and a pair of oversized glasses made her eyes look like cannons ready to fire. She wore a continuous smile that seemed genuine.

"We've got to get Pius XII beatified, Johnny," she declared. "The man was a saint." Johnny? I hadn't been called that since fifth grade. And, in fact, there was something about this scene that reminded me of my parochial school education. Picking a slim hardcover book from the pile, she continued, "This is my latest. I had to write it, with the smear campaign going on against this good man. I gave a copy to the pope the other day." It was titled simply *Pope Pius XII* and laid out the case that the late pontiff had prudently and quietly helped the Jews, opposed Hitler at every turn and practiced the virtues of a saint. As I paged through it, I glanced at the other books, all written by the nun—*Pope Pius XII: Architect for Peace; Consensus and Controversy: Defending Pope Pius XII; Shepherd of Souls: A Pictorial Life of Pope Pius XII*—and wondered whether I would be given a guided tour through each of them.

"Do you have children? They'll love this," she said, pulling out a copy of *Pius XII: The Children's Pope*, a biography in easy-to-color line drawings along with a brief narrative. I turned to a page titled "The Holocaust" and read: "In Germany, Adolf Hitler killed thousands of Jewish people and others. The pope saved many by hiding them in the Vatican and in convents and monasteries. He also provided them with money, food and clothing." Another page recalled how Pius once found an injured bird in the Vatican Gardens and nursed it back to health. It would perch on his shoulder during mealtimes, hopping down to eat from its own dish of seeds and keeping him company.

"It's all true," Sister Margherita said, looking over my shoulder. "People forget what a beautiful human being this man was. How many children do you have—three? Take one for each of them, dear." She had plenty on hand.

I asked her how she had become interested in the subject. She explained that she had been talking one evening with some older members of her order in New Jersey. The nuns had been in Rome during World War II and described how they would hide Jews in their convents, saving many lives. They knew of other convents and parishes that had done the same. Sister Margherita became intrigued and decided to spend some time in Rome researching the issue. A retired university professor of Italian language and literature, she had written books on Thomas Jefferson and Philip Mazzei, among others, so she knew her way around archives and memoirs, and she appreciated the value of firsthand witnesses. She had two big advantages in Rome: First, she had been born in Italy and knew the language; second, she knew the ecclesial terrain, and her religious habit opened all the right doors. Her research method was simple: Keep asking, keep pressing and don't take no for an answer.

The result was a 1997 book titled *Yours Is a Precious Witness: Memoirs of Jews and Catholics in Wartime Italy*. Despite its ponderous title and its clearly partisan defense of Pius, the book quickly became required reading among historians of the period. Sister Margherita had done what others had never bothered to do: talked to the real people—including many elderly residents of Rome convents—who had sheltered Jews and liaised with the Vatican under German occupation. This was no generic apologia; she provided the names of refugees hidden in the Vatican and in Rome's Pontifical Seminary. She documented more than 160 religious houses that had provided safe harbor and listed the number of Jews who'd stayed in each one. Some were places where only one or two people were concealed from the Nazis, while at others hundreds were hidden away. Many were cloistered convents, so offering refuge involved bending their own religious rules, but they did so out of charity and because they felt the pope expected no less of them.

But was Pius really the hidden architect of this heroic effort? Or was it a case of the church's foot soldiers risking their lives to help the Jews while the pope and his officials stayed above the fray? Sister Margherita's argument was that it was impossible for Pius not to have known of this great humanitarian effort in his own diocese and that the lack of written papal orders was a logical precaution under Nazi occupation. When I asked whether there existed one letter, one papal memo, one Vatican memoir that could have demonstrated Pius's direct involvement, the nun showed me an old photograph of Pius's bedroom at his summer residence in Castel Gandolfo, captioned "The Nursery." She pointed to the papal coat of arms on a tapestry and the figures in the photo: Jewish mothers holding their infants. The pope had given up his own quarters to be used as a birthing room for pregnant refugees. "Do you think Pope Pius didn't know about any of this? Of course he knew. He made it happen," Sister Margherita said.

Her book had launched her on the Pius punditry circuit, and more than once she found herself on radio or TV face-offs with *Hitler's Pope* author John Cornwell, a man she considered a mendacious hack. She was bothered by the fact that, because of her religious habit, her opponents tended to dismiss her or, worse, be nice to her. "The trouble is, nobody comes and fights me. I'm waiting for the opportunity, because I've got the documentation for everything," she told me.

With relish, Sister Margherita told me how she had met with John Paul II a few days earlier and told him bluntly: "Your Holiness, almost fifty years have passed. When will Pope Pius XII be beatified?" In reply the Polish pope smiled and said some complimentary things about Pius, but didn't commit to a date. So, with less decorum, she pressed a number of papal aides with the same question. It irritated her to hear answers that carefully avoided controversy.

Now was the time for action, she insisted. In the public relations campaign Pius was again winning some battles, but the war would be lost unless the cause for his sainthood quickly took some decisive steps. She already had a timeline in mind: In the fall of 2008 the church would celebrate the fiftieth anniversary of Pius's death. That would be the perfect moment for his beatification.

"It would make waves. But it's time to make the waves," Sister Margherita said.

In May of 2007 I was waiting in the Rome airport with fifty other journalists, preparing to board Pope Benedict's plane for Brazil. Andrea Tornielli, a well-informed Italian *vaticanista* who wrote for the Milan newspaper *Il Giornale*, sidled up to me and whispered something about Pius's finally getting the green light. Tornielli had been a strident defender of Pius and had a direct line to promoters of the sainthood cause. The day before, he told me, the thirteen bishop and cardinal members of the Congregation for the Causes of Saints had unanimously endorsed a decree stating that Pius XII had heroically lived the Christian virtues. In the calculus of saintmaking, "heroic virtues" plus a miracle equals beatification. The congregation's decree, if approved by Pope Benedict, would mean that beatification could take place once a miracle was attributed to Pius's intercession. And after beatification, approval of a second miracle would bring canonization.

I noted a couple of unusual things about this latest twist in the Pius wars. First, the congregation's vote, supposedly confidential, had leaked out within twenty-four hours. Second, we soon learned the congregation's decision had been without dissent and without much internal debate, which might have been expected in such a controversial case. As the pope's plane took off for São Paolo, Father Peter Gumpel, the man in charge of documenting the cause, was telling our Rome bureau that the vote was "unanimous and totally positive." Clearly, Pius supporters were going public to bring pressure on the pope: To stop this beatification, Benedict would have to go against a clear mandate from his own top administrators.

The congregation had based its decision on a six-volume, three-thousand-page *positio*, or position paper, prepared by Gumpel with meticulous detail. He claimed to have covered everything in his report—the good, the bad and the neutral. The *positio* included sworn testimony from witnesses, historical documents and a review of literature about the Vatican's activities during World War II. Because of his crucial task, Gumpel had also been given access to material in the secret archives; part of his assignment was to make sure there were no ugly surprises waiting in the basement boxes marked "Pio XII."

The beatification cause was waiting on Benedict's desk when he returned from Brazil, but the pope was in no hurry to make a decision. Weeks went by, and then it was summer, when work slows to a crawl at the Vatican. Fall arrived, and still nothing came down from the papal offices. At the Congregation for the Causes of Saints, officials suddenly realized that the fate of Pius's beatification might not be known until mid-December, when the bishops and cardinals on the congregation returned to Rome for their twice yearly meeting. If the pope had approved the "heroic virtues" decree for Pius XII, they would learn about it then—as would the whole world, since it would be among the decrees the congregation published at the end of the meeting. If not, some sort of explanation would have to be made.

The day of the congregation's plenary session arrived on December 17, 2007. The cardinals and bishops filed into the congregation offices and took their seats at a long, oval table. They were each handed a sheet of paper with the names and brief biographical data of fourteen individuals, the causes that had received Pope Benedict's formal approval. At the top of the page were miracles attributed to the intercession of six men and women. The lower half listed eight names who had lived "heroic virtues": Italian missionaries, the founder of a religious order, a Lebanese priest, a Spanish layperson, even a Roman girl called Nennolina who had died of bone cancer at age six. Pope Pius XII was not among them. The pope was going to beatify Nennolina, a child who wrote sweet and innocent letters to Jesus, and not Pius XII, the man who had steered the church through a world war, who had quietly and skillfully resisted its ideological enemies, who had opened the church to science, who had launched liturgical reform, who had written a spiritual masterpiece on the mystical Body of Christ and who had suffered the slings and arrows of partisan critics.

As the congregation members sat in stunned silence, they were informed that the pope had taken their unanimous approval of Pius's cause under advisement. In the meantime, he was appointing a commission to study the issue. Few details were offered about the commission; its members were not fully identified, and it wasn't clear when they would meet, or complete their assignment. It wasn't even stipulated what they would study. It crossed everyone's mind that this commission, like the one appointed to "study" the beatification cause of Father Léon Dehon, was simply a stalling tactic, one that could operate indefinitely.

There was one small shred of hope: Pope Benedict was clearly worried about the effect of Pius's beatification on Catholic-Jewish relations. That, in fact, was the only thing that could be "studied" at this point, since the congregation had already determined that Pius was a holy man. But what if it could be demonstrated that a sufficient number of Jewish experts considered Pius a quiet hero? That this was a question that not all Jews agreed upon? That perhaps a majority of Jews considered the naming of saints an internal Catholic question, an issue that didn't concern them? And that many Catholics wouldn't stand for a saint to be held hostage to interfaith dialogue? What if all this could be accomplished during the next ten months, culminating in the celebration of the fiftieth anniversary of the death of Pius XII, on October 9, 2008? That was now the target date, the deadline. Pope Benedict would celebrate a memorial Mass in Saint Peter's on that day and under those circumstances could not ignore the sainthood question. The pope had found a way to neutralize the thirteen prelates of the congregation, but he could hardly disregard a campaign that included cardinals, historians, Jewish leaders and rank-and-file Catholics. After years of small battles, it was time to mobilize for something bigger. The Pius crusade was just getting started.

Sister Margherita Marchione sat waiting for her ride in the foyer of her convent, just down the street from Saint Peter's Square. Through the big picture window she could see squirrels scuttling along the arbor that ran up the back side of the Janiculum hill. It was a beautiful October day in 2008, and the late afternoon sun bathed the neighborhood in a golden light. In a few minutes the nun would be off to yet another appointment—the presentation of the Italian edition of her latest book, *The Truth Will Set You Free: Commemorating the 50th Anniversary of the Death of Pope Pius XII*. As author, she would be the star attraction in the company of a number of other luminaries. Senator Giulio Andreotti would be there, as would Andrea Riccardi, the head of the influential Sant'Egidio Community, a historian and a relatively new voice in the pro-Pius chorus. Cardinal Tarcisio Bertone, the Vatican secretary of state, had written the introduction to her book. That was gratifying enough, but even more amazing was that the Vatican newspaper, *L'Osservatore Romano*, had published the cardinal's introduction in today's edition under the headline "Action, Not Lament," which began by stating, "Over the last decade, Sister Margherita Marchione has gathered documents that prove Pope Pius XII was neither silent

nor an anti-Semite; he was prudent." She had already bought several copies
of the newspaper to take back to New Jersey.

In a certain sense this had been her victory tour. But at age eighty-six
she was exhausted from all the events and attention. Her small frame
seemed to have shrunk a little, and her full-throttle energy level had ta-
pered off. She kept telling people this was her last trip to Rome. She'd said
as much before, but this time she thought she meant it. After nine books
and countless speaking engagements, she felt that she had completed her
work, as far as the subject of Pius XII was concerned: "I don't know what
more I can do. But sooner or later the truth will be known."

For Sister Margherita "sooner or later" was the following day, October
9, when the fiftieth-anniversary memorial Mass would be celebrated in
Saint Peter's Basilica. Like others, she felt confident Pope Benedict would
make the big announcement, declaring—finally—that Pius XII had lived
the Christian virtues heroically, thus opening the way to his beatification.
Certainly all the signs were favorable, she thought.

Early in the year a petition asking that the beatification of Pius XII
"proceed without delay" had been quietly circulated in the United States by
the Catholic League and the Society of Catholic Social Scientists. When it
was sent to Pope Benedict in March, the appeal had some fifteen thousand
signatures. Father Gumpel, from his Jesuit headquarters in Rome, had
helped them frame the request in language that was suitably humble but
not without force, concluding, "We urge that you honor this holy and brave
pontiff at the soonest possible date."

Church leaders in Rome, meanwhile, announced a series of major conferences and exhibits leading up to the fiftieth anniversary of Pius's death.
Among them was a symposium on Pius's influence on the Second Vatican
Council—an effort to move the discussion away from World War II and
spotlight Pius as a multifaceted leader. A biographical photo exhibit was
arranged at the Vatican, and many of the images were strikingly at odds
with the common public perception of the man: Pius standing among the
Vatican bakers as they readied emergency bread deliveries to wartime refugees in Rome, Pius meeting with Jews who'd escaped deportation in 1943,
Pius petting two lambs at his Castel Gandolfo villa, Pius with a pet canary
perched on his finger.

As the anniversary approached, *L'Osservatore Romano* began publishing full-page articles lauding every aspect of the late pontiff's character and papacy. Many editions contained more information about this dead pope than the living one.

But the most important event of the year, the one designed to remove any lingering doubts about beatification in the mind of Pope Benedict, was organized not by the Vatican but by an American Jew, Gary Krupp. Krupp, a medical businessman from Queens, had grown up hating Pope Pius, thinking the pontiff had done nothing to stop the slaughter of six million Jews. Then he began reading about Pius, and the more he read, the more he became convinced that the late pope was getting an unfair hearing from critics. He became one of Pius's most vociferous defenders, and the Vatican appreciated this unusual ally. In 2000 Pope John Paul II invested Krupp as a Knight Commander of the Pontifical Equestrian Order of Saint Gregory the Great. In 2007 Pope Benedict upgraded that with a silver star. Krupp was honored with the Servitor Pacis Award in 2006, presented by the Vatican ambassador to the United Nations. He wore his Vatican medals and his knight's uniform with pride. In 2003 he and his wife, Meredith, had founded the Pave the Way Foundation with this ambitious objective: "To enable all the world's religions to mutually realize that extremism, politics and personal agendas must not be allowed to poison the true benevolent message common to all faiths."

In mid-September of 2008 Krupp held a Pius XII symposium in Rome, which he envisioned as a kind of showdown. The program featured Catholic and Jewish speakers—including Father Gumpel—and video footage of interviews with people who had been saved from the Holocaust through the church's intervention. Krupp's innovation was to have invited about seventy guests who had been suspicious or negative toward Pius's wartime role, including rabbis and other Jewish representatives. The idea was to show that if Pius's legacy could survive this critical audience, there was simply no reason to delay his beatification any longer. The move was considered brilliant by Vatican officials, who arranged a papal audience for participants.

Krupp himself left no doubt where he stood. Pius, he said, had wisely refrained from high-profile actions on behalf of Jews because he'd correctly surmised it would lead to even greater Nazi persecution. Instead, Pius worked secretly through the church's pastoral network to save hundreds of thousands of lives. It was that simple, and Jewish critics of the late pope should be "ashamed." The time had come, Krupp said, for the world "to forgive Pius XII for not talking the talk but truly commend him for walking the walk."

The three-day symposium was hardly a completely open debate. Some of the most critical Jewish groups wanted nothing to do with Krupp and his pro-Vatican agenda and declined his invitation. Representatives from three major Jewish museums did not participate, even though Krupp had offered to pay for a live video feed if they were unable to travel to Rome. But many of the Jews who did attend seemed genuinely impressed at the evidence marshaled in support of Pius. David Nekrutman, executive director of the Israeli-based Center for Jewish-Christian Understanding and Cooperation, was perhaps typical. He said he'd arrived at the symposium not knowing much about Pius XII, but "whatever I knew, it was definitely bad." Ever since seeing an exhibit on Pius's wartime failures at the Yad Vashem Holocaust Memorial in Jerusalem, Nekrutman had written off the Catholic Church. But in Rome the symposium program had convinced him that Pius did indeed help the Jews. "What I am now trying to discover is to what extent," Nekrutman explained—exactly what Krupp and the Vatican were hoping for.

Among the first to arrive at the Mass for the fiftieth anniversary of the death of Pope Pius XII was Sister Margherita Marchione. Worried that Saint Peter's Basilica wouldn't fill up on a Wednesday morning, she had phoned friends and relatives the day before in her hometown south of Rome, urging them to get on a bus and come to the Mass. As she looked around she saw her fears had been unfounded: The church was already packed. Cardinal Angelini sat in the red hat section, and Father Blet was nearby. Senator Andreotti presided over a significant group of political leaders. Two and a half years earlier they had all met for the conference at the Lateran University, united in a cause. Today they would find out whether the pope was on their side.

The remarkable fact was that few people inside the Vatican really knew what Benedict had in mind, and even for those at the highest levels of the Roman Curia, his intentions were extremely difficult to read.

Benedict began his sermon, as usual, by reflecting on the day's Scripture readings. It so happened that the Old Testament reading was from the Book of Sirach: Those who intend to follow the Lord, it said, must be prepared to face trials and suffering, and need patience lest they lose heart. Benedict was obviously drawing a parallel with the trials and sufferings endured by Pius XII, but it crossed the minds of beatification boosters that his words—especially the word "patience"—might also be intended for them.

Soon enough Benedict was describing Pius's actions during World War II. He hit all the right notes: Pius's unceasing acts of charity to the persecuted, regardless of religious affiliation; his personal sacrifice of food, heating and other comforts in order to share the distress of the population in Rome; his public statements against those "destined for death" because of nationality or race—a clear allusion, Benedict said, to the deportations and extermination being perpetrated against the Jews.

He then turned to the encyclicals written by Pius, the theological insights, the innovations in ecclesiology. Then, suddenly, it came.

"Dear brothers and sisters, while we pray that the cause of beatification of Servant of God Pius XII may proceed successfully, it is good to remember that holiness was his ideal, an ideal he did not fail to propose to everybody," the pope said.

And that was it. No announcement, no decree of heroic virtues, no timetable—just a brief allusion to the beatification cause, and the prayer that it might turn out well. Considering that Pope Benedict was, at this point, the only obstacle to beatification, what kind of prayer was this? Another appeal for patience? Another indefinite delay? The pope didn't seem to realize that the situation had gone too far for that.

To the larger public it was not immediately apparent what had happened at the commemorative Mass. But among the dignitaries seated in the front rows of the basilica, the disappointment was palpable. Sister Margherita left clutching her Mass booklet and prepared for her trip back to the States. Instead of going home in triumph, she was just going home. "He should have done it. This was the time," she said later. "The Vatican's afraid of the Jews."

✦ ✦ ✦

The world headquarters of the Jesuit order lies in a block of nondescript buildings on Borgo Santo Spirito, tucked into the base of Janiculum Hill about a hundred yards from Saint Peter's Square. From the window of his second-floor office, Father Peter Gumpel enjoyed a vista of the garden that covered the hillside behind the complex with orange trees and flower beds. To this panorama had been recently added a tall silver flue that carried exhaust from the Jesuit laundry. "It rather ruins the poetry of the view," Father Gumpel said with the barest hint of regret.

I went to see Gumpel shortly after the grand celebrations for Pope Pius XII had come to an end. The man who had shepherded the cause sat before me in a thick wool sweater, straight as a stick and just as thin, frankly acknowledging his frustration at the delay in beatification but avoiding any direct criticism of Pope Benedict.

"Would you like a cigarette?" he asked hopefully as soon as I sat down, pointing to a pack of Rothmans on his desk. No thanks, I said, but knowing his habit I invited him to indulge. He declined, saying he smoked only if his guest smoked. This was a man who made no exceptions to the rules, even when they were his own. Gumpel spoke softly in a German accent. He had recently celebrated his eighty-fifth birthday, and his sallow face was creased with lines. The deep grooves on the sides of his chin made him look like a wooden puppet when he talked, an impression strengthened by his glassy-eyed gaze. He had retired years earlier from the Congregation for the Causes of Saints, but kept working on an unofficial basis. His job was to document sainthood causes, a task he undertook with rigor and exactitude. His office was spare, and I noticed that the thick red *Annuario Pontificio*—an essential tool, but an expensive one—was last year's edition. It crossed my mind that Gumpel probably operated on a budget close to zero. His vast wooden desk was a landscape of books and mementos. At its center a small metal crucifix was laid flat, surrounded by porcelain figurines of dogs that looked sadly upon the crucified Christ, a bizarre but touching little tableau.

I asked about his life story, and it soon came out that Gumpel was not his real name. He had been born in Germany to a wealthy noble family that fell victim to the Third Reich. It was a biographical chapter he did not enjoy exhuming, and his chin trembled with emotion as he recounted the events.

First, his grandfather was taken away and presumably killed; they never found his body, but his gold cuff links turned up in a woods. Then, in 1938, when he was fifteen years old, his uncle called to tell him his mother had been arrested on trumped-up charges and something terrible had happened. "Is she dead?" the boy asked. "Yes," he was told. That turned out to be premature, as he soon found out; she was going to be shot at five a.m. the next morning. He went to a phone booth, assuming their home phone was tapped, and made calls to important people that he knew through family connections. Then he waited up all night for news. Amazingly, his mother was spared execution at the last moment, and was later released. He and his sister were sent immediately to Holland for safety, and he never lived in Germany again. When he joined the Jesuits in 1944, he gave his name as Peter Gumpel. Given his own family's suffering under Hitler, it did bother him that some critics had characterized him as insensitive to the evils of Nazism, simply because of his defense of Pius XII.

Gumpel collated evidence for Pius's sainthood cause with scholarly zeal, and he frequently defended the late pope's record. He became a favorite among journalists because he was so quotable: Pius's critics were "woefully ignorant," their research was "historically shabby and superficial," Jewish groups were "menacing and practically blackmailing the pope." He sometimes gave American detractors of Pius a discount for inexperience and innocence: "These Americans, they have never lived in a police state. Therefore, they simply haven't got the feeling about what could be done, what was feasible, what was opportune. They just have to see this from dry documents, but they haven't lived in it."

Pope Benedict had long hoped to make a pilgrimage to the Holy Land, and in late 2008 that trip began to take shape behind the scenes. For reasons that included international public relations and its religious tourism industry, Israel strongly desired to host the pontiff. The Vatican was hoping the prospect of such a visit would help prod Israel to complete a long-pending agreement on the legal and financial status of Catholic agencies and properties. There was also endless negotiating to be done over where the pope could go, who would meet with him and how much the Israeli government would do to make the trip a success. The politics of all this was complicated, but one thing was certain: Eruption of a Catholic-Jewish conflict over Pius XII could only hurt the outcome. Pius's beatification, therefore, would have to remain in a state of suspension.

It was at that point that Father Peter Gumpel knocked this delicate diplomacy into disarray. In an interview with the Italian news agency ANSA, Gumpel took aim at a photo display at the Yad Vashem Holocaust Memorial in Jerusalem, which stated, "Even when reports about the murder of Jews reached the Vatican, the pope did not protest, either verbally or in writing." The display had long irritated the Vatican and nearly caused a diplomatic incident the year before. Now Gumpel asserted flatly that the caption was "an obvious historical falsification" and that as long as it remained in place, a papal visit to Israel "would be a scandal for Catholics."

Within minutes Gumpel's comments had caused a firestorm in Israel and deep concern at the Vatican's Secretariat of State. Officials on both sides realized that the Jesuit was single-handedly trying to scuttle the papal visit and open a new offensive in the Pius wars. Normally the Vatican allows such incidents to play themselves out, but on this occasion the Vatican spokesman, Father Federico Lombardi, also a Jesuit, issued a terse statement a few hours later contradicting Father Gumpel. Lombardi said the Yad Vashem display was indeed inaccurate, but that it would not prevent Pope Benedict from visiting Israel. Lombardi went even further, saying publicly that the pope, for the moment, was not signing the decree of heroic virtues for Pius XII because he wanted to continue the period of "study and reflection" on the question. The Vatican statement ended with the following: "In this situation it is not appropriate to exercise pressure on him in one direction or the other."

Those six words—"in one direction or the other"—were astonishing. That the Vatican would defend Pius XII from critics was to be expected, but now it was effectively telling the pro-Pius lobby in its own ranks to cease and desist.

As it turned out, Benedict was simply being Benedict, proceeding with such unhurried deliberation that even his strongest supporters were driven to distraction. Timing was everything.

The pope did make his pilgrimage to the Holy Land, in May 2009, and just as John Paul II had done in 2000, Benedict visited Yad Vashem, stood at the Western Wall, met with the chief rabbis and prayed at the Holy Sepulchre.

Pope Pius XII was never officially mentioned during the papal pilgrimage. Benedict's strategy—putting the sainthood cause on hold—had effectively defused the issue, and his Israeli hosts had no interest in raising it.

When he returned to Rome, the pope asked to see the file on Pius XII. Seven months later, in December of 2009, he finally signed the decree of heroic virtues, surprising just about everyone. Pius's backers in Rome were quietly ecstatic. In effect sainthood was now only a miracle away. Jewish groups were predictably outraged, but their criticism was mitigated by the fact that, on the same day, Benedict had signed a similar decree for Pope John Paul II. It was a classic Vatican balancing act: John Paul II was the best friend the Jews had ever had on the papal throne, even if Pius still exasperated them.

To take the edge off, the Vatican also offered what amounted to a disclaimer. The written statement came from Father Lombardi, the Vatican spokesman, and it made three points: First, sainthood was a measure not of papal performance and decision making, but of holiness and inner virtue. Second, if Pius XII were to be beatified, it would not represent an endorsement of all the choices he made during World War II. Third, given Pope Benedict's respect for Jews, his signing of the heroic virtues decree for Pius "should in no way be seen as a hostile act against the Jewish people." In effect, the Vatican was distancing itself from Pius's actions even as it moved him closer to beatification.

All that mattered now, however, was finding a miracle attributed to Pope Pius's intercession. As even his strongest supporters were aware, that might not be easy.

One of the traditional signs of sainthood, still very much taken into account by Vatican experts, is the existence of a "popular cult"—evidence that people pray to the person in the years following his or her death. The six-year-old Nennolina, for example, who was soon to be beatified, was this kind of grassroots saint. Her friends, neighbors and relatives kept the fame of her sanctity alive by publishing her letters, reporting her holiness widely and praying to the little Roman girl.

If the fact that Pius XII was a pope gave his sainthood cause some in-
herent advantages, in other ways it made perceptions of his holiness less
immediate and less personal. He was for most Catholics a remote figure at
the far end of the hierarchy. History would ultimately be his judge, and it
always struck me that whatever "popular cult" he did have seemed to be
centered in and around the Vatican.

Because Pius was born in Rome, I decided to visit the neighborhood
where he grew up. Looking at the map, I realized that I walked past his
birthplace every day yet had never been aware of it—I had never seen a
marker or memorial, or heard a word about Pius from the shopkeepers and
residents there. A few minutes later I was standing at number 34 Via degli
Orsini, an elegant five-story palazzo tucked into the warren of streets that
run west from Piazza Navona to the Tiber River. A uniformed doorman
glanced out from his cubbyhole, where he was reading a book by Oriana
Fallaci. "Dica," he said. I asked him whether this was the birthplace of Pius
XII. "Si, si," he replied with no elaboration. I asked whether one could visit
the pope's apartment. He shook his head no. Any memorial marker? I
asked. He nodded toward an inner courtyard where, near a trickling fountain, a marble plaque confirmed that, indeed, Eugenio Pacelli, later Pope
Pius XII, had been born in this very building. A well-dressed woman walking a Chihuahua came from the courtyard, and I asked whether the pope's
birthplace ever drew visitors or interest. No, she said. The Pacelli family
hadn't lived there long, and they were renters—it wasn't as if this was their
ancestral family home. At 19 Via della Vetrina, Pius's second home in
Rome, it was the same story: no sign, no memories, no apparent interest
among the residents. The people working at the building's ground-floor
tanning parlor had no idea Pius had ever lived there (and perhaps had no
idea who he was). The elementary school run by Sisters of Divine Providence, where young Pius spent his formative years, had been closed long
ago. At Chiesa Nuova, where Pacelli served as an altar boy and later worked
as a young priest, I combed the church and found no reference to Pius, save
for a tiny brass plaque that had recently been affixed to a baroque wooden
confessional. The Pacelli family's connections, it dawned on me, were all
with the Vatican—his father and brother were lawyers in the Vatican's Sacred Rota tribunal, while his grandfather had been an important minister

to two popes and had helped found the Vatican newspaper, *L'Osservatore Romano*. The Pacellis were *papalini*, a term used by Romans—often with disdain—to refer to everything managed or influenced by popes in their city. From the day of his birth, Eugenio Pacelli had been more at home in the Vatican than in Rome.

I had a few other places to visit on my pilgrimage. The first was the main Rome convent of the Religious Teachers Filippini, Sister Margherita Marchione's order, where the nuns had hidden more than sixty Jewish women and children during World War II. It's a large four-story building on Via delle Botteghe Oscure, adjacent to the old Jewish ghetto and across the street from Italy's former Communist Party headquarters. I had no appointment, but was met at the door by the black-bonneted Sister Carmella. I explained that I had heard about the Jewish families that had been concealed here, and wondered if there was anything to see—an inscription, for example. No, she explained, there was no inscription, but she did summon another nun and asked her to show me a few things.

Eighty-year-old Sister Teresa took me to a third-floor vestibule, where we stood in front of a plaster statue of Mary. The statue, she said, had been a gift of the Jews who had survived the war here. "It seems a little strange that they would choose the figure of Mary, since Jews don't believe in that. But you see, they knew we would like it," she said. On a shelf nearby was a seven-branched Jewish menorah. I asked if this was where the clandestine refugees had been hidden. Oh, no, she explained. Not up here—that wouldn't have been safe.

She led me down to the ground floor and across a courtyard, explaining cheerfully that she had not yet entered the convent during the war, but had heard the stories from the older nuns. We entered a kitchen, at one side of which was a door leading to the cellar. A fluorescent light buzzed to life, and we descended to a gray concrete labyrinth of underground chambers. It looked like a modern catacomb. It was here that the Jews had stayed, many of them for more than a year during the period of 1943–1944. Keeping them safe was not so simple, Sister Teresa told me. They had to be fed, and spies in fascist Rome were always on the lookout for anyone buying an excess amount of food. So the nuns would go out one by one, every day, to different parts of the city to buy the extra groceries.

One day Nazi soldiers had come to the complex and began banging on the front door with their rifles. The nuns inside feared the worst, and gathered to pray around a statue of Saint Joseph Labre. This eighteenth-century figure, known as the beggar saint, had lived a life of poverty and devotion on the streets of Rome, surviving from charity and sharing what little he had with others. Every morning, he would come to this same Filippini convent for a bowl of soup. When he died at age thirty-five, children in the neighborhood ran through the streets shouting, "The saint is dead! The saint is dead!" Now, 160 years later, a group of nuns invoked his protection as the Nazis pounded louder on their door. And remarkably, Sister Teresa recounted, after a while the pounding stopped. The soldiers gave up and went away. They never came back.

I asked again why there was no inscription in the convent to commemorate what had occurred here. She shrugged, saying there was no need to advertise good deeds. Then, as an afterthought, she blurted out: "And they say Pius XII didn't do anything! He gave the orders to open our doors!" Whatever documents historians had uncovered or failed to find, there was no doubt in her mind about the heroism of the late pope.

As she led me out, the nun mentioned that a Jewish baby girl hidden in the convent's basement now ran a shop a block away. Intrigued, I crossed the Via delle Botteghe Oscure and stepped into the neighborhood still known as the Jewish ghetto, a cramped residential area stretching about four blocks toward the narrowest part of the Tiber River. It was a sixteenth-century pope, the much hated Paul IV, who had confined Jews here, excluded them from all but the lowest occupations and made them wear a distinctive yellow hat. I soon found my way to the tiny children's clothing store where Ornella della Torre was sitting behind a counter. Yes, she told me, she was the one saved by the nuns' generosity. She remembered nothing firsthand because she was only an eighteen-month-old infant at the time, but the details had been told to her many times. At dawn on October 16, 1943, Nazi troops swept through the neighborhood, going house to house and rounding up Jewish men, women and children. Ornella's mother, then twenty-five, grabbed her baby daughter and slipped into the back alleys before the soldiers reached her apartment. They lived on the street for a while, then heard from others that the Filippini convent had become a safe haven.

The nuns took them in and harbored them for the coming months. Ornella spoke affectionately of the sisters and admired them for putting themselves at risk to save the lives of others. As for Pope Pius XII, she said it was likely he knew and approved the fact that Rome's religious houses were hiding so many Jews. "But," she said, and paused to choose her words carefully, "he's an ambiguous figure for me. I was a baby, so I can't judge what happened. The question is, could he have done more? Maybe he could have."

Do you think he was a saint? I asked. "Oh, no! Other popes, perhaps, not him," she said, reaching inside an accounts book to pull out a large color photo of Pope John Paul II, who had visited the Rome synagogue in 1986. "You don't know how much I liked *this* pope," she said. "But for me, when it comes to Pius XII, that question mark remains."

I had one more stop to make. Just past the synagogue I crossed the narrow Ponte Fabricio, the oldest bridge in Rome, to Tiber Island, and walked into the small Church of Saint Bartholomew. In recent years the church had been dedicated to contemporary Christians who died for the faith, and there was one chapel in particular that I wanted to see. It was marked by a handwritten card that read, "New Martyrs of Nazism." On the tiny altar of the chapel was a letter in a gilt frame. It had been written by Franz Jägerstätter, an Austrian Catholic who in 1943 was executed for refusing to serve in Hitler's army.

Jägerstätter had seemed an unlikely conscientious objector. He was a farmer and a simple man who as a youth rode a motorcycle and chased after girls. He had apparently once fathered a child out of wedlock. But after marrying a local woman named Franziska Schwaninger, his life changed. The couple came to Rome for their honeymoon in 1936 and went to Saint Peter's Square for a blessing from Pope Pius XI. Back in Austria, they read the Bible together and he began going to Mass daily. A devoted father to their three young daughters, he was conspicuous in his village for pushing the baby stroller—not something most men would do.

When Hitler came to power, Jägerstätter began to take a close look at what the Catholic Church taught about war. Gradually, he began a personal program of noncooperation, even quitting the local volunteer fire department when they took up a collection for the National Socialist Party. At one point Jägerstätter wrote down a series of questions about the morality of the Nazi war effort and went to discuss them with his bishop, only to find the bishop afraid to confront the issues. In 1943 his exemption from military service as a farmer ended, and when he was called to active duty, Jägerstätter decided he could not serve Hitler in good conscience. Local church leaders and most of his Catholic friends tried to talk him out of his decision. Think of your wife and daughters, they told him. You'll be executed, and they'll be left alone. Jägerstätter was not swayed, though it pained him to think of the suffering his death would cause his family. From his prison cell, he wrote tender letters to Franziska, telling her, "I thank you once more from the bottom of my heart for everything that you have done for me in my lifetime, for all the love and sacrifice that you have borne for me: and I beg you again forgive me if I have hurt or offended you, just as I have forgiven everything." Franz Jägerstätter was beheaded by guillotine on August 9, 1943. "I am convinced that it is best that I speak the truth, even if it costs me my life," he wrote before his sentence was carried out. A prison chaplain who witnessed his final moments remarked, "I can say with certainty that this simple man is the only saint I have met in my lifetime."

Jägerstätter might have gone unnoticed by the rest of the world if the U.S. sociologist Gordon Zahn had not stumbled upon his story in the 1950s while researching in Germany and written a biography of him. Jägerstätter's sainthood cause was introduced at the Vatican a few years later, but it didn't make much progress. In early 2007 three U.S. pacifists quietly called on the Vatican to inquire about the cause and received some good news: Pope Benedict was about to declare Jägerstätter a martyr. A few months later Jägerstätter was beatified. He had gone from the slow track to the ranks of the blessed in the blink of an eye. In late 2008, Franziska Jägerstätter, now ninety-five, traveled to Rome with her three daughters. Pope Benedict welcomed them to the Vatican and embraced them warmly. Then they came to the Church of Saint Bartholomew to remember and honor Blessed Franz. One daughter, Maria, said her absolute earliest memory was "the whole family sitting around the table and Mother reading the letter that my father had been beheaded. Everyone cried." Maria was four years old at the time. "We never felt he abandoned us," she said. They believed he was protecting them from heaven. Maria added: "Our father was always a saint to us. If you read his last letter, you would know he was." In that letter,

Franz said that now he understood how Jesus must have suffered on the cross, knowing that his mother was there watching him die.

A longer letter considered his "spiritual testament" is the one in the gilt frame, and it draws visitors from around the world who wish to see the little shrine dedicated to Franz Jägerstätter and others who stood up to the Nazi machine. Fifty-five years after his execution, this peasant farmer who put his faith before the fatherland was making a connection to Catholics and non-Catholics, young and old, people from every continent.

As I left the church and crossed back over the bridge, I pondered why Franz Jägerstätter's beatification had been such an easy process, and why the case of Pius XII was still sitting on the bench. The differences were numerous, of course. Martyrdom makes things simpler for the saintmakers: Jägerstätter had one crucial life-or-death decision to make, while Pius had to make hundreds of judgments that affected millions of people. Jägerstätter had also been forced to explain himself, and had documented a moral and spiritual struggle not to history, but to the flesh and blood around him, beginning with his own family. Pius, as supreme pontiff, never had to explain or justify his actions to anyone, nor was he expected to do so. There were hints that he, too, endured doubts and anguish, but for the most part he kept them to himself. His struggle was not part of the written record—even, apparently, among the millions of pieces of paper still locked in the Vatican archives. I felt certain that one day Pius XII would be beatified. But for now he remained for most people an enigmatic and distant figure. My brief historical pilgrimage was over. From the sidewalk leading out of the Jewish ghetto I saw the white dome of Saint Peter's Basilica come into view, floating on the horizon, majestic and remote.

CHAPTER EIGHT

HEMLINES AND
BANANA PEELS

FOUR DAYS after his election in 2005, Pope Benedict held an audience for the approximately three thousand international journalists who had covered the death of Pope John Paul II and the conclave that had chosen him as the 265th pontiff.

I took my seat in the modernistic Paul VI Audience Hall and heard colleagues express their surprise that the pope's first major audience should go to them. As Cardinal Joseph Ratzinger, the pope had spent a lifetime avoiding the press pack, preferring to work with journalists one-on-one, often in book-length interviews that were subject, of course, to his own editing. I felt certain this encounter was someone else's idea, a PR move designed to evoke a similar meeting some twenty-six years earlier when the newly elected Pope John Paul II held a freewheeling press conference with reporters.

Benedict gave a brief talk, slipping easily from Italian to French to English and his native German, and then, instead of inviting the journalists to question him, as his predecessor had, he asked them to stand and pray the Our Father. And with that it was over, the entire event having lasted seventeen minutes. As we stood around and watched from afar, Benedict greeted only a few bishops and priests who had been allowed access to the stage.

From the point of view of the pope and his aides, the meeting had gone well. But there was a problem, one that was noted in whispers during the audience and in much harsher tones later in the Vatican press hall and Roman Curia corridors. Years later, in fact, the single detail that would be remembered from this encounter was one seemingly unrelated to journalism: The hemline on the pope's white cassock was at least three inches too short. The garment looked as if it had shrunk in the wash. This fashion faux pas was duly noted by CNN and other major media, though the most strident reaction came from the pope's own aides. "My God, can't they get it right? You could see his socks!" one Vatican functionary complained afterward.

+ + +

Vatican protocol is more a mind-set than a rule book. It covers everything from papal dress to ambassadorial seating charts. Virtually nothing that happens in the Apostolic Palace, where the pope lives and works, is without a traditional form: prayers, private audiences, speeches, even such things as posture, lighting and gift giving. The pomp and circumstance move into high gear whenever a foreign dignitary arrives. It is a world where no event is unscripted, and where the little things—like the burnt red color of the pope's shoes—carry much weight. Yet it's also a world in which something can, and often does, go wrong.

Imposters have breached the front lines of papal ceremonies. Visitors have tossed leaflets, books and rocks at popes. Prime ministers and their wives have worn the wrong clothing and brought inappropriate gifts. Papal aides have been caught smoking behind the papal library. Pope Paul VI once entered Saint Peter's Basilica for a Mass and found his portable throne abandoned on the ground when his chair-bearers had gone off for coffee.

If a history of Vatican gaffes is ever written, Massimo Sansolini would be the one to do it. I met him in 1999, just after reading his book, *Io, Sediario Pontificio*—"I, Pontifical Chair-Bearer." The volume had a low print run even in Vatican City, yet it remains one of the most revealing behind-the-scenes accounts of daily life in the papal palace. The chair-bearer's job, a centuries-old tradition, was phased out in 1978, when Pope John Paul II refused to be carried aloft through the crowds, to the great disappointment of the *sediari*. Now they're known as "papal gentlemen" and function as ceremonial ushers, rarely hoisting anything heavier than a silver trayful of rosaries.

Sansolini remembered the day he lost his old job. The Polish pope walked into Saint Peter's for the first time, and as someone in the crowd called for the pope to be raised up, the pope shouted back: "No! Not in the chair!" Thus ended a centuries-old tradition.

Sansolini took to this new position with a vigilance that some might regard as extreme. He considered himself an arbiter of style and class; in his view, the Vatican's gentlemen constituted a kind of Praetorian Guard of good taste, protecting the pope from inelegant situations or outright embarrassment. He had a particularly keen eye for ecclesial attire: A well-groomed man with a regal bearing, Sansolini had been a fashion designer before joining the chair-bearers in 1964. Although his job brought him in frequent contact with the supreme pontiff, he cared little about the power of the papacy. But give him a swatch of the best *doupioni* silk and his eyes would dilate. He had a penchant for copes and capes, especially the *cappa magna*, the greatest of liturgical cloaks—unfortunately out of favor after Vatican II—with its train of scarlet silk stretching some thirty feet. It pained him that Pope Paul VI had progressively done away with these magical splashes of vestments and accoutrements. In Sansolini's eyes, the world of the papacy had passed from royal red to a pedestrian beige—quite literally: Paul VI had even replaced the burgundy damask wallpaper in Vatican offices with a mousy taupe wall carpeting. Ugh.

Whenever a world leader arrived for a papal audience, Sansolini was there, dressed in his tuxedo-style uniform with a row of ribboned medals on his lapel. Sansolini watched the VIPs scrupulously, taking mental notes. Afterward, he would pass judgment—and in Sansolini's court of fashion, there was no appeal. European royalty acquitted themselves quite admirably. Meeting Pope John Paul in 1980, Queen Elizabeth was elegance personified, right down to the jeweled "E" on the sash that draped from her shoulder. Heads of state, on the other hand, were more prone to blunders. French president Valéry Giscard d'Estaing had earned high marks until he crossed his legs during the pope's speech, a breach of protocol that Sansolini could hardly believe. The Eastern Europeans were even worse. When Polish premier Lech Wałesa and his wife walked hand in hand down the Vatican corridor on their way to see the pope, they looked to Sansolini like a couple strolling on their honeymoon. And what was that on her head? Some kind of military beret? When Raisa Gorbachev showed up to see the pope wearing red instead of the traditional black, and no veil, it pained Sansolini to give her demerits, because she seemed otherwise like a classy lady.

U.S. presidents were habitually the worst violators of the unwritten rules. Jimmy Carter struck Sansolini as someone who had just stepped out of the Georgia backwoods, smiling too much, making too much noise and moving his arms like windmills. The Americans always seemed baffled by the array of Vatican uniforms, unable to match the rank with the garb. One U.S. president, flush from a papal audience, greeted a long line of Vatican dignitaries and then, with a flourish, turned toward the Vatican's elevator operator—whose uniform featured shoulder loops and silver buttons—and gave him a snappy military salute.

The Wednesday general audience was less than an hour away, and already the Paul VI Audience Hall was filling up. It was a splendid October morning, and Pope John Paul II, just back from a trip to the United States, would draw another standing-room-only crowd. Massimo Sansolini was on duty, helping a bishop take his place in front of the pope's chair. He looked at the prelate's pectoral cross and winced. The cross itself was an acceptable silver design, but it was bouncing all over the man's chest. Bishops no longer pinned the cross to the third button, its rightful place, but wore it on a long chain, where it swung from armpit to armpit. Another unfortunate sign of the times.

It was nearly ten thirty, and Sansolini had a sudden pang of hunger. He turned to his friend Gianfranco, another papal usher, who always brought small chocolate bars, the good bitter kind. But today Gianfranco shook his head. "Sorry, no chocolate. I've got two beautiful ripe bananas in my overcoat, but I don't know where we can eat them with this crowd." Sansolini surveyed the hall as Gianfranco went to the cloakroom and returned with the bananas under his uniform. They ducked into a side passage, then through a series of private chambers, greeting Swiss Guards along the way. The tiny last room was empty, and here they could finally eat their bananas in peace. Sansolini peeled his and took a big bite—and then, to his horror, the door opened. A group of VIP pilgrims entered and rushed through on their way to the hall. The two papal gentlemen stood at attention, the bananas hidden behind their backs, their mouths full. Luckily, no one noticed; eating on the job was a faux pas that would not be forgiven at the Vatican. They wolfed down the rest of their bananas, stashed the peels and hurried back to the auditorium.

By now the crowd was seated, and in a few minutes the pope would walk in, prompting an explosion of camera flashes and jockeying for position among the pilgrims. Sansolini scanned the crowd for signs of trouble. Technically, papal ushers don't deal with security at these audiences, but they often end up protecting ceremonial dignity from a certain fringe element. Sansolini had seen it all: men and women who rushed the pope for an autograph, couples who set their infants free to roam toward the papal stage, individuals caught up in spiritual seizures. One woman showed up demanding a front-row seat, declaring loudly and repeatedly, "I am the mother of the baby Jesus!" The ushers headed off embarrassment by telling her, "Listen, dear, your baby is hungry, and you'd better go home to feed him." She immediately got up and, thanking them, left the hall.

Sansolini's most memorable encounter in the audience hall still haunted him. He had noticed a strange group of people enter, carrying a woman on a stretcher and looking for seats close to the papal stage. One of his superiors whispered to him: "Keep them back. Not near the front. And block them if they try to move up." Evidently this ensemble was already known to the higher powers. When Sansolini approached them, he was even more amazed: Two priests and a Carabinieri official were in front, followed by two men who bore the stretcher and two others who carried little footstools. A man with two children completed the tableau. The woman lay in a semiconscious state, moaning quietly. She looked pale and distressed, and both her hands were heavily bandaged. As her companions slowly unwound the bandages, Sansolini understood what was happening: The woman bore the *stigmata*, the bleeding wounds of Christ. When one of the priests lifted her hat—Sansolini noticed it was an old-fashioned French-style bonnet with a pleated ruche—he saw that her forehead was covered with numerous small wounds that oozed fresh blood, as if they had been produced by a crown of thorns. The woman, Sansolini was told, was the mother of three children and had suffered the *stigmata* for two years. She no longer ate, nourishing herself solely by eating daily the consecrated host of Communion. She wanted desperately to greet Pope John Paul.

Sansolini had seen his share of sham mystics at papal audiences, but he felt instinctively that this woman was genuine and decided to intervene. The order to keep the group away from the pope had come from Archbishop Dino Monduzzi, prefect of the Papal Household. Monduzzi ran the show at the general audience, and there was no arguing with him. A grizzled, chain-smoking Italian who barked out orders in monosyllables, he didn't like surprises. Now he stood and listened to Sansolini plead the woman's case, all the while watching the door for the pope's imminent arrival. Monduzzi looked irritated; he had no intention of moving the group to the *prima fila* and risking public embarrassment. Then he had an inspiration and muttered, "The Room of the Green Divan." Sansolini nodded and led the group to the small chamber where the pope could greet people privately just before he entered the big hall of the auditorium. As they disappeared the woman turned her head on the stretcher and gently thanked him.

Today Sansolini stood in the front of the hall and glanced carefully over the *prima fila* section. The guests here were granted not only a front-row seat but a close encounter with the pope afterward. *Prima fila* tickets were rare and valuable, usually obtained through connections. But as Sansolini knew only too well, not everyone who managed to get into this section had done so legitimately. Imposters would sometimes dress in ecclesiastical garb so they could meet the pope, maybe even kiss his ring and have their picture taken. Over the years, Sansolini had removed false nuns, priests and even bishops from the *prima fila*. He felt he could spot a ringer instantly just by looking at their clothing. And now his gaze was fixed on an older prelate, apparently a South American, who had a counterfeit air about him. His attire seemed in order—a buttoned black cassock with the violet piping and waistband proper to his rank—but then Sansolini's eyes fell on the bishop's feet. He was wearing white socks! Within minutes the team of ushers had gently intervened and moved the pseudo-prelate to a seat at the back of the audience hall, over his strong objections.

That day Sansolini helped identify four other fake bishops. One wore a cassock that was tinted a dark gray instead of black. Another showed up in a "clergyman" black suit instead of a cassock—a mistake no real bishop would make. Another had on a fine Oriental-style suit that was a telltale purple, and still another had swirling long sleeves more appropriate to a kimono. Bogus, each and every one of them. Fashion was the final arbiter. They sat in the back.

The zealous pursuit of imposters by papal ushers might seem exaggerated, but frauds and phonies have long gained access to the front lines of papal ceremonies. In 1997 a well-groomed Spanish-speaking man showed up in the audience hall with his wife and two small children, declaring himself the new ambassador of Mexico. They greeted the pope personally and quite warmly, then slipped back into the crowd before anyone noticed that the real Mexican ambassador was working in his office a few blocks away.

But the most notorious hoaxster, one who made headlines when he was caught in 1988, was a figure out of Woody Allen's *Zelig*. Police picked up Ugo Ferrari, a forty-eight-year-old man with a history of mental problems, for suspected arson in four Rome churches. An odd series of events had led authorities to him. At one of the fire-damaged churches, a Vatican official had recently been invested as a cardinal. The pastor there became suspicious after a Vatican photographer called him to identify a thin, elegantly dressed man who appeared prominently in several photographs. The pastor recalled that the man had several weeks earlier presented himself as a Vatican security agent for a "check" of the church. During the ceremony the pastor never questioned his presence, and Vatican personnel assumed he was a local guest of honor.

This was, in fact, Ferrari's standard operating procedure. He sometimes dressed in elaborate uniforms, which he found would open many doors, and had an obsequious, "curial" demeanor, frequently falling to his knees before bishops and other ecclesial authorities.

When police arrested him, they discovered a scrapbook of newspaper photos showing him with Pope John Paul II and other church personalities. There he was walking in procession behind Polish Cardinal Józef Glemp; at Cardinal Achille Silvestrini's side during his investiture; kissing the hand of John Paul II—a photo that ended up on the front page. Police searching Ferrari's room at a Rome boardinghouse also found a drawerful of notes and telegrams from various bishops who had apparently answered his correspondence.

The church fires Ferrari allegedly set were small ones, enough to send the pastor scurrying for help while Ferrari looked for money and valuables in the sacristy. But the fact that Ferrari had so easily impersonated a Vatican security agent was cause for some alarm. Vatican security had a reputation for being discreet but highly effective, yet that aura of invincibility was strictly an image, as its own officials knew only too well. Ferrari had exposed the Vatican for what it was: a theater where anyone in the right costume could take center stage.

The Swiss Guard at the Bronze Gate saluted me and stamped his boot so hard that it echoed like a gunshot. I climbed the three flights of steps toward the Cortile di San Damaso, the heart of the Apostolic Palace, where a picket of Swiss Guards was assembling and a worn red carpet was being rolled out. The sun was beating down hard, and the men were already sweltering in their uniforms. I walked across the courtyard and flashed my pass at a guard *commandante*, then entered the main building and stepped into the elevator, which took me to a gleaming marble hallway where a small crowd of monsignors and ushers was milling around, ready to go into the usual drill when a foreign dignity arrived—in this case, the president of Rwanda.

It was my first time as a participant in a reporting pool at the pope's library, and I was duly impressed. Weren't those Raphael's frescoes on the ceiling of the loggia? Ahead of me was a telescoping series of rooms, each more sumptuously decorated than the next. In the Clementine Hall another row of Swiss Guards stood at attention, halberds at the ready. This was the route the visiting president would walk, escorted by a legion of Vatican attendants.

I was led to a chamber that housed a statue of Mary and Jesus and an antique clock ticking out the seconds on a magnificent walnut table.

With me were three pool photographers, one of whom began chatting to a colleague until our minder, Marjorie Weeke, silenced him with a withering glance. She eyed him closely for a moment, looking critically at his purple tie and unkempt collar. "Next time wear something decent," she barked. He had been let off lightly; more than once Marjorie had ejected journalists from papal events for improper attire. "What is it they don't understand about 'dark suit'?" she would complain. A thin, wiry woman who used her elbows to move through a pack of journalists, she had a sharp tongue and a keen eye for anything that might appear indecorous at a papal event. She commanded respect from Vatican guards and the pope's protective circle, no little accomplishment for an American. Her unique talent was in knowing how to deal with the media, especially TV people. She understood how important it was for the cameras to get their perfect shot, but she also recognized that reporters had to be as invisible as possible at the Vatican. If you were a camera operator or a photographer, you didn't want to get on Marjorie's bad side, because she controlled position at papal events. And she had a long memory.

Marjorie was queen of the caustic remark, but she was not humorless. She stood next to me now, looked at her watch and muttered out the side of her mouth: "Ten minutes late. I suppose they'll blame it on the traffic." She gave a little harrumph of a laugh and shook her head. Silence returned to the room, and the ticking clock now seemed to be scolding the late arrivals. Then someone rang a tiny bell, and the choreography began.

In a few moments the president and his entourage appeared and made their way to the papal library at a processional pace. As soon as they had passed, Marjorie pushed us quickly through a small door and herded us down a back passageway, a shortcut to the antechamber of the library. "Come on, move it," Marjorie ordered a straggling photographer, whose camera lenses swung against the narrow walls of the corridor. We arrived just in time to see the president round the corner and Pope John Paul come out to greet him. Handshakes, smiles, a photo op that lasted ten, fifteen seconds at most, and then they went inside.

We traipsed back into the warren of hidden passages and into a tiny holding room on the far side of the papal library. The photographers sat on an old wooden bench and looked up at the frescoes, saints framed by distorted arabesques. In strolled Monsignor Stanisław Dziwisz, the pope's secretary, who smiled and made small talk with everyone in the room. Two reporters from Rwanda had joined us, and Dziwisz now went to get them some papal rosaries to take to their friends and relatives back home. I made my way to a small service window that overlooked a dimly lit courtyard. A prelate in full regalia stood in front of me, dragging deeply on a cigarette and blowing smoke out the window. Archbishop Monduzzi, gatekeeper for papal appointments, kept an ashtray here for these crucial nicotine breaks in between audiences. He chatted with an usher and was soon lighting up another smoke, which he had to suddenly stub out a few moments later when a loud buzzer rang: The pope had a little button under his desk that he'd press when he wanted to end a private audience, a signal for Monduzzi or others to come in. Today the meeting had run its course in less than ten minutes. The door to the library opened. Monduzzi stuffed the pack of cigarettes in the pocket of his soutane and straightened his sash. The ushers stacked medallions on a tray to hand out to the president and his entourage. Then we all paraded inside, where the pope stood chatting with his guest in front of a painting of the risen Christ.

I could see immediately that the pope's library was not really a library, but a ceremonial meeting room. The members of the visiting entourage had been ushered in and were seated in beige chairs flanking an Oriental carpet. We stood on the opposite side of the room, the photographers clicking away while we print reporters tried in vain to hear snatches of conversation between the pope and the president. They exchanged gifts, the pope said thank you very much and it was over. Dziwisz saw them all to the door, and the press corps was sent back the way we'd come in. The entire event had lasted less than twenty minutes. I looked at my notebook on the way back to the Vatican press office. It was empty save for "painting of Africa," the gift presented to the pope. My briefing to fellow reporters lasted thirty seconds. As far as I know, no one outside of Rwanda wrote about the event.

Over the years I've witnessed papal audiences with major leaders and minor functionaries, with dictators and Nobel Prize winners, with saints and sinners. I was present when Mikhail Gorbachev arrived for his historic meeting with John Paul II in 1989 as the future of Eastern Europe hung in the balance. I watched Yasser Arafat enjoy his papal moment, laughed when John Paul tried on Bono's sunglasses and observed Pope Benedict zone out during countless audiences with heads of state. The papal encounters with American presidents have always been the most entertaining, and offer the clearest proof of a culture gap between the hierarchies of the Vatican and those of the United States. Briefly stated, Americans are backslappers and chitchatters; Vatican officials from the pope on down are ring kissers and speech givers.

In June of 2007 President George W. Bush arrived for his first meeting with Pope Benedict.

This was a somewhat tense moment in U.S.-Vatican relations, and the issue was Iraq. Four years earlier Bush had dismissed Pope John Paul's cautionary warnings about war during the buildup to the invasion of Iraq, leaving deep resentment at the Vatican. In the aftermath of Saddam Hussein's demise, as terrorism, factional fighting and anti-Christian attacks increased, the Vatican said, essentially, "We told you so." When Bush subsequently came for a meeting with Pope John Paul in 2004, it had been a masterpiece of Vatican staging. The pope and president each delivered speeches in the ornate Clementine Hall. Normally when a president came to visit, the Vatican filled the hall with American clergy, seminarians and others lucky enough to be invited for the event. It inevitably produced a pep rally mood and good feelings all around. But on this occasion few Americans were included, and the velvet chairs were mostly empty. The mood was somber, and turned positively sour when the pope began to speak. In a strained and halting voice, and with every ounce of energy he could muster, the ailing Pope John Paul gave Bush a dressing-down that he would not soon forget. He reminded the president of the Vatican's opposition to the war and declared that things were going poorly in Iraq: terrorism. "Grave unrest." The lack of political reorganization. What Iraq needed now, he insisted, was to get its sovereignty back, preferably under some kind of international framework. John Paul referred to the "deplorable" disclosures of abuse of Iraqi prisoners by U.S. soldiers and said it undermined the fight against terrorism. Bush squirmed on his oversized chair and looked like a schoolboy being told his grades were failing.

Now, three years later, Bush was hoping to turn the page with the new pope. Unfortunately, however, Benedict was not being particularly cooperative. Earlier in 2007, at his Easter "Urbi et Orbi" address from the balcony of Saint Peter's, the pope had bluntly declared that "nothing positive comes from Iraq, torn apart by continual slaughter as the civil population flees." That sent officials of the U.S. embassy to the Holy See into a damage-control frenzy. Publicly they insisted that the United States and the Vatican were essentially in agreement when it came to rebuilding Iraq. Privately they met with Vatican foreign policy experts and let it be known that the pope's remarks were "not constructive"—about as harsh a phrase one can use in Vatican diplomacy.

So today the stage was set once again for diplomatic drama. I expected Benedict to be a bit easier on Bush than his predecessor had been. Iraq would be mentioned, but it would not dominate their meeting. The reason was that Bush and Benedict aligned on pro-life issues, and that weighed as much or more with the German pope.

As soon as the president and his entourage had passed, we hustled through the back corridor toward the papal library, where we were allowed to witness the president's arrival. Even before Bush entered the room, I heard his voice call out to a papal aide, "How ya doin'?" Then he rounded the corner and greeted His Holiness warmly: "It's good to be with you, sir." That "sir" would be duly noted, and points taken off. Bush then sat down across the desk from the pope, leaned back comfortably in the gilded chair and crossed his legs. I scanned the room to see if Massimo Sansolini had noticed.

Before we were chased out, I heard the pope ask Bush about his meeting earlier in the week in Germany, a summit of the G8, the heads of the major industrialized countries. Bush called it "successful," but when the pope pressed for details, the president kept his answer short. "It was, you know, a lot of different opinions. But it was good. It was good." The pope stared unblinking at the president. As the door to the library closed, leaving the two of them alone, I could only wonder what they would talk about for the next half hour.

When we returned for the gift giving and the picture taking, I immediately noticed the roughly carved walking stick. It lay on the table that separated the journalists from the ceremony, which Benedict and Bush were now approaching. I've always thought that selecting a gift for the pope must be a tough assignment. What do you give him? American artwork? He has warehouses full of art. A book? Equally redundant, given the Vatican's vast libraries. President Lyndon B. Johnson came up with a novel idea in 1967 when he presented Pope Paul VI with a bronze bust—of LBJ, apparently leaving Paul VI speechless. Now Pope Benedict, standing a few feet in front of the journalistic pack, picked up the walking stick and examined the lettering that wound around its length. "The Ten Commandments?" the pope asked. "The Ten Commandments, yes, sir," Bush replied. The president explained that it had been carved by a homeless man in Texas, whose talent had been discovered by some friends in their local church. Thanks to the sales of his walking sticks, the man had managed to get himself off the streets and into an efficiency apartment. It was, in short, an American success story, one that combined charity and initiative, without the interference of the welfare state.

As we were led out of one door of the library I turned back and saw the papal gentlemen holding up the walking stick and looking at its rather crude lettering. For a pope who had a closetful of silver pastoral staffs, this might have seemed an odd bequest. But it was not scorned. As one usher told me later, "The spirit of the gift was very simple and direct. Very American."

President Bush returned to the Vatican in the summer of 2008 for what he knew would be a farewell audience with the pope. The president's planners wanted something big, something special, and they felt Benedict owed them one. A few months earlier the president had hosted the pope at the White House in an extravagant ceremony. With thousands of Washington's movers and shakers in attendance on the South Lawn, Bush greeted Benedict with the words "*Pax tecum*" and then gave him a welcoming speech that was flattering even by Vatican standards. That event set a tone of welcome and respect that carried through the rest of the pope's U.S. visit and helped make it a success.

White House aides were now thinking the pope could reciprocate by hosting the president in the Vatican Gardens. It would be an unusual break with protocol, but the less formal setting would put the president at ease. The meeting would also burnish Bush's "world leader" credentials a few months before he left office. When they floated the idea, Vatican organizers were not enthusiastic, but finally agreed. The two leaders would meet in a medieval tower at the far end of Vatican City, then take a stroll through the picturesque gardens. The whole event was designed as a rolling photo op.

The trouble with photo ops, though, is that they don't really produce much hard news. I watched the live coverage on Italian TV, and the event appeared to be little more than a series of awkward handshakes and nods. The stroll in the garden looked especially strained for both participants. It was only later in the day that I was able to piece together through the Vatican's video footage some of the conversation that had taken place between Bush and Benedict, and I understood just how little substance there had been behind the theater.

The video showed a picture-perfect June day at the far corner of the Vatican Gardens, where the pope stood in front of Saint John's Tower and waited for his guests. When the president arrived, he bounded out of his limousine with an enthusiasm that was clearly absent in his host. The pope smiled and responded in monosyllables to the president's expressions of amazement at the tower, the gardens and the weather. Bush quickly attached himself to the only American in sight, Archbishop James Harvey, addressing him loudly and mistakenly throughout the visit as "Your Eminence"—the standard address reserved for cardinals—instead of "Your Excellency." Harvey, a soft-spoken prelate who organized papal appointments, had been brought in to act not so much as a translator but as a buffer between the pope and the president.

"You look great!" Bush told the pope as they entered an elevator for what must have been a long ride to the second floor of the tower.

"*Ja*," the pope replied.

The cameras were turned off for their private meeting and picked up again when Benedict, Bush and Harvey went back into the elevator to catch the panoramic view from the tower's parapet above.

"Your Eminence, you're looking good!" Bush informed Archbishop Harvey, who kept his eyes to the ground. As the three gazed out over the Vatican Gardens, the president grew animated and asked how much land they had. The pope let Harvey answer: 109 acres. "Not quite as big as Texas," Harvey added. "But more important," Bush retorted, prompting them all to chuckle. This was the kind of repartee the president enjoyed.

From the other side of the tower they looked down upon the ancient Vatican walls. Bush cogitated in silence, then asked, "So do people patrol from up here?" Benedict stared blankly and let Harvey field this one, too. "They can," the archbishop said. "Do people try to break in? I mean, try to?" the president wanted to know. "There's not too much of that," Harvey said wearily as Pope Benedict turned and began heading back to the elevator.

The gift-giving scene was predictable, with the pope giving Bush a framed photo of their recent meeting at the White House, and the president presenting Benedict with a framed photo of the same event. Pope Benedict also included a big picture book of the Vatican, telling the president, "Perhaps you will now have time to read a little." Bush thought for a moment, then agreed heartily, "I bet we do!"

Next came the stroll in the garden, the kind of staged event the Vatican does not do well. Vatican theater works best when performed under a baroque altar canopy or in the sumptuous halls of the Apostolic Palace, where dozens of bit players contribute to the choreography and where the supreme pontiff is the protagonist—the man who can push the button under his desk and have his guest ushered out. Out in the Vatican Gardens, a news helicopter buzzed overhead as camera operators and photographers crouched behind the trees lining the footpath. Papal and presidential aides followed fifty paces behind at a slow pace, moving like a phalanx of zombies. Benedict seemed uncomfortable, and Bush looked as if he was still trying to kick-start a real conversation with the pope. He swung his arms, turned his head, smiled and pointed to things—the trees, the walls—while the pope mostly stared straight ahead.

Finally they reached a grotto where the Sistine Chapel boys' choir—the Vatican's answer to the fife and drum corps at the White House—would sing two songs. An Oriental rug had been placed on the cobblestones, where President Bush, Mrs. Bush and the pope took seats on three wooden deck chairs. Afterward Bush went up to greet the boys, peppering them with questions in English, which none of them understood. The pope was already in departure mode. The president's armored limousine pulled up. Bush's final good-bye to the pope was a nod and a wave; he appeared to consider going back for a warm handshake in front of the photographers, thought better of it and climbed into the car.

I had been watching the video with a Vatican employee, who turned to me afterward and noted the time.

"One hour, four minutes," he said. "It seemed longer."

CHAPTER NINE

SEX

THE VOICE at the other end of the phone was gaining speed, straining my note-taking skills, and the speaker's heavy Tuscan accent didn't make things any easier. But what he was telling me held me spellbound.

"When they write about AIDS, reporters talk about the church's 'moral doctrine' against condoms, or a Vatican crusade against condoms. That's simply not true. We've never published a document on this, and for good reason. Some individuals have made remarks, but that is not the same as an official position," he said.

I tried to get a question in, but he was talking too fast to stop.

"I maintain that there can be situations in which the use of the condom is licit—not as an exception but licit in itself—because it is used with the goal of health protection. For example, if you have a Catholic couple, married, and one of the spouses has the virus. This is not hypothetical, you know. Pastors have to deal with these questions. In places like Nigeria, there are hundreds, maybe thousands, of Catholic couples where one of the partners is HIV positive. Many of these couples would like to have children, but they risk death if they have sexual relations without a condom. In such a situation, you can make a case for using the condom. Clearly the couple's intention is not contraception, which is what the church finds morally objectionable about the condom. It's a case of protecting human life. In fact, it may be a form of self-defense," he added.

The year was 2003, and the voice on the phone belonged to an Italian theologian, but not just any theologian. Father Maurizio Faggioni was an expert on bioethics, a medical doctor and, most important, a key adviser to the Vatican's Congregation for the Doctrine of the Faith, then headed by Cardinal Joseph Ratzinger. If what Faggioni was telling me was accurate, the doctrinal congregation had refrained from making a pronouncement on the use of condoms to protect against HIV/AIDS precisely because its own experts were engaged in a theological debate on the issue. It was a debate that most Catholics would never have imagined taking place inside the Vatican.

I knew from experience that this was a hot-button issue—often *the* hot-button issue—in the minds of many Americans, including those inside and outside the church. Whenever I returned to my home state of Minnesota or gave a talk somewhere in the United States, I was inevitably asked: How can the church justify its no-condoms policy when it's killing people? For years I had been responding that, despite the public impression, no pope had ever stated that using condoms to prevent AIDS was morally wrong, that the new and encyclopedic Catechism of the Catholic Church was silent on the matter and that the whole question remained a gray area. Yes, several Vatican officials did believe that condom campaigns were not the answer, and in fact were concerned that they might give people a false sense of security. But this was far different from proclaiming it sinful. All of which, I am sure, made me sound like a hairsplitting apologist for the Vatican's position.

Now I was listening to one of the Vatican's own specialists—one of a handful of theologians who could actually claim to be shaping policy—tell me that the use of condoms was an open question.

"The doctrinal congregation has looked at many aspects of the problem. But the fact is, there are no easy answers. There is no new 'doctrine' for AIDS, you understand, just classic moral principles that need to be applied in individual circumstances. That's why we haven't published a document on this: We don't need one. The real moral problem is dealt with at an individual level, in concrete cases, not by abstract pronouncements," he said.

"But what about the various cardinals who've gone on record as saying condoms are inherently bad? Aren't they leaving the opposite impression?" I asked.

Faggioni sighed audibly. "These aren't official positions—they're personal opinions. And it amazes me that the press doesn't know the difference. This question has shadings and nuances that need to be kept in mind, but the press just wants to roll it into one big homogeneous mass: 'The Vatican says.' 'The Vatican' is not any cardinal who opens his mouth."

I went back to the question of condom campaigns, often supported by governments and international health agencies. "What's the problem with that?" I asked.

"Look, you have to begin by acknowledging that the condom is not one hundred percent effective. In a percentage of cases—seven, eight, maybe ten percent—the condom does not protect completely. That means, from a personal point of view, it doesn't offer absolute security. But from the standpoint of health care policies, it's still clear that use of condoms reduces the spread of the disease. So from this perspective, health officials can argue that it's better to promote condom use and lower the rate of infection. For the church, this presents a problem—which is why the church recommends abstinence. But it's one thing to advise abstinence, and another thing to demand it," he said.

I wondered if Faggioni was a lone reasonable voice on all this, or if he represented a strong faction inside the Vatican. I later called another adviser to the doctrinal congregation, Monsignor Ángel Rodríguez Luño, an Opus Dei priest and moral theologian at Rome's Pontifical University of the Holy Cross. He said he thought the trouble with condom campaigns was that they tended to promote sexual permissiveness—a commonly held viewpoint in the Vatican.

Many people assume that because the condom is a contraceptive device, the church's condemnation is automatic. But Luño explained that it was a mistake to think that for the church this was primarily a birth control issue. For one thing, he noted, sexual relations outside of marriage, whether homosexual or heterosexual, are already considered immoral by the church, so whether a condom is used is beside the point. "The church does not have a doctrine on the various ways to carry out immoral acts," he observed with a slightly ironic tone. The point was that sinful sex was no more or less sinful with a condom—indeed, a condom under these circumstances might simply be prudent.

What struck me about these theologians was that they seemed virtually invisible in the ever percolating media storm over the Vatican and HIV/AIDS. As World AIDS Day approached on December 1, 2003, the head of the Pontifical Council for the Family, the late Colombian Cardinal Alfonso López Trujillo, said in a televised interview with the BBC that the latex used in condoms was porous enough to allow the HIV virus to pass through—a claim that prompted scientific ridicule and political condemnation. Even inside the Vatican, Cardinal López Trujillo was known as a loose cannon, but for that very reason journalists loved him and were eager to use him as a spokesman for the Catholic Church. For weeks the story generated headlines: "Activists Blast Vatican Stand on Condoms," "Catholics Should Challenge Church's AIDS Claim," "UN Official Slams Vatican" and "In the Fight Against AIDS, Catholics Can Only Be Ashamed."

I wrote a story based on what Faggioni and others had told me, and it did raise a few eyebrows. As one journalistic colleague told me, however, it was ultimately "too theological." My piece did nothing to diminish the widespread perception that the Vatican was anti-condom, pure and simple. Moreover, I later learned that one effect of my article was that Father Faggioni had been asked not to give any more interviews.

Clearly the condom debate among Vatican theologians touched some raw nerves. One day I went to the John Paul II Institute at Rome's Lateran University to interview two specialists in sexual ethics who also had influence at the Vatican. When I voiced Father Faggioni's arguments, they looked aghast and then pounced with surprising vehemence. The condom, said Father José Noriega, is always a technical solution that risks "deforming" the value of married love as taught by the church. Seconding that opinion was Father Jean Laffitte, who like Father Faggioni was an adviser to the doctrinal congregation. I sat in their office, a brightly lit cubicle enclosed by cheap partitions, and listened as these two theologians explained to me the facts of life and love in such platitudes as "The church views married love as a form of self-giving that may require sacrifices." An awareness of the real-life problems of married couples, so evident in Father Faggioni's arguments, never seemed to enter their minds.

Before I left, Father Laffitte added a more practical consideration: If the church approved of condoms for HIV/AIDS protection, he explained quietly, many Christian couples would question why contraceptives were not also justified in other serious circumstances. Yes, I thought, this was the real issue here. For the conservative camp this debate was not about the life-and-death issue of infection but the Catholic vision of sexuality. Since the 1968 encyclical *Humanae Vitae*, that vision had been inextricably bound to the church's teaching against birth control—the insistence that every act of married love be open to procreation. These theologians now feared that this precept, weakened by decades of dissent and indifference, was so tenuous that admitting just a single exception—condom use against AIDS—would undermine it completely.

When Cardinal Ratzinger was elected pope in 2005, I wondered whether this hero of Catholic conservatism might just surprise everyone. After all, if Ratzinger was willing to entertain a theological debate on condoms and AIDS within the doctrinal congregation, maybe he recognized the need to clarify the issue publicly once and for all.

And in fact, during his first year in office, Pope Benedict appeared to be laying the groundwork for just this kind of shift. It was supposed to be secret, of course, but in 2006 Cardinal Javier Lozano Barragán, a talkative Mexican who headed the Pontifical Council for Health Care Ministry, disclosed that the pope had asked a commission of scientific and theological experts to prepare a document on condom use and HIV/AIDS prevention. The cardinal said that his own council had sent over a two-hundred-page report to the doctrinal congregation, and he was expecting a final document to be made public soon. Barragán was among the few Vatican officials who defended the morality of condom use by married couples when one spouse was infected with HIV, and now it seemed that this line of thinking was gaining a foothold.

The announcement made headlines around the world, but reporters spent little time exploring its theological subtleties—the moral reasoning over circumstances and intentions that was at the center of the Vatican's study. Instead, the dominant journalistic take was much simpler: In the face of global opposition, the Vatican was reversing itself and moving toward a historic overturn of its "ban" on condoms. Some media were already touting the Vatican study as a harbinger of a wider shift on contraception. This, of course, was just what the conservative camp had feared and predicted. Cardinal Barragán's interview triggered alarm inside the Vatican, and officials scrambled to limit the damage. Two days later the chagrined cardinal was marched before the microphones of Vatican Radio to issue a "clarification." He said now that this was simply the first stage of a study, and that he didn't know whether any document would be issued. It was clear that any movement on condoms and AIDS would meet with deeply entrenched resistance in the Roman Curia.

Three years later the Vatican's "condom study" had all but faded from memory. It was April 2009, and Pope Benedict was making his first trip to Africa, a continent ravaged by AIDS and HIV infection. The pope planned to meet with the press aboard the six-hour flight to Cameroon, and reporters were asked to submit questions in advance. I presumed—wrongly—that any queries about condoms would fail to make the cut.

When the pope strolled into coach class an hour into the flight, flanked by his usual coterie of aides, Philippe Visseyrias, a correspondent for the French TV channel France 2, asked him about people who considered the church's position on HIV/AIDS prevention "unrealistic and ineffective." The pope started to answer in French, but when reporters howled in protest he switched to Italian. As always in his off-the-cuff comments, Benedict spoke rapidly and without much expression, his eyes rolled slightly upward, as if he were taking dictation directly from God. For this topic he had a mental checklist: First, the church works on the front lines of AIDS care around the world. Check. Second, you can't solve the problem only with money and programs; you need a spiritual dimension. Check. Third, you can't solve the problem by distributing condoms; on the contrary, they make the problem worse. At that the reporters looked at one another in shock. The pope had already moved on to discuss other aspects of the AIDS epidemic and the need for the "humanization of sexuality," but the story was clearly in the statement he had just given to us: Condoms help spread AIDS. By the time Benedict had landed a few hours later in Yaoundé, Cameroon, wire services were running headlines that would overshadow his entire six-day African trip: "Pope Tells Africa: Condoms Wrong." "Pope: Condoms Increase AIDS." "Pope Reaffirms Ban on Condoms." As usual, the headlines reflected some mistaken journalistic preconceptions. The pope, for example, had not even addressed the question of whether condom use in certain circumstances was morally illicit or licit, so to speak of a "ban on condoms" was inaccurate. Instead, and rather amazingly, he had focused exclusively on the practical question of efficacy—hardly his area of expertise.

The vehement negative reaction to the pope's remarks came from all quarters. Benedict was denounced by government ministers in France, Belgium and his native Germany for endangering public health. A World Health Organization official defended condom use as effective against the spread of HIV/AIDS. In the United States, Harry Knox, soon to be named an adviser to President Barack Obama on faith-based initiatives, said the pope was "hurting people in the name of Jesus" by spreading "blatant falsehoods." A *New York Times* editorial blasted the pope, saying he "deserves no credence when he distorts scientific findings" about condoms. Even some Catholic leaders, including a bishop in Hamburg, Germany, distanced themselves from the pope's analysis.

The impression was that the pope had managed to outrage much of the civilized world. The following day the Vatican again moved to limit the fallout. I was working in a crowded Cameroon press center when I spied Father Federico Lombardi, the Vatican spokesman, slip in the door. We were on him like a school of piranhas. Lombardi had one basic talking point: The pope, he said, was simply cautioning against "excessive or absolute trust in condom distribution" as a way to stop the spread of HIV/AIDS. I decided to press Lombardi on something I'd noticed on the Vatican's Web site. In the "official" transcript of the pope's airborne press conference, entire phrases had been modified to soften his remarks, including the money quote: "One cannot overcome the problem with the distribution of condoms. On the contrary, they increase the problem." That line now read: "One cannot resolve the problem with the distribution of condoms. On the contrary, there is a risk of increasing the problem." In fact, as anyone who took the trouble to check the original video on YouTube could learn, the pope had not spoken of a "risk" of making the problem worse—he had been categorical in his rejection of condom distribution. I asked Lombardi if the Vatican was still rewriting what the pope actually said. And he rather sheepishly said yes. Even though it had been noticed—and ridiculed—on previous occasions, a monsignor back at the Secretariat of State routinely tweaked the pope's public statements before they ended up in the history books. It was part of the great communications disconnect at the Vatican.

In the coming days the Vatican would cite studies to demonstrate that the most effective anti-AIDS campaigns in Africa were based on efforts to promote abstinence and fidelity in sexual relations. They even found one high-profile ally, Edward C. Green, director of the AIDS Prevention Research Project at the Harvard Center for Population and Development Studies, who said that "the best evidence we have supports the pope's comments." Green's own argument was that condoms led to riskier sexual behavior, including multiple and concurrent sexual partners.

Criticism of Pope Benedict continued for weeks, but it was clear that losing popularity points was of secondary concern to him. He wanted to send a signal, a strong one, that he was not in agreement with whatever a handful of pastoral workers or theologians or even cardinals might be saying about the need to accept condoms as a first line of defense against HIV/AIDS. Most people presumed this closed the Vatican's internal debate on the topic. After the Africa trip, one priest assured me, the Vatican's study on condoms would never be resurrected, but I wasn't convinced of that. It was possible that Benedict was going on record against the practical value of condoms, knowing that a document on moral exceptions for condom use was still in the Vatican pipeline and would eventually be released—maybe in a year, maybe in ten years. In that case he was simply making a preemptive point: that any exceptions admitted by moral theology represented a cautionary yellow light, not a green light, for condoms. Or to put it another way, just because it's permissible doesn't make it a good idea.

Then, in the fall of 2010, Pope Benedict blindsided everyone. In his book-length interview *Light of the World*, German journalist Peter Seewald asked whether it wasn't "madness to forbid a high-risk population to use condoms." The pope's answer began with the requisite criticism of overreliance on condom campaigns to stop the spread of HIV/AIDS. But then the pope said that for some people—he gave the example of a prostitute—using a condom to reduce the risk of infection might actually be a step toward moral responsibility.

Seewald asked: "Are you saying, then, that the Catholic Church is actually not opposed in principle to the use of condoms?"

The pope answered: "She of course does not regard it as a real or moral solution, but, in this or that case, there can be nonetheless, in the intention of reducing the risk of infection, a first step in a movement toward a different way, a more human way, of living sexuality."

In a few nuanced sentences Pope Benedict had shifted the church's outlook on condoms and in the process set off a chain reaction of praise, criticism and confusion. The mainstream media hyped it as a "revolutionary" change in church teaching. In fact, Benedict had not altered church teaching but had merely stated what his own Vatican theologians had been saying quietly for years. The World Health Organization took the pope's remarks as general acceptance of condoms and as being "in line with evidence that condoms are highly effective in preventing infection with the HIV virus." That made Vatican officials cringe, and they insisted that the pope was talking about individual moral choices and not public policy—which was a real distinction, though it all seemed to lead to the same conclusion: Using a condom could be justified to prevent disease.

The most anguished response came from the Catholic right, the bloggers and self-appointed watchdogs of orthodoxy who were convinced that Benedict could not have meant that condoms were ever truly acceptable. The conservatives were especially worried about erosion of the birth control doctrine. They argued that the pope must have been referring exclusively to male prostitutes in his condom example, because if a condom was used in sex with a female prostitute, it would effectively be an act of contraception. This absurd notion demonstrated, once again, that the church's teaching on birth control was widely misunderstood. Even Catholic right-wingers seemed to forget that *Humanae Vitae* spoke of responsible sexuality in marriage—and did not try to impose an across-the-board ban on birth control in every act of nonmarital sex. As one Vatican official told me: "My God, do these people think the church wants sex with a prostitute to be 'open to life'? That's ridiculous!"

Clearly, both for the church's critics and its most ardent defenders, the condom had become an icon in the religious culture wars, a symbol either of papal intolerance or sexual mayhem. The pope had now tried to stake out a small plot of middle ground. Some commentators viewed Benedict as naive for exploring the issue in an informal interview with a journalist, yet that had been precisely his strategy. After years of study, the Vatican was not yet ready to make a formal pronouncement on the morality of condoms to prevent AIDS. What Benedict wanted to do was put down a marker suggesting that there was, in fact, some moral leeway regarding a subject that, for many people, was a question of life and death.

Before long, prominent Catholic conservatives were calling for a clarification from the Vatican's doctrinal congregation—in effect, asking for a correction to the pope's comments. Luke Gormally, a leading British bioethicist and a member of the Pontifical Academy for Life, led the charge, insisting that any sexual intercourse with a condom is morally wrong. Gormally laid out his argument in clinical detail: A minimal condition for proper marital intercourse is that "a man ejaculates into his wife's reproductive tract." In Gormally's view, it didn't matter if a couple used a condom with the intention of preventing disease rather than preventing reproduction—it was still a sin against nature. Other theologians on the right chimed in, claiming that the pope must have been misunderstood, because that line of reasoning—condoms are acceptable for prostitutes, because the sex they engage in is already sinful—would lead the church to support the use of condoms for all "fornicators," including sexually active teenagers. A few weeks later, the Congregation for the Doctrine of the Faith did issue a clarifying note, but it was not what Catholic conservatives wanted. The statement dutifully expressed indignation over "manipulation" of the pope's words and proclaimed that the church's teaching against birth control remained intact. But at the heart of the three-page text was confirmation that, at least in the context of prostitution, it was acceptable for those infected with HIV/AIDS to use a condom to avoid spreading the disease. In effect, it asked: Why would you risk killing another human being with your own immoral behavior? For those paying attention, this was a remarkable shift. The condom was no longer out of bounds.

By this time, however, many of my colleagues in the mainstream media were losing interest in the moral arguments, and figured their readers wouldn't care, either. "This is getting too inside-baseball," one reporter for a major wire service complained. The story line they picked was simpler: The Vatican was again being forced to clarify the pope's words, proving that it doesn't really know how to communicate and could really use a more sophisticated PR operation. "They're cleaning up the pope's mess again," my wire service friend declared. He failed to see that the real story was immensely more interesting and unusual: A conservative pope, to the horror of his loyalists, was opening a public debate over sexual morality and in the process exposing deep fault lines in the Catholic Church.

♦ ♦ ♦

In the late 1990s I learned that the Vatican had for years been studying the question of whether homosexuals should be ordained to the priesthood. Not surprisingly, this discussion—held in the utmost secrecy, of course— had never led to any results. As far as I could gather, top Vatican officials were pretty much evenly divided. Some wanted to pursue the issue, convinced that the priesthood was turning into a refuge for gays; others felt that celibacy, not sexual orientation, was the more important factor in a priestly vocation. Both sides probably recognized that any Vatican initiative to vet homosexuals would look like a witch hunt, and so nothing was done.

My queries on the subject drew stony silence from the usual Vatican suspects, but at the end of 2002 I stumbled onto a scoop. After phoning around to some of the lower-level officials of the Congregation for Catholic Education, which oversees seminaries around the world, I learned not only that the study was going forward but that the first draft of a document was being passed around. A second source, after insisting on anonymity, confirmed that a document was in the works and said that it would contain clear directives against admitting homosexuals to the priesthood. He had his argument well primed: "The document's position is negative, based in part on what the Catechism of the Catholic Church says in its revised edition, that the homosexual orientation is 'objectively disordered.' Therefore, independent of any judgment on the homosexual person, a person of this orientation should not be admitted to the seminary and, if it is discovered later, should not be ordained."

I wrote a story the same day, and it provoked a typical reaction: great interest—pro and con, but mostly con—among readers, alarm among many priests and a quick backtracking effort by the Vatican. Roman Curia officials stated that no such document had been written, and that these were simply discussions, all implying that the journalist (me) had gotten carried away. A month later, Polish Cardinal Zenon Grocholewski, the head of the Vatican's education congregation, was asked at a press conference whether a document banning gays from the priesthood was being drawn up, and he said rather lamely that he didn't know yet. Then he took a swipe at what he called "a certain type of journalistic sensationalism."

News stories about the document probably slowed down its publication, because a lot of opposition came to the surface. In subsequent months I spoke to several bishops who were uneasy with the idea of banning gay men from the priesthood and troubled by the report of an imminent document. They let Grocholewski's congregation know of their objections. There was actually a strong vein of resistance inside the Vatican, too. To casual observers, the idea of having no gays in the priesthood might seem fully in line with the Vatican's logic—beginning with the premise that homosexuality itself is "disordered." But in fact many Vatican officials worried that any effort to identify homosexual seminarians through psychological testing would threaten the entire vocations picture. Once psychologists set the standard of what was "normal" in sexual orientation or practice, there was no telling what would happen. Was celibacy "normal," for that matter? Routine testing, the Vatican officials argued, would sow unnecessary doubts and make it appear that the shrinks were now the gatekeepers to the priesthood. And at a time when priest shortages were reaching record proportions, did the church really need any more reasons to reject candidates?

What gave the no-gay movement an unexpected boost was the sex abuse scandal, which was now unfolding in sordid detail in the United States. Many experts and several U.S. bishops had warned against scapegoating homosexuals for priestly sex abuse, arguing that gay men were no more likely to engage in pedophilia than straight men. But Vatican officials kept pointing out in private conversations that a large percentage of the abuse victims were teenage boys. Our news agency decided to pose the question to the Vatican's highest-ranking U.S. official, Cardinal J. Francis Stafford, and his answer was stunning. Cardinal Stafford, who headed the Pontifical Council for the Laity, said the vast majority of the abuse cases involved homosexual activity by priests, not child abuse in the strict sense. "I think it's a misnomer, really, to call it child abuse. I think it's more of an acting out homosexually." He said the cases of pedophilia, or attraction to prepubescent children, were a significant minority, and to focus on them was to "blur the reality." The cardinal's message was clear: The "reality" was that the church had a gay problem.

In February of 2004 the Vatican held a closed-door meeting with psychology and psychiatry experts to come up with ways to identify potential sex abuse perpetrators. It was the Vatican's first comprehensive effort to examine the psychological causes and types of abuse, as well as screening procedures, recidivism rates, effects on child victims and the possibility of successful therapy for abusers. During the encounter Roman Curia department heads asked the experts about the idea of banning homosexuals from the priesthood as a strategy against sex abuse. In response, some dutifully noted that homosexuality does not cause sexual abuse. But others were less categorical. Dr. Martin P. Kafka, a psychiatry professor at Harvard Medical School, said he thought homosexuality, while not a cause of sex abuse, was a "likely risk factor" that deserved further study. He stated that in comparison with the general population, abuse cases in the church disproportionately involved homosexual male adults who'd molested adolescent males. The no-gay-priests faction did its best to ignore the fact that Dr. Kafka had also wondered whether celibacy could also be considered a "risk factor" in sexual abuse.

Soon afterward, the Vatican faced a series of embarrassing disclosures at an Austrian seminary in the town of Sankt Pölten. One of the seminary's students had been arrested on charges of child pornography after authorities found some forty thousand incriminating images on his computer, including scenes of sex with children. Police also found pictures of seminary staff members and students kissing and fondling each other. The local bishop, the notoriously conservative and unpopular Kurt Krenn, at first downplayed the seriousness of the photos, claiming they were part of a prank during a Christmas party. But to some officials in Rome, the incident bore the distinctive earmarks of the "gay subculture" thought to exist in many modern seminaries. In this case the Vatican acted with unusual speed. A month after the scandal came to light, the two-hundred-year-old seminary was closed down, and Bishop Krenn resigned shortly afterward.

Six months later, in February 2005, the Vatican's Congregation for Catholic Education summoned its bishop members from around the world for a major meeting. The number one agenda item was discussion and approval of a document titled "Instruction Concerning the Criteria for the Discernment of Vocations with Regard to Persons with Homosexual Tendencies in View of Their Admission to the Seminary and to Holy Orders." Cardinal Grocholewski betrayed a sense of urgency as he tried to guide the document to the finish line. His major concern was that Pope John Paul II had just been taken to the hospital with breathing problems. It was essential to wind up this project and close down debate before the ailing pope took a turn for the worse. Grocholewski knew that a change in pontiffs could permanently derail the document, and from his Polish sources in the papal household he knew that John Paul's prognosis did not look good. Exhorted to action, the congregation duly gave its stamp of approval, despite a few misgivings among some of the bishops. But then the pope was rehospitalized and underwent a tracheotomy; until he improved, John Paul would be unable to personally review the text of the document and have the final say on its publication.

Grocholewski feared the worst, and when John Paul died on April 2, all Vatican documents in progress were officially suspended, with no guarantee that they would be carried over into the subsequent pontificate. Their fate would depend entirely on the next pope. Grocholewski entered the conclave with 114 other cardinals on April 18, and when they emerged the following day a smile had returned to his face. Cardinal Joseph Ratzinger had been head of the Vatican's doctrinal congregation for twenty-four years and, although only a handful of Curia insiders were aware of it, a hidden architect of the document on homosexuality and the priesthood.

A few months later, in the first major publication of Pope Benedict's pontificate, the Vatican finally issued its document banning gays in the priesthood. Contrary to rumors, the text did not take an ambiguous line, but ruled out priestly ordination for men who had been active homosexuals, who had "deeply seated" homosexual tendencies or who supported the "gay culture"—whatever that was. It called on seminary directors to, in effect, screen gay men before they got in the door. It made no accommodation to homosexuals who were celibate. The strong message was: If you're gay, go away. The foundational argument for the new policy was the church's teaching that homosexual acts are gravely sinful and that homosexual tendencies are "objectively disordered." A homosexual orientation alone would impair a priest's ability to carry out his pastoral ministry in a healthy way, it said. In a vague reference to cases of sex abuse by priests, the document added that the pronouncement was "made more urgent by the current situation."

The last line of the text stated: "The Supreme Pontiff Benedict XVI, on

31 August 2005, approved this present Instruction and ordered its publication." Strangely, much of the media treated the document as a holdover from John Paul II's reign, and not as an opening sally from the new pope. In fact, it had been Cardinal Ratzinger's doctrinal congregation that first suggested such a document as early as 1996. Although carried out by the Congregation for Catholic Education, Cardinal Ratzinger reviewed its work every step of the way, including a first draft in 1998, a second draft in 2002 and the final version in 2005.

But the document might never have survived had Cardinal Ratzinger not been able to engineer a small editing change—just seven words—in the Catechism of the Catholic Church. The new catechism had been published in various modern languages in 1992, after a wide consultation with bishops and experts around the world. Cardinal Ratzinger was then put in charge of preparing the definitive Latin edition of the text, and he used the opportunity to make more than one hundred changes in wording. When the Latin edition was unveiled in 1997, a new concept had been introduced in the section on homosexuality. In its original version, the catechism stated: "The number of men and women who have deep-seated homosexual tendencies is not negligible. They do not choose their homosexual condition; for most of them it is a trial." The new version read: "The number of men and women who have deep-seated homosexual tendencies is not negligible. This inclination, objectively disordered, is a trial for most of them."

The modification marked a significant shift of emphasis in the church's teaching. The church had long taught that homosexual acts were "intrinsically disordered" and always immoral by their very nature. Now it was declaring that the homosexual inclination itself constituted a tendency toward an intrinsic moral evil. That didn't mean that same-sex attraction was sinful, but that it could never lead to anything good. And despite protests to the contrary by theologians, the term seemed to imply that homosexuals were defective in the eyes of God.

Eight years later, the catechism's wording change became the basis for the church's ban on gay priests. What many people wondered was how the Vatican could realistically enforce its new rule, or whether it really wanted to. An Italian colleague from RAI TV voiced a common reaction when he snickered and told me, "This document will be put in a drawer and forgotten. If they really went after gay priests, they'd empty out half the Vatican."

Priestly celibacy falls into one of those gray areas of church teaching: less than a dogma but more than a tradition. It has become, however, a flagship issue of recent popes and their advisers, a principle that's been staunchly defended despite the global priest shortage and the fact that many clergy have trouble leading celibate lives. The more celibacy has come under question, the more the Roman Curia has closed ranks, making it an unofficial litmus test of loyalty.

This position may seem strange, given that the Catholic Church already does have married priests—thousands of them, fully functioning and happily sharing the connubial bed with a spouse. Most are clergy of the Eastern Catholic rites, which have been allowed to keep not only their particular liturgical customs but their tradition of a married priesthood. These men live and work in many countries, including the United States and, of course, Rome. The Eastern rites, however, represent a minority in the church, and Rome has made it clear that the practice of married priests is tolerated as an exception to the rule because of historical peculiarities. Yet that argument has been undermined in recent years, as the Vatican has allowed former Anglican priests who are married to be ordained as Catholic priests in the Latin rite. In effect, despite rhetorical flourishes in favor of celibacy, the Vatican itself has been reestablishing the married priesthood in the Western church.

Over the years some Catholic leaders, including bishops, have spoken out on the celibacy issue, pushing for wider change. Almost always they are brought to heel, and in some cases their ecclesial careers have run aground. In 2006 Brazilian Cardinal Cláudio Hummes was one of Pope Benedict's more surprising choices for a top Vatican post. A Franciscan known for his social justice activity, Hummes was head of the immense São Paolo archdiocese when Benedict picked him as prefect of the Congregation for the Clergy. The appointment shocked the pope's conservative friends. Hummes had for years been a strong supporter of Brazilian labor unions, which is how he became friends with union boss—and later Brazil's leftist president— Luiz Inácio Lula da Silva. To many in the Roman Curia, that association alone made Cardinal Hummes suspect. Now, at the relatively advanced age of seventy-one, he would be coming to Rome to oversee policies for the world's four hundred thousand priests. The appointment was widely seen as a move to bring a moderate Latin American voice into the Roman Curia.

In early December, shortly before Cardinal Hummes was due to arrive at the Vatican, a Brazilian newspaper published an interview in which he carefully staked out a more liberal position on married priests. "Even though celibacy is part of Catholic history and culture, the church could review this question, because celibacy is not a dogma but a disciplinary question," he explained. He characterized the modern shortage of priests as a real challenge and said that in response the church should not be "immobile." The first step, he said, would be to "discuss whether it is necessary to review the norms on celibacy."

By the time the interview landed on the desk of the Vatican's secretary of state, Cardinal Tarcisio Bertone, Cardinal Hummes was already en route to Rome. Major Italian newspapers had picked up the story overnight and were suggesting that Benedict's new appointee was about to steer the church toward a historical shift on celibacy. Cardinal Bertone and his top aides were alarmed. What Hummes had said was impeccable on a doctrinal level, but it went against Vatican policy. Only a month earlier, after Zambian Archbishop Emmanuel Milingo had ordained four married men as bishops against papal orders, the pope had convened top Vatican department heads to strongly reaffirm priestly celibacy. Hummes was now publicly embarrassing the Roman Curia.

I discovered from a usual round of sources that the Brazilian cardinal was already persona non grata in some Vatican quarters. When I learned that Hummes's plane was supposed to land in Rome that morning, I phoned over to the Domus Sanctae Marthae, the Vatican's guesthouse, and asked in my best clerical voice if *Sua Eminenza* had arrived. A woman receptionist responded: "Not yet. Is this the secretary of state again?" I said nothing. "He knows he's supposed to call you as soon as he gets here," she continued. Okay, I said. The man was clearly in hot water.

A few hours later, having arrived in Rome, Cardinal Hummes was forced to issue what was essentially a retraction. His statement, distributed at the Vatican press office, declared that priestly celibacy was an ancient value in the church and was not up for discussion. "It is based on a consolidated tradition and strong theological-spiritual and practical-pastoral arguments that have also been backed up by popes," the statement said. Hummes noted that most bishops at the 2005 Synod of Bishops had determined that relaxing the celibacy rule would not resolve the problem of priest shortages, and concluded, "This question is therefore not presently on the agenda of church authorities." I had never before witnessed such a public arm-twisting by the Roman Curia. Welcome to Rome, Cardinal Hummes.

Two months later a full-page article appeared in *L'Osservatore Romano* under the headline "The Importance of Priestly Celibacy." "Priestly celibacy is a precious gift of Christ to his church, a gift that must continually be meditated upon and strengthened, especially in the deeply secularized modern world," it affirmed. The author was Cardinal Cláudio Hummes.

For Vatican officials one of the most deeply resented arguments against priestly celibacy is that it tends to screen out emotionally healthy candidates. During the wave of priestly sex abuse disclosures in 2010, Pope Benedict repeatedly had to confront the issue head-on, insisting that celibacy was a sacrifice that configured a priest to Christ, not a warning sign of sexual perversion. In his *Light of the World* interview with Peter Seewald later that year, the pope expanded his thoughts on the subject. In particular, he took aim at homosexuality in the priesthood, calling it "one of the miseries of the church" and expressing the hope that gay priests "must at least try not to express this inclination actively.

"Homosexuality is incompatible with the priestly vocation. Otherwise, celibacy itself would lose its meaning as a renunciation. It would be extremely dangerous if celibacy became a sort of pretext for bringing people into the priesthood who don't want to get married anyway," the pope said. He defended the Vatican's 2005 document against ordaining homosexuals. It was important to select priestly candidates very carefully, he said, "to head off a situation where the celibacy of priests would practically end up being identified with the tendency to homosexuality."

Never before had a Vatican official voiced so bluntly what so many of them feared privately: that the priesthood was turning into a gay ghetto.

✦ ✦ ✦

In October 2007 Italian TV viewers were treated to an unusual episode of the equivalent of *Candid Camera* inside the Vatican. The network LA7 was broadcasting a special on gay priests, using footage obtained with a hidden video camera. This particular segment showed a young man going to an appointment with a Vatican monsignor, who welcomed him into his Roman Curia office. The faces were blurred beyond recognition and the voices distorted, but it was clear that the priest was coming on to the young man. At one point the camera showed the priest with his hand on the back of the youth's leg. They spoke briefly about sadomasochism.

"You're cute. You're too cute," the priest said, sitting down next to him on a couch.

"Thank you. But you're about to commit something with me that is a sin in the eyes of God," the young man replied.

"No, I don't consider it a sin," the priest said, unsuspecting that he was being set up.

When the youth questioned how an ordained minister could ignore the church's rules on homosexuality, the priest responded curtly, "We're not going to do anything because you have too many limitations." He then asked the young man to leave the building and to be careful on the way out. "Now I'm going to put you in the elevator. If someone stops you, don't say anything to anyone, okay? If you want, call me or send me a message," the monsignor said. Then he added the phrase *"Quanto sei bbono,"* slang perhaps best rendered in English as "You're sooo hot."

Several Vatican officials were watching the program with interest, and the phone calls began immediately after it aired. One bishop recognized the office in the video clip—and the white couch on which the youth was sprawled—as that of Monsignor Tommaso Stenico, a section chief at the Congregation for the Clergy.

Stenico was a handsome priest, sixty years old but looking younger, and a familiar face to viewers of the Catholic TV station Telepace, where he sermonized regularly. Now his photo was plastered over the front pages of Italian newspapers under the headline "Gay Encounter Inside the Vatican." Stenico had also been a regular contributor to the conservative Catholic Web site Petrus, and the site's director became the first to denounce the priest, saying it was "scandalous, shameful, ignoble, blasphemous and de-monic" that a priest would attempt to have sexual relations at the Vatican, "where Saint Peter was martyred."

When I spoke privately with Vatican officials about Stenico, I found little sympathy for the man. He was derided as vain and imprudent—someone who had besmirched the Roman Curia by not being careful enough.

Monsignor Stenico's defense was feeble even by Vatican standards. He said he was the victim of a trap—which was true enough, in a sense—but then added that he had posed as a homosexual only to gain information and not to engage in gay sex. He claimed he had long been suspicious of a gay campaign to manipulate priests with homosexual tendencies, so he decided to use his training as a psychologist to investigate, posing as a "thief among thieves" in the homosexual world.

"In this manner I discovered that it is true. There really is a diabolical plan by groups of Satanists who target priests," he said.

No one at the Vatican bought it. The Vatican spokesman, Father Federico Lombardi, soon announced that Stenico had been suspended from his Vatican position and that his case would be treated with "severity and determination." Stenico portrayed himself as a martyr. "I'm on the cross, together with Jesus Christ." But a few days later the Italian magazine *Panorama* reported that Stenico had taken out an insurance policy of sorts: He had prepared a "detailed dossier" of every homosexual cleric at the Vatican, including high officials of the Roman Curia. Stenico was said to have outlined his information in a letter that was making the Vatican "tremble."

The Stenico scandal got a great deal of attention in conservative blogs like *Rorate Caeli*, which was widely read inside and outside the Vatican. "It is unavoidable to conclude that the Vatican is infested with active homosexuals—who are only suspended from their functions when they are arrested with transsexual male prostitutes . . . or found looking at homosexual pornography Web sites . . . or shown on national television as they bring their dates to their Vatican offices," the blog lamented.

The case of Monsignor Cesare Burgazzi, an official at the Secretariat of State, was another embarrassment for the Vatican—all the more because Burgazzi had for years also served as a *ceremoniere* in Saint Peter's, standing on the altar with the pope. According to the newspaper *La Repubblica*, in May 2006 the forty-eight-year-old priest was approached by plainclothes police as he cruised an area of Rome notorious for transsexual prostitution. It was after midnight, and his priest's collar, police said, had been tossed into the backseat of his Ford Focus. The monsignor, either alarmed at being found out or, as he later told a court, frightened by the approach of unidentified men, rammed the police car and fled the scene. After a twenty-minute chase during which Burgazzi hit two more police vehicles, he was finally stopped. Three policemen suffered minor injuries when they had to subdue the prelate with force. In this case, the Vatican responded at first by denying the story. A statement calling the article a complete fabrication was posted on the Vatican Web site. That statement was removed several days later and never reappeared. Burgazzi was not charged with soliciting prostitution but with resisting and injuring the police officers and damaging the cars. A prosecutor wanted to send him to prison for a year and a half. It took the Italian court three years to process the case, and in the end it acquitted Burgazzi on the grounds that "the facts do not constitute a crime." A church official said Monsignor Burgazzi's "Calvary" had ended with his honor restored. Two years later, in November 2011, Pope Benedict promoted Burgazzi to the position of section chief in the Secretariat of State.

The many gay priests who worked in the Roman Curia were distressed at public indiscretions precisely because this recklessness drew unwanted attention to the issue of homosexuality. Their motto was the Latin proverb *Si non caste, saltem caute*—If not with chastity, at least with caution. The Vatican's tendency to protect its own provided a safe haven for all kinds of behavior, but landing in the police blotter was asking for trouble to say the least. It fed the growing public perception that the Vatican preached one thing and practiced another.

Many remembered the backlash that followed publication of a tell-all book in 1999—a book that had been read, with relish or alarm, by nearly every priest who worked at the Holy See. Titled *Via col vento in Vaticano*— *Gone With the Wind in the Vatican*—it recounted in tantalizing detail tales of corruption, careerism and homosexual scandal inside Vatican offices, often with telltale clues about the identities of protagonists. The author was given as "I Millenari," or The Millennialists, but insiders soon figured out that was probably an anagram for "Marinelli." In fact, even as the book was selling out its hundred-thousand-copy first print run, Monsignor Luigi Marinelli, a retired and somewhat embittered Curia official, admitted that he was one of the authors and defended the work, saying it was healthy for the church to own up to its failings. Disciplinary proceedings were immediately brought against Marinelli, adding to the widespread opinion that the Vatican would pursue anyone who dared tell the truth about its less savory secrets. One of the book's chapters, "The Javelin of Homosexuality," claimed that a predilection for young men was a subtle but near constant factor in the typical Vatican superior's relationship with his staff of priests. Homosexual favors were a sure way to quickly climb the Vatican career ladder, it asserted. The chapter also compared the situation within the Vatican walls to the biblical description of a divine punishment of Israel: "And he will give them child princes and the effeminate will rule over them."

Monsignor Marinelli had worked in the Roman Curia for forty-five years, but he quickly became an untouchable. He was summoned to a hearing at a Vatican court but refused to attend. He confirmed to reporters that not only was everything in his book true, but his team of authors had decided to leave out the most salacious episodes. Marinelli said 80 percent of the Roman Curia officials and staff were good people, but 20 percent were greedy, vile and morally deficient—and they were the ones who seemed to rise to the top. The Vatican court ordered the sequestering of the book and prohibited its translation, a move that was ignored by the Italian publisher and that, inevitably, only boosted sales. Meanwhile, church authorities were quietly considering suspending Marinelli from his priestly ministry. He left his apartment near the Vatican and returned to his hometown of Cerignola in southern Italy. As it turned out, the prelate was dying of cancer. When he passed away the following year, his family requested a funeral in the local cathedral, but it was refused for scheduling problems.

In March 2010, the Vatican was shaken by Italian press reports that a Nigerian member of a Vatican choir had arranged multiple encounters with male prostitutes for Angelo Balducci, a "papal gentleman." Papal gentlemen are supposedly professional men of "high moral standing" who serve as ceremonial ushers in their spare time. In fact, the office was routinely handed out to the political and business friends of powerful prelates at the Vatican Secretariat of State. Balducci, a former executive who had recently come under investigation in an Italian corruption inquiry, was said to have discussed the gay liaisons in wiretapped conversations, and the transcripts ended up in a Rome newspaper. Balducci was immediately suspended from his duties at the Vatican, and the Nigerian chorister was also dismissed.

A few months later another Vatican sex scandal erupted when *Panorama* ran a long investigative report on gay priests. Under the headline "Le Notte Brave dei Preti Gay" (The Wild Nights of the Gay Priests), the magazine recounted the sexual exploits of three priests who frequented gay clubs, slept with casual acquaintances, joined online gay chats and paraded around half naked in their priestly vestments. A hidden camera recorded video of the activities, including "dirty dancing" with some well-oiled male escorts. One of the priests asserted that 98 percent of his priest friends were gay and said that only an intransigent wing of the church refused to acknowledge and accept this fact. Predictably blogs and other media quickly picked the story up, asking, "Are 98 percent of Vatican priests gay?"

That got the Vatican's attention; the pope is, after all, head of the Diocese of Rome, and this report made a mockery of the city's clergy. The day the article appeared the Rome diocese put out a statement that, in effect, invited actively gay priests to leave the priesthood and stop embarrassing the church. "They should know that no one is forcing them to remain priests. Consistency demands they should come out into the open," the statement declared, adding that those leading such a "double life" should never have been ordained.

The Diocese of Rome could not refrain from attacking *Panorama*, too. The magazine was engaging in a campaign to "defame all priests" and discredit the church, the diocese argued. It did not escape the attention of Vatican officials that *Panorama* belonged to the media empire of Prime Minister Silvio Berlusconi. For them, the article had the telltale signs of payback.

In the summer of 2009 the government of Silvio Berlusconi was under fire. The seventy-two-year-old premier, hair-plugged and face-lifted, had a soft spot for young women, to no one's particular surprise. But when he presented an aspiring lingerie model, Noemi Letizia, with a gold and diamond necklace on her eighteenth birthday, it began to look unseemly even in the eyes of the very tolerant Italian public. Then it came out that paid escorts furnished by an underworld figure routinely adorned Berlusconi's dinners and parties, and sometimes spent the night with him. The prime minister blandly defended himself by saying, "Italy has a lot of beautiful girls, and I'm no saint." It was a line that seemed to resonate with a significant percentage of Italian men, but not with Berlusconi's wife, Veronica, who announced she was divorcing him and suggested he was suffering from sex addiction. When magazines published photographs of nude men and women at Berlusconi's pool, including an older gent sporting an erection, the whole thing began to resemble something between a soap opera and *Satyricon*.

As the scandal built, *Avvenire*, the newspaper of the Italian bishops' conference, began to criticize Berlusconi in comments penned by the newspaper's editor, Dino Boffo, raising eyebrows at the Vatican. The Vatican and Italian church leaders, as well as the Vatican newspaper, had been keeping a prudent silence on the matter, knowing that Berlusconi's center-right coalition was an ally on issues like aid to private schools, the morning-after pill and same-sex marriage. Vatican secretary of state Cardinal Tarcisio Bertone was the architect of this see-no-evil policy, and in late summer he decided to invite Berlusconi to a meeting and dinner in Aquila, to celebrate the city's traditional "feast of forgiveness." While it offered the perfect setting for a rehabilitation of Berlusconi's image in the eyes of the church hierarchy, it left some Catholics disgusted with the Vatican. Vito Mancuso, a leftist theologian, wrote in *La Repubblica* that Cardinal Bertone preferred to dine at the table of Herod instead of denouncing his sins. He added that while the Vatican consistently railed against postmodern "nihilism," it seemed incapable of condemning it in practice. The "forgiveness" dinner was abruptly canceled, however, when the morning newspapers arrived on Cardinal Bertone's desk. The lead headline in *Il Giornale*, owned by Berlusconi's brother, read, "Sexual Incident of *Avvenire* Director: Supermoralist Is Charged with Harassment." The story was a personal attack on Dino Boffo, claiming he was a homosexual who had been fined by a court a few years earlier for making harassing phone calls to the wife of the man who was his lover.

The newspaper, edited by Berlusconi loyalist Vittorio Feltri, kept up its campaign for days on end, calling Boffo and his defenders hypocritical liars. Boffo represented the church's hierarchy in the Italian media, and such an attack was unprecedented. It was also effective. While the Vatican and bishops rallied round Boffo and condemned Feltri and *Il Giornale*, the man in the street figured there must have been something to the story. After all, a court had ruled against Boffo, and although the court records were confidential, Boffo could have chosen to disclose them—but didn't.

Meanwhile, *Il Giornale* stepped up its attacks, now denouncing the duplicity of church figures with "weak flesh" who preached sexual morality but couldn't keep their own lives in order. A week later Boffo resigned, and *Il Giornale* chanted victory. The Vatican quietly began trying to patch things up with Berlusconi's government, and Berlusconi went back to his young women and his parties. In the eyes of the public, it was just one more example of Vatican hypocrisy. As one commentator put it, the episode seemed to prove the old adage that "the more rigid the moral pronouncements, the more faults one is hiding."

The Vatican had been dragged into a political street fight, one that it never wanted, and even Pope Benedict was ultimately drawn into the scuffle. In a staged move designed to demonstrate the pope's concern, he was briefed on the incident in a phone call with Cardinal Angelo Bagnasco, the president of the Italian bishops' conference.

Il Giornale got in a parting shot that was remarkable in its tone of derision toward the Vatican: a front-page commentary titled "If I Were Pope I'd Tell My Aides: No More Hypocrisy About Sex." The article, mocking Pope Benedict's academic approach to sexual matters as well as his German accent, proposed a papal speech in which the pontiff might "set aside the pastoral documents that explain the principles of love and that distinguish wisely between *eros* and *agape*, and instead enter into the scabrous material of sexuality." It accused the church and its ministers of "trafficking in sex" for centuries and said the priestly pedophilia cases were just the most recent examples. The article's basic contention was that the church's own performance demonstrated why it would always fail to enforce its teachings on sexual morality.

The article concluded by affirming that the true Catholic "is neither a

Puritan nor a sexophobe. He is a realist and shows indulgence with sins of the flesh."

The Boffo affair appeared to end there, but five months later it resurfaced in a way that caused even more tremors inside the Vatican. At the Ristorante da Berti in Milan, over plates of *ossobuco con risotto*, Vittorio Feltri and Dino Boffo met one afternoon and enjoyed an amiable lunch together. During the meal Feltri apologized to Boffo. He had learned, he said, that his newspaper's attack on the *Avvenire* editor was based on false documentation. But Feltri had something else to get off his chest, and indeed this was the real reason he had invited Boffo to lunch. The false dossier, he said, had been hand delivered to him by a Vatican official who was "beyond suspicion." In other words, the bringing down of Boffo had been an inside job, a Vatican plot that, in its deviousness, was worthy of the notorious Borgia papacy.

Feltri then went public with his apology, insisting that it had been the Vatican that had set up Boffo and himself. He hammered on his theme, dropping hints about who the Vatican emissary might be, until he had all but named the two prime suspects: Cardinal Tarcisio Bertone, the Vatican secretary of state, and Gian Maria Vian, the editor of *L'Osservatore Romano*. According to scenarios reconstructed with delight by Italian papers, Bertone and his sidekick Vian had singled out Boffo as a way to weaken Cardinal Camillo Ruini, who had appointed Boffo and remained his protector. All this was supposedly part of a grand plan by Bertone to assume control of the Italian bishops' conference.

The Vatican finally reacted to the sniping. A statement issued by Bertone himself called the accusations baseless, but by then the impression in most people's minds was that the whole episode was part of a secret war in the church's hierarchy. Italians tend to prefer intrigue over innocence any day, and they gave little credence to the Vatican's proclamation that Pope Benedict had taken a personal interest in the case and that he viewed the scandal as an attack on the papacy. This was clearly an Italian turf battle, and the German pope was probably irritated but not terribly troubled over it.

A monsignor with decades of experience in the Vatican offered me three impressions of the matter. First, if Pope Benedict really was devoting any time to this kind of Italian mudslinging, then something was wrong with the universal church. Second, the Italian cardinals had come off as virtual mafiosi, and had probably ruined their chances in the next conclave. Third, the Vatican's political skills had clearly been slipping, because politics in the modern age depends as much on media savvy as backroom maneuvering.

I found myself nodding in agreement, and then bounced a final thought off my source. I found it curious, I told him, that neither the Italian media nor the public seemed to take a great interest in the sexual aspect of this scandal. In the United States there would have been endless poring over the lurid details. But in this case, despite accusations involving call girls and naked parties and homosexual affairs, even the Vatican seemed to view the key dynamic as more about power than sex.

The monsignor laughed at my naïveté. "My friend, for the Vatican, sex is *always* about power."

CHAPTER TEN

THE REAL BENEDICT

✠ THE FIRST THING I noticed was the twitching leg. It was dark backstage, but I could make out the slight figure standing at the edge of the platform. He wore a black suit with a white stripe running down the side, and his right leg was jerking up and down involuntarily. It had to be Dylan. And he must be nervous, I thought. Singing for the pope was not an everyday thing.

A few moments later Bob Dylan and his band took the stage, and ripped into "Knockin' on Heaven's Door." A roar went up from the vast fairgrounds in Bologna where more than 350,000 young people got to their feet. They had come not only to hear Dylan and the assorted rock bands that performed that evening but to witness an encounter of two cultural icons. Pope John Paul II sat in an alcove on the right of the stage, chin in hand, listening as Dylan segued into "A Hard Rain's A-Gonna Fall" and closed with "Forever Young."

Then Dylan walked over to the pope, beige cowboy hat in hand, and—after nearly tripping over a step—bowed and shook the Polish pontiff's hand. The pope spoke into Dylan's ear and smiled.

In the press perch, I sat next to Phil Pullella of Reuters and watched all this in a state of awe. It was 1997, and both John Paul and Dylan seemed genuinely moved. The entire event sounded like something a PR agent might dream up but would never come to pass: Dylan, the born-again minstrel who was just recovering from a near fatal illness, performing at a Eucharistic Congress where a giant cross dominated the stage; the pope then offering a verbal riff on "Blowin' in the Wind," using the lyrics to evoke the action of the Holy Spirit.

The concert, broadcast live by Italian state television, was hailed by just about everyone. Church organizers were ecstatic. It had pushed the limits of John Paul II's interaction with popular culture, but in the end it worked.

What better way to connect with young people today? There was one strongly dissenting voice at the Vatican, though. Cardinal Joseph Ratzinger, the Vatican's doctrinal watchdog, let it be known that he thought letting an increasingly frail and ailing pope share the stage with a group of rock and pop stars was a bad idea. Ratzinger argued that Dylan and his musical confreres had a completely different message than the pope. They were "false prophets," and showcasing them at a Eucharistic Congress was the ultimate folly.

When Cardinal Ratzinger was elected to succeed John Paul eight years later, I remembered this episode—minor in itself, but a clue to reading the mind-set of the new pope. For years I had figured that Ratzinger, a piano-playing Mozart aficionado, simply didn't like modern music. But as I watched Pope Benedict operate, I realized that his views were more complicated than that. To Benedict, Dylan was the quintessential symbol of the 1960s protest movement, with an antiauthoritarian bent that made him dangerous. He represented an open challenge to the old order of things. And while some of Dylan's songs may have been inspired by Christianity and the Bible, this type of music lacked the gravitas of a requiem or even a decent liturgical hymn. It was artistic, but it didn't harmonize with tradition. Ergo, it wasn't to be trusted.

As became increasingly apparent after his election, this perspective on popular culture was typical of Pope Benedict. He felt safe only within a very circumscribed ecclesial environment, the sheltered realm of faith and church. Outside those borders, there were no real answers, and nothing really to be learned. To Benedict, the outside world was full of impurities and illusions that, unfortunately, had seeped into some sectors of the Catholic Church. And although he would never have said it aloud, part of the reason had been Pope John Paul's penchant for reaching out and making connections with people who had little to do with the faith—journalists and sports heroes, aboriginal dancers and rock stars. It bought the church publicity, but at what price? With Benedict, the era of slumming with the stars would come to an end.

The Vatican's annual Christmas concert was one of those crossover events that, in Pope Benedict's view, had brought the church more harm than good. For thirteen years pop and rock stars had been coming to the

Vatican to perform in a benefit and share the limelight with Pope John Paul; past luminaries had included Whitney Houston, Dionne Warwick, Gloria Gaynor, John Denver, Tom Jones and Lionel Richie. B. B. King had even given the Polish pope one of his electric guitars. It was primarily a feel-good event, though there had been occasional controversies. In 2003 the American singer Lauryn Hill had stunned the concert audience when she asked church leaders to "repent" for the abuse of children by priests. (The Vatican dismissed her impromptu outburst as a "sour note.") In late 2005, as Pope Benedict prepared to host his first Christmas concert, organizers received word that Brazilian singer Daniela Mercury might use her Vatican slot to promote the use of condoms against AIDS. She was immediately dropped from the program. When Benedict learned of the controversy, he decided not to meet with any of the concert performers that year. It just wasn't worth the trouble. The following year the concert was discontinued altogether. It was a small step in Benedict's great program for the church, a program that might be summed up in a single word: decontamination.

As often happens on days when reporters find their stories aren't getting any play and TV correspondents are told not to bother with any stand-ups, the mood in the Munich press center was turning unpleasant. It was day three of Pope Benedict's "homecoming" visit to Bavaria in 2006, and the trip had already dropped off the media radar. Victor Simpson, the AP reporter who had covered papal trips since the early days of John Paul II, coaxed me outside, where he was taking a cigarette break. We both observed that this visit was not generating much interest. "And you know why," Victor said. "No emotion. I mean, he comes back to his roots and—nothing. He acts like he's going through the motions."

Earlier in the day I had stood and listened to Benedict address the crowd at the picturesque Marian sanctuary in Altötting—a place he had visited frequently as a child, though he didn't even mention that fact. When the pope walked past the house where he was born in Marktl am Inn, he barely looked at it, seemingly eager to get through the afternoon schedule. The photographers and camera operators who had waited hours outside the house for a poignant visual came away empty-handed. It was not much better for us print people, desperate for a story line. When we spied Austrian Cardinal Christoph Schönborn standing on the sidelines, we quickly descended on him and asked why Pope Benedict was so intent on depersonalizing the papacy. Schönborn, who had known Ratzinger for thirty-three years, told us that he had characteristically been very discreet about his personal feelings. "He always looks at what is behind the apparent and the emotional for something deeper," Schönborn explained. That may have been true, but it didn't help us much. This was a pope who didn't feel obligated to emote in public, and whose speeches and sermons in Bavaria were as flat as stale beer.

The most revealing biographical information about Pope Benedict came from the pope himself in *Salt of the Earth*, a book-length interview he gave to Peter Seewald in 1996. Rereading its pages in Munich, I realized that Joseph Ratzinger had been shut off from the world at a very early age. He was an altar boy along with his older brother, Georg, and after receiving Communion from a cardinal one day he announced that he wanted to be a cardinal, too. (On the other hand, as Georg Ratzinger recalled, after they watched a man painting the walls of their house, Joseph had said he wanted to be a housepainter.) His vocation was determined in 1939 when, with war impending, both boys were enrolled in a minor seminary. Joseph was twelve years old then and, except for a brief stint in the army, from that moment the church was his entire life. Even in the seminary young Joseph had a tendency to seclude himself. He found it hard to study in a roomful of sixty students. As one of the smallest and weakest boys in the class, he especially hated the two hours of sports each day, which he described as "true torture." His best friends were his books, and his academic ability soon earned him the degree of privacy he sought. After ordination in 1951, he pursued advanced studies in theology and philosophy and began a career as a professor. He thrived within the walls of academia, but in the late 1960s the student unrest that spread across Europe turned this intellectual sanctuary into a battleground. Ratzinger was on the Catholic theology faculty at the University of Tübingen, where he witnessed increasing Marxist influence and radicalization, culminating in the protests and riots of spring 1968. By all accounts that experience gave his worldview a permanent shift to the right. The radical movement and the growing disrespect for authority among his students confirmed to Ratzinger that even in the university's theological faculties, the faith was in jeopardy of ideological distortion. Tübingen was no longer a safe environment, and in 1969 he took a teaching position at the much smaller and less prestigious University of Regensburg, where he eventually became vice president and served as a theological adviser to the German bishops' conference. When he was named archbishop of Munich in 1977, he had had virtually no experience as a pastor; his appointment as head of the Vatican's doctrinal congregation in 1982 took him even further away from the day-to-day reality of most Catholics. This was a man who had found a refuge in the church from social conflict, criticism and doubt. Unlike John Paul II, who had had experience as a factory worker, an actor, a poet and a university student, and who had fought continual political battles as a bishop under communism, Benedict shied away from the world. To him it was a dangerous place.

During the Bavaria trip, the venues and program of events highlighted the stages of the pope's ecclesial and academic career, but little else. Prayer followed prayer, and the most exciting item on the agenda was the blessing of a new church organ. It was like being in a pious bubble for six days, untouched by the surrounding social and political and economic reality. As a result, Pope Benedict seemed ever more two-dimensional. Major international wire services could not keep dispatching reports about prayers to Mary. My colleagues were already under pressure to justify the time and expense involved in covering this trip. And now their editors were cutting their stories down to briefs. In an era of failing newspapers, this was an unforgivable waste of journalistic resources.

Even the celebrity status of the pope—which should have guaranteed his place on the rotating roster of newsmakers—was in jeopardy, a topic that came up that evening at dinner, when the talk turned to the pope's dismal performance on his homecoming tour. At the table were Victor Simpson, Phil Pullella, ABC's Phoebe Natanson, Ian Fisher of the *New York Times*, and Andreas Englisch, the *Bild* reporter who seemed to know everything about Benedict. In the consensus view at the table, the pope's media problem was that he hadn't defined himself, a failure that had handicapped reporters tremendously. To sell the pope as a story, he had to have a persona—good or bad, but a figure with global impact.

From the day of his election, the media had been searching for a Benedict persona, but nothing had stuck. The pope had immediately shed the *Panzerkardinal* image that had attached to him as the Vatican's doctrinal watchdog. Benedict had made it clear that he had a different agenda as pope, telling one aide, "It was easy to teach the doctrine. Helping a billion people live it is quite another thing."

Reporters quickly latched onto the image of "Benedict the Gentle," making much of his supposed love of cats, birds and other animals. We were assured by Cardinal Tarcisio Bertone that, as cardinal, Benedict not only had fed the stray cats around the Vatican but also had spoken to them, probably in Bavarian dialect. There were even rumors of a big tabby hiding out in the papal apartment, but our sources told us the pope had no cat: Vatican rules prohibited pets in the papal quarters, and Benedict was no rule breaker. His longtime adviser Ingrid Stampa finally divulged that he'd never kept cats, except for two porcelain ones on a bookshelf.

Another rumor held that Benedict loved teddy bears. According to Georg Ratzinger, his brother had a great sensitivity to living creatures, so he was always receiving toy animals for Christmas. His teddy bear was supposedly his favorite. While taking an "In the Footsteps of Benedict" tour in Bavaria, a CNS stringer chatted with Franz-Xaver Zeiser, who had lived next door to the Ratzingers as a young boy. Zeiser, who is nine years younger than Joseph Ratzinger, said that as a teenager the future pope had "a giant teddy bear back then, and he often used it to scare me." Zeiser decided one day he'd had enough and left a large hammer outside the Ratzinger house. "When Joseph came at me with his teddy bear again, I raced outside and grabbed the hammer. Then we stood, grimly facing each other, me gripping the hammer and him his teddy bear. Eventually we both put down our 'weapons,' and that was the end of that," said Zeiser. I loved this story, because it made the pope more human. At the same time, it was becoming clear that Benedict as Saint Francis of Assisi was not going to stick.

"Benedict the Bold" was another short-lived creation of the journalistic imagination. In this version of the German pope, he would move quickly to undo the liturgical changes of the Second Vatican Council, beginning with restoration of the Tridentine Mass. But although the pope did lift some restrictions on celebrating the old rite and added a few candlesticks to the papal altar, he did not launch a liturgical revolution. And despite early rumors of a Roman Curia temple cleansing, Benedict ended up leaving the vast apparatus of Vatican offices relatively untouched. As rumors of a curial shake-up evaporated, some of his most ardent supporters were left disappointed. They could not have imagined, however, how difficult it would have been—even for the supreme pontiff—to reduce the Vatican bureaucracy. Benedict had discovered the same resistance faced by previous popes: Whenever he suggested a major innovation or radical reform, aides would whisper, "But, Your Holiness, this *cannot* be done." Eventually he decided that, given his age, any attempt to reshape the Roman Curia simply wasn't worth the effort.

Benedict as "the green pope" caught on for a brief spell. This image was primarily based on the installation of solar panels above the Vatican's audience hall—a project Benedict had approved but by no means instigated. Then, in 2007, the U.S. company Planktos and its Hungarian partner came up with a reforestation project that would add to the pope's green aura. They announced they would create a Vatican Climate Forest in Hungary, planting enough trees to offset Vatican City's greenhouse gas emissions. Nearly 125,600 oak, white willow, black poplar and wild fruit trees would be planted over the next eighteen months along the Tisza River, making the Vatican the first carbon-neutral state in the world. It was good publicity for Planktos and for the Vatican—a win-win situation, Pope Benedict was told. But three years later the Vatican discovered that not a single tree had been planted. Planktos had gone out of business, and its Hungarian partner had no intention of following through with the plan. Benedict, meanwhile, had been giving speeches that didn't play particularly well to his new environmental fans, as he made it clear that his vision of "human ecology" included protection of the unborn and rejection of gay marriage. Quickly and quietly, Benedict was retired from the media's roster of environmental champions.

What did seem genuinely high on the pope's agenda was a teaching mission about the relationship between God and humanity. For reporters, that was another hard sell as news. To make matters worse, Benedict appeared to avoid any current or topical issues. More and more often his talks focused on the spiritual lessons of early church fathers and saints. I noticed that after a few months many of the Vatican beat reporters were no longer showing up in the Sala Stampa.

In southern Germany we were getting a typically heavy dose of the pope's "Catholicism 101": The importance of devotional practices. Ancient Bavarian prayers. Saint Augustine. Saint Corbinian. A spiritual explication of his coat of arms.

When our dinner finally broke up, the prevailing view was that on this trip Benedict had—perhaps permanently—taken himself out of the news cycle. That assessment would change dramatically a few hours later, when, at five a.m., we were handed the papal speeches for day four of the trip, which included a major address at the University of Regensburg.

Jeff Israely was excited, and that was something worth noting at six thirty a.m. in the Platzl Hotel elevator. We were on our way to breakfast, and Jeff had already skimmed ahead to the Regensburg speech. What had caught his eye were the phrases that would soon fuel headlines around the world.

"He talks about jihad. Look at this," Jeff said, pointing to his underlined text. "In Islam 'you will find things only evil and inhuman.' It's a religion 'spread by the sword.' This is gonna piss people off."

Jeff, who was covering the trip for *Time* magazine, fully recognized that Benedict was quoting a medieval critique of Islam, and not exactly endorsing that critique. Still, the pope had left enough ambiguity to allow people to jump to that conclusion. On a very intellectual level he was taking on Islamic extremists, with language that would almost certainly offend Muslims. As NPR's Sylvia Poggioli remarked, "Come on, he uses the name Mohammed!" To be fair, the speech also threw down a finely reasoned challenge to Western secularism, arguing that the "crisis of faith" and the marginalization of religious values had effectively made it impossible for the West to engage in a real dialogue with Islamic culture. But that part of the speech was just too complex for most news stories.

By eight a.m., when our *Volo Papale* bus reached Regensburg, the press center there was buzzing. Reporters had already phoned in alerts to editors for the afternoon speech. We invited Father Federico Lombardi, the Vatican spokesman, to come and explain the pope's remarks in advance—in a sense, offering the Vatican a preemptive defense. But Lombardi seemed disinclined to run interference for Benedict, and commented merely that the pope did not intend to describe Islam as a "violent" religion. That did nothing to neutralize the news stories that had already been written at this point, and when the pope delivered his speech to an audience of German intellectuals, smiling and looking at ease in the safety of academia, reporters hit the "send" button.

In retrospect, Vatican officials would blame the Regensburg incident on a series of unfortunate circumstances. It was Father Lombardi's first foreign trip, and it came during a transition period: Cardinal Angelo Sodano was being replaced by Cardinal Tarcisio Bertone as secretary of state in a few days, and in the meantime no one was minding the store. Sodano, who had accompanied the pope to Germany, said he'd had no idea what the speech was about until he listened to the pope deliver it. No Vatican official, it turned out, had vetted the papal texts for phrases that might provoke misunderstanding or protest. The Vatican's coordinator of dialogue with Muslims, Archbishop Michael Fitzgerald, had been sent off to Cairo as a papal ambassador a few months earlier, and his replacement had not yet been named. The few lower-level aides who had seen the pope's speeches were apparently too intimidated to say anything. In terms of communications breakdown, it was a perfect storm.

Within a few days Benedict's speech had provoked the "wrath of Islam," as predicted in the first news reports from Regensburg. Few people had actually read the speech, but most had seen the headlines. Islamic gangs set churches afire in the West Bank. Iranian officials said the pope was part of a "Western conspiracy" against Islam. In street protests in Pakistan, Turkey, Indonesia and India, Benedict was burned in effigy while demonstrators chanted, "Crucify the pope!" Morocco recalled its ambassador to the Vatican, and other countries called for a papal apology. In Iraq, al-Qaeda groups reportedly promised war against "worshipers of the cross." Before the end of the week, an Italian nun would be shot dead in Somalia.

On the pope's return trip to Rome, as the protests were beginning to take shape, the mood in the press section of his plane was decidedly more lively. We had a major news event on our hands, one that would keep snowballing. And more important, we finally had a papal persona. While much of the initial coverage from Regensburg had a scolding tone—how could the pope have failed to anticipate the reaction?—the story line was already shifting: Far from committing a gaffe, Benedict had said what needed to be said to the Islamic world. He had done so deliberately and directly, adopting a less compromising style of dialogue. And in two months, he could take that tough new message directly to the Muslim world when he visited Turkey.

I was skeptical of "Benedict the Crusader," and even before the Turkey trip that image, like so many previous ones, began to unravel. To quell the firestorm the pope publicly expressed regret that his words had offended Muslims, emphasizing that he did not share the assessment of Islam that he had quoted. He then invited Muslim leaders to Rome and assured them he was not backtracking on interfaith dialogue. All this was to his credit, as Benedict seemed genuinely humbled to learn that an ill-considered phrase from the lips of the pope could have life-or-death consequences in the world outside the Vatican. But fellow journalists were divided on what this ultimately meant. Had Benedict really been that tone-deaf to Muslim sensibilities in Regensburg? Or had he been poking the beast?

In the Vatican press office one day, Ian Fisher, the *New York Times* correspondent, told me he suspected the pope's modus operandi was passive-aggressive. I could see his point. As a cardinal and then as pope, Benedict had a history of making provocative comments and then protesting that he had been misunderstood: Other religions were "gravely deficient." Protestant communities could not properly be called "churches." Catholics were "waiting for the moment when Israel will say yes to Christ." Priests should sometimes deny Communion to pro-choice politicians. Science can help people see the "intelligent design" of creation. In each of these instances the pope—or some representative—had been forced to explain and downplay his words in the face of public reaction. The same dynamic was at work now, as one Muslim leader after another held a "reconciliation" audience with Benedict.

Journalists, however, were loath to let go of this new image of a cultural warrior, a man who didn't mince words. A week before his trip to Turkey, Benedict appeared on the cover of *Time* under the headline "The Pope Confronts Islam." The story proclaimed that, unlike his predecessor, Pope

Benedict was a "hard-knuckle intellect" who was "unlikely to clothe himself in a downy banner of brotherhood." For much of the Western media, the stage was set for an interreligious showdown in Turkey.

But in Turkey, true to form, Benedict shifted gears. The first surprise came on the plane from Rome, when he told reporters that Turkey was engaged in important changes that brought it closer to Europe, leaving us to wonder whether he was signaling approval of Turkey's bid to join the European Union. A few hours later, in Ankara, after a private meeting with Benedict, Turkish prime minister Recep Tayyip Erdoğan said the pope had told him he supported Turkey's EU membership request. The initial response among Vatican reporters was skepticism; Erdoğan was probably just spinning the pope for political advantage. But when we asked Lombardi and other Vatican officials, they confirmed that as long as Turkey met EU human rights requirements, the Vatican looked with favor on its membership bid. This was a rather stunning development and—as WikiLeaks cables later demonstrated—one that was being closely tracked by U.S. diplomats. Most Europeans opposed Turkey's entry into the European Union, fearing that a populous Muslim nation with political and cultural ties to the East would permanently alter Europe's cohesiveness. A year before his election Pope Benedict had famously supported that point of view, observing that, in a cultural sense, Turkey had always represented "another continent, in permanent contrast with Europe." When I asked a Vatican diplomatic source what accounted for the about-face, he said simply, "In 2004, the pope was giving his personal opinion. Now he's speaking for the interests of the whole church." In other words, Benedict—the "hard-knuckle" straight shooter—had adopted the Vatican's diplomatic agenda.

In Turkey the pope turned down the rhetoric on Islam. He gently made the point that human rights and religious freedom must be the measure for Christian-Muslim relations. But above all he expressed his deep respect for Muslim believers. The crowning moment came on the third day of the trip, when Benedict made a "surprise" visit to the Blue Mosque in Istanbul—an event that had, in fact, been planned for some time. The setting was sublime: Built by Sultan Ahmet I in the early 1600s, the Blue Mosque, with six minarets and cascading domes, is one of the most famous religious buildings in the world. The pope entered the carpeted prayer hall after taking off his shoes and donning a pair of white slippers. He seemed genuinely interested as Mustafa Çağrıcı, the grand mufti of Istanbul, explained the religious significance of the architecture. Benedict looked up and admired the arabesque designs of the dome.

When they came to the mihrab, the carved marble niche that points the way toward Mecca, the mufti told the pontiff, "In this space everyone stops to pray for thirty seconds, to gain serenity." When the mufti announced that he was going to pray, Benedict, his arms folded over his pectoral cross, stood next to him and began moving his lips, as the Turkish TV cameras zoomed in for a close-up of the two figures.

"He's praying!" an Italian reporter shouted in the press center.

"No! He can't be praying—he's in a mosque!" came a protest from the other side of the room.

Thus ensued a bitter and very loud debate among the journalists, settled a few minutes later when our pool reporter, Serena Sartini, returned from the mosque with a papal quote. When the two men had turned away from the mihrab, she said, she clearly heard the pope tell the mufti, "Thank you for this moment of prayer."

To top it off, the pool reporter told us, the pope had received a gift from the mufti before leaving the mosque, a ceramic tile inscribed with the word "Allah" in the form of a dove.

As I rewrote the lead of my story, I thought, *What a great moment.* With one gesture Benedict had defused a religious confrontation and cast off the role of crusader. With a few seconds of prayer he had reminded the world that Christian-Muslim relations cannot be reduced to politics—that God is always part of the equation.

An hour later I packed up my laptop and headed to the lounge of the Hilton Hotel, where I passed Jeff Israely, who shook his head in what looked like grave disappointment. The journalists holding court in the bar had already passed sentence: The pope had wimped out. Instead of challenging the Muslims on their home turf, Benedict had turned the other cheek. And frankly, he had tried their patience. Once again, he had backed away from the persona that he, after all, had created. Someone who keeps walking off the stage was not going to get good reviews from this audience.

Ian Fisher broached the topic directly a few days later in a *New York Times* story that began, "Has the pope gone wobbly?"

The lightning-rod issue when discussing the "real" Benedict is priestly sex abuse. To his supporters, the pope has been the Vatican's quiet voice of conscience, having worked for years behind the scenes to establish new rules that would make it easier to defrock abusive priests. To critics, Benedict has been part of the problem, dutifully expressing moral outrage but failing to follow through where it really counts—i.e., firing bishops who cover up these crimes and dispelling the climate of clerical privilege that allows them to happen.

A week before John Paul II died in 2005, Cardinal Joseph Ratzinger delivered a talk that probably earned him the papacy. It was the annual Via Crucis procession at the Rome Colosseum, and Ratzinger was standing in for the ailing pope, pronouncing a meditation at each of the fourteen stations. Reporters received the text early, and it read like a prophetic warning: "How much filth there is in the church, and even among those who, in the priesthood, ought to belong entirely to him. . . . Lord, your church often seems like a boat about to sink, a boat taking in water on every side." To insiders it looked as if Ratzinger was setting an important marker: If elected pope, he would conduct a much needed housecleaning. This was a man who, as head of the Vatican's doctrinal congregation, had actually read the case files of the worst sex abuse cases. He had been outraged, we were assured, and would take action.

And as pope, he did take action. But it seemed to lack the sense of urgency felt outside the walls of the Vatican. His painstakingly slow investigation of Legionaries of Christ founder Marcial Maciel Degollado was a prime example. By the time the church determined that Maciel had abused seminarians, fathered children and paid off Vatican officials, the man was dead and buried.

Benedict's methodology was patience, and his primary objective was to protect the institutional church.

In 2010 an avalanche of new sex abuse disclosures surfaced in Ireland, Germany, Belgium, Austria, Switzerland and the Netherlands. In many ways it reprised the 2002 scandal in the United States: Bishops had moved abusive priests around, failed to act on allegations and rarely reported crimes to civil authorities. Most of the cases were decades old, but that did not stop the media drumbeat. Increasingly the blame was laid at the doorstep of Pope Benedict. Among the various "smoking guns" claimed by reporters was the fact that, in the early 1980s, a German priest accused of sexually abusing a child had been allowed to return to pastoral work in the Archdiocese of Munich when it was headed by Cardinal Joseph Ratzinger. The Vatican's defense was that Cardinal Ratzinger hadn't been aware of the priest's reassignment—the decision had been made by a subordinate, who publicly assumed all responsibility. There were hundreds of priests in the Munich archdiocese, church sources said, and the future pope couldn't be expected to keep track of them all. To most of us in the Vatican press room, that seemed reasonable, if perhaps compromised by Benedict's own recent exhortation to Irish bishops to always "be attentive to the spiritual and moral lives of each one of your priests."

Like other reporters, I wrote story after story on the new wave of sex abuse revelations. Most of the attention focused on old correspondence, archived letters and memos made available by U.S. lawyers involved in abuse lawsuits. For the lawyers, finding a trail of responsibility that led all the way to the pope would bolster the argument that the Vatican itself should be held liable for the damage done to their clients. For the media, it launched another version of the real Benedict, this time cast in the role of hypocrite: When it came to abusive priests, he spoke firmly in public but eventually gave priority to the church's corporate interests. Much was made of the fact that, under Benedict, the Vatican still did not support mandatory reporting of all suspected cases of sexual abuse to civil authorities, unless required by law. The Vatican's argument was that making bishops and priests reporting agents for the state would undermine the confidentiality necessary to their pastoral role. Church officials pointed out that other professionals, including doctors and teachers, had similar reservations about mandatory reporting. Nevertheless, in the court of public opinion, this policy now weighed heavily against Benedict and his aides. A Pew Research Center study found that the pope's approval ratings in the United States had plummeted: In April of 2010 only 12 percent of respondents thought that Benedict had done an excellent or good job in addressing the sex abuse scandal—a drop from 39 percent two years earlier.

No evidence was ever found, however, to suggest the pope had actively covered up sex abuse crimes. The Vatican, meanwhile, launched an information counteroffensive, publishing previously confidential policy documents and spotlighting decisions made by Benedict, both as pope and when he was head of the doctrinal congregation. The aim was to demonstrate that, over the previous decade, this pope had quietly added force to the church's abuse policies. For one thing, he had convinced Pope John Paul to establish a "shortcut" method of laicizing abusive priests.

But as often happens at the Vatican, this public relations campaign was abruptly derailed by the unorchestrated interventions of two papal loyalists. During Holy Week of 2010 the New York Times published a frontpage story reporting that in 1996 then Cardinal Joseph Ratzinger had failed to defrock a Milwaukee priest, Father Lawrence C. Murphy, who had molested as many as two hundred deaf boys. Vatican officials were incensed at the article, noting that it was only in 2001 that Cardinal Ratzinger's congregation took over the handling of sex abuse cases. The attempt to attribute this to Pope Benedict, they said, showed how low the Times had sunk.

This sense of being victimized by the media apparently inspired Father Raniero Cantalamessa as he prepared his sermon for the Good Friday prayer service in Saint Peter's Basilica. For thirty years Father Cantalamessa, a buoyant and bearded Capuchin friar, had served as "preacher of the Papal Household," a job that includes sermonizing to the pope and Roman Curia officials at various times of the liturgical year. Cantalamessa had long been involved with the charismatic renewal movement, and the gift of the Spirit seemed to pulse through his homilies, which skipped thematically from contemporary music to Old Testament passages to what was on TV the night before.

Cantalamessa's free-style approach to research had occasionally landed him in trouble. Preaching at the pope's Lenten retreat in 2009, he had reflected on President Obama's continued references to the utopian writings of the medieval mystic Joachim of Fiore, who had prophesied a time when the church would be unnecessary. The problem was, Obama had never actually cited Joachim of Fiore—it was a journalistic hoax that had taken root on the Internet. When Cindy Wooden of our office asked Cantala-messa where he had gotten his information, he was painfully candid: "Typing 'Obama Joachim of Fiore' into Google produces all of the news on which I based my speech."

Now, a year later, he decided to take a Good Friday walk through the sex abuse minefield. His approach was unusual: He suggested that the Catholic Church was being unfairly attacked, and that Jews—who "know from experience what it means to be victims of collective violence"—should sympathize. As Benedict and his aides sat expressionless next to the altar of Saint Peter's, Cantalamessa then read a letter from a Jewish friend, who said the current criticism of the pope and other church leaders reminded him of "the most shameful aspects of anti-Semitism." With that phrase the Holocaust alarm bells went off in newsrooms everywhere. The papal preacher seemed to be comparing the programmed extermination of six million Jews, who were innocent victims of a racist ideology, to some bad press endured by Catholic Church leaders, who had, in some cases at least, actually covered up sexual abuse by priests. No sooner had the pope processed out of Saint Peter's than Jewish groups around the world were protesting, and many Catholics were shaking their heads in disbelief.

Among those surprised by Father Cantalamessa's remarks were officials of the Vatican's Secretariat of State. About an hour after the sermon was delivered, Vatican spokesman Father Lombardi publicly disowned it, stating, "I don't think it's an appropriate comparison." He added that Cantala-messa's opinion was his own, and that his homily was not an official Vatican statement. The last thing the Vatican wanted was to escalate the sex abuse story by offending the Jews.

But by the time Lombardi spoke, the story was leading online news tickers. The next day it ran on page one of the *New York Times* and many other newspapers around the world, under headlines such as "Vatican Equates Criticism on Sex Abuse with Holocaust." The sermon was seen as evidence that Vatican insensitivity ran so deep and on so many levels that the pope and his aides were hopelessly disengaged.

Pope Benedict, however, had been as blindsided by the Good Friday sermon as everyone else. Strangely—unbelievably, to outsiders—the papal preacher had neglected to submit his text to anyone at the Vatican before pronouncing it to the pope and the world. Cantalamessa explained that no one had ever looked at his sermons ahead of time; essentially, he had an open mic every time he spoke.

But even as this episode was fueling more criticism of the Vatican, a small group of cardinals met to devise another public relations maneuver that would backfire. Cardinal Angelo Sodano was upset at the headline in the Saturday edition of one Rome newspaper: "Comparison of Attacks on Pope to Anti-Semitism Sparks Outrage." The worst part, for Sodano, was that Lombardi had practically disavowed Cantalamessa. Was it a crime now to defend the Holy Father? Something needed to be said, and Cardinal Sodano, as dean of the College of Cardinals—a position that gave him some leverage—saw a unique opportunity. He laid out his idea to the other cardinals, who nodded in assent: At the start of Easter Mass the following morning, he would deliver a brief "greeting" to the pope. It was an unusual gesture, but Sodano believed he could easily convince Vatican liturgists to make it happen. His talk would be a verbal vote of confidence in the supreme pontiff, certain to draw applause from the faithful in the square. The pope needed to know that he had their moral support, no matter what the media were saying.

In the Vatican press office the next morning, reporters were mystified but not particularly interested when Cardinal Sodano began to speak. It was raining, and Saint Peter's Square was a sea of umbrellas. Sodano called the pope "the untiring rock of the holy church of Christ" and thanked him for his strength, courage and great love. The world's cardinals, bishops and "four hundred thousand priests who generously serve the people of God" supported the pope, Sodano went on. By now Benedict had a wary look, as if he wondered where this was going.

"Holy Father, the people of God are with you, and they do not allow themselves to be impressed by the current petty gossip, or by the ordeals that occasionally strike the community of believers," the cardinal declared. The reporters suddenly perked up. Had Sodano just called coverage of the sex abuse scandal "petty gossip"? Sodano quickly wrapped up his message and walked over to the pope, who rose and embraced him. Benedict had a faint smile on his face, but he must have been concerned about the wisdom of this ecclesial pep rally. Sodano had not shown the pope his text before-hand; once again, Benedict had been in the dark.

Catholic News Service had been the only agency in the Vatican press office to record Sodano's *fervorino*, and soon our booth was crowded with reporters who wanted the exact quotes. The Italians kept repeating the key word, *chiacchiericcio*, and the Americans were arguing about how best to translate it: "petty gossip," "idle gossip" or "idle chatter." In the end the exact translation didn't much matter, as its meaning was clear. Cardinal Sodano later exacerbated the situation by telling the Vatican newspaper that the "unjust attacks on the pope" were motivated by opposition to church teaching on the family and on human life.

Not surprisingly, Sodano's remarks got more news coverage than anything the pope said that day, leading some to complain that the Vatican couldn't stay on message even at Easter. In the United States criticism came from all quarters, including some influential conservative Catholics who were frustrated with the Roman Curia's "ongoing out-of-touchness," as *New York Times* columnist Ross Douthat put it.

Even more galling was the fact that Cardinal Sodano himself had helped put the church and the pope in such a defensive position to begin with. For years Sodano had been the chief Vatican protector of Father Maciel, the disgraced Legion of Christ founder. If new reports published by Jason Berry in the *National Catholic Reporter* were correct, Sodano was also among those who'd received payments from Maciel in exchange for his favors. Young Legionaries, Berry reported, would routinely visit Roman Curia department heads and hand them envelopes full of cash, Mafia-style. Berry's articles were read by Vatican officials, who began to wonder whether making Sodano dean of the College of Cardinals was another of Pope Benedict's mistakes: If Benedict should die, Sodano would be the one to preside over the funeral and organize the conclave. In effect he would be the church's face to the world.

The backlash to Cardinal Sodano's "petty gossip" speech spread through other quarters, too. Diplomats wondered aloud why Benedict allowed himself to be caught unawares by his underlings, and why he didn't grab the reins of authority. The pope seemed to have lost control of the Roman Curia. A sense of uneasiness percolated through Rome.

All of which set the stage for what happened two weeks later in Vienna. Cardinal Christoph Schönborn was talking to a small group of newspaper journalists in an "informal" meeting—i.e., off the record, at least in Schönborn's mind. Asked about the sex abuse scandal, the cardinal opened fire on Sodano, saying he had deeply offended victims of clerical sex abuse by his "petty gossip" remark. Moreover, Schönborn said, it was Sodano who in 1995 had blocked a Vatican investigation of the late Cardinal Hans Hermann Groër—Schönborn's predecessor in Vienna—on allegations of sexual abuse of seminarians. Groër was forced to resign as archbishop but never admitted guilt. Sodano had used his influence as secretary of state to block then Cardinal Joseph Ratzinger from making a formal inquiry into Groër's actions, Schönborn claimed.

Cardinal Schönborn's comments were, of course, eventually reported and were viewed with fascination by observers who had never witnessed open warfare among cardinals. Some thought Schönborn was positioning himself as a *papabile* for the next conclave. More likely, Schönborn was trying to subtly defend his old friend Joseph Ratzinger—underscoring the fact that, under John Paul II, Ratzinger had tried to aggressively pursue sex abusers but had been thwarted by Roman Curia enablers.

But if that was his aim, Schönborn had miscalculated badly. An infuriated Cardinal Sodano went directly to the pope and convinced him not only to call Schönborn in to clarify the matter, but to make the Austrian cardinal undergo a virtual auto-da-fé and public humiliation. In June of 2010 appeared a remarkable one-page Vatican *bollettino* that described, in detail, Schönborn's trip to the woodshed. First Benedict and Schönborn had a private discussion, and then Cardinal Sodano and Cardinal Bertone were brought in. The Vatican statement was unusually blunt, saying Schönborn had been asked to explain his criticisms of Sodano and he had dutifully expressed his "sorrow" over the public reaction. It clarified Sodano's use of the term "petty gossip"—which, according to the Vatican, had been completely misinterpreted as a lack of respect for sex abuse victims. The bottom line was this: "It should be remembered that in the church, when there are accusations against a cardinal, the competence rests solely with the pope; others may have an advisory role, always with the proper respect for the person." This was Schönborn's sin: He had broken ranks. One cardinal must never criticize another in public, using the media as his messenger. Cardinal Schönborn left Rome and maintained a prudent silence for months to come.

The journalists in the Sala Stampa reported this as yet another effort to muzzle criticism in the church. Vatican officials spun it differently, citing it as an example of greater transparency. Pope Benedict, they argued, had identified a conflict, brought in the key players and straightened things out—and then made it all public. But it wasn't convincing, as hands-on management and disciplining subordinates were simply not Benedict's style. And the supposed urgency he had displayed in neutralizing criticism of a Vatican cardinal was something he had never shown in other matters, including clerical sex abuse cases. As a manager, Benedict was in fact rather passive; he seemed to think time would heal all problems, or perhaps make them irrelevant.

The sex abuse scandal had by now affected everything the pope did, and had become an undercurrent present in every trip he made, every bishop he appointed, every priest he ordained. It had begun to negatively affect church finances, as more and more dioceses declared bankruptcy in the face of lawsuits and as fewer dollars were sent to Rome. It emboldened critics and even some bishops to question the church's rules on celibacy. It left the church's corps of priests dispirited, and parishioners more and more wary.

To his credit, Benedict quietly strengthened the rules for dealing with abusive priests, met with abuse victims in several countries and professed a deep sense of shame at these cases. But his main public response was to declare a vague period of "penitence" for the entire church. He spoke increasingly about moral relativism as the root cause of sexual abuse, as if the church had been infected by changes in the outside world rather than by the structural weaknesses in the church itself. He failed to acknowledge that the prevailing ecclesial model of authority and secrecy and clericalism had allowed abusive priests to be protected for decades. In short, he had no intention of dismantling the system, and he was convinced the church could weather the storm with its own resources. He didn't trust civil law, psychological professionals or—least of all—the media to provide real answers. True reform would come from prayer and conversion, he kept insisting. It would not come from whistle-blowers like Cardinal Schönborn. Benedict's methodology was to protect the institutional church, the church that had protected him from the age of twelve.

By 2011 the real Benedict was beginning to look a little like Charlie Brown, convinced he couldn't win in this world but plugging away regardless, with a demeanor that often seemed either dispirited or wistful. As a concession to the crowds and the cameras, the pope occasionally forced a smile. He launched what he hoped would be his legacy project, a Vatican agency to promote "new evangelization" in traditionally Christian countries. The agency played to the pope's primary theme of rediscovering the rightful place of God in personal life and in society. But Benedict had no illusions about its success, speaking openly about the dominant "culture of death," the powerful pull of materialism, the seemingly unbridgeable chasm between rich and poor and the fact that Catholics in Europe and the Americas were leaving the church in droves. Benedict appeared resigned to the idea that the church was condemned to struggle against the cultural mainstream, perhaps as a minority—even in places where it had once shaped civilization.

The pope operated with such detachment that one might legitimately have suspected him of having given up hope on the sorry state of earthly affairs. Visiting a Rome parish one day, he probably shocked his listeners when he posed these dark questions: "If we look around the modern world, where God is absent, we have to say that it is dominated by fear and uncertainty: Is it good to be a human being or not? Is it good to be alive?" In the end, of course, the pope would always come down on the side of hope and insist that giving up was not a moral option, that Christians were obligated to work to improve this world and, specifically, to engage in acts of charity. If "God is love," as he wrote in his first encyclical, then people best share in that love through acts of kindness and self-sacrifice to others.

Unsurprisingly, this was a message that barely moved the needle on the journalistic news meter. Although Benedict made occasional symbolic appearances with the needy, it was difficult for people to view him as a living example of charity in action. His aides insisted that the pope maintained a very simple lifestyle, but the sumptuous setting of every photo or video from the Vatican gave a different impression. Benedict did preside over a "poor people's event" once a year. In late 2010, when he hosted 350 homeless from the Rome area for a post-Christmas luncheon, he sat at the head table and conversed at length—remarkable for a man who rarely invited guests to lunch or dinner at the papal apartment. Benedict generally preferred to dine alone, and sitting at the table and making small talk was perhaps a form of penitence. He needed his private life for time to think, to pray and to write—activities best conducted in solitude.

In public the pope cut back on his interaction with large crowds. At the beginning of his pontificate, he accepted the idea that pressing the flesh was part of the modern papal job description. At the start of his weekly general audience, he would walk down the main aisle through the multitude, his nervous smile lit up by thousands of camera flashes, extending his hands and then having to yank them from the grasp of well-wishers. He soon stopped running the pilgrim gauntlet, however, which seemed to him a distraction.

Sometimes the distractions came to him, in the most awkward manner. In December of 2010, I sat in the Vatican press office watching the pope at his general audience on the room's big monitor. The sex abuse scandal was still the biggest story of the year, and the crowds in the audience hall seemed smaller. The pope had finished his routine greetings in seven languages when four young men dressed in white costumes assembled directly in front of the pontiff. This was the annual "circus audience" day, when performers from a local circus were given five minutes to show off their talents—usually juggling or acrobatics. We gathered around the monitor in the press room with mild interest, but what happened next prompted groans and guffaws. On cue, the men peeled off their shirts Vegas-style, revealing tanned muscular torsos, and performed a supple pyramid balancing act. Pope Benedict looked mildly embarrassed, but the audience loved it, and a few appreciative whistles could be heard. The video became a YouTube favorite, under titles like "Surprise Strippers in Vatican!" and "Pope Captivated by Shirtless Male Acrobats." The image of four men stripping in front of the pope was not one the Vatican wanted in circulation, but once again, no one had previewed the acrobats' performance.

A few weeks later the pope ended his audience by meeting with costumed members of the Cologne Carnival, a traditional seasonal celebration in Germany. The video showed Benedict warmly greeting an amply endowed figure in blond pigtails. But as the camera zoomed in, it became apparent that the lipsticked lady was actually a man. Once again the press room erupted in laughter, though there was a logical explanation: In the Cologne Carnival, the figure of the *Jungfrau*, or "maiden," is always portrayed by a man dressed as a female. But, tradition or not, it looked to most people as if the pope were consorting with a drag queen.

There were security incidents, too. On Christmas Eve in 2008, a deranged Swiss woman in a bright red hoodie jumped the barriers in Saint Peter's Basilica and nearly reached the pope as he processed into the church. Incredibly, the same woman showed up a year later—wearing the same red sweatshirt—and this time managed to knock Benedict to the marble pavement. The pope was fine and carried on as if nothing had happened, but a French cardinal broke his hip in the chaos that followed. The barriers were immediately moved farther from the pontiff.

As an astute observer of contemporary culture, Benedict knew that to get a hearing in the modern world, one had to firmly take hold of the microphone. Yet his low-key approach to the papacy, which guaranteed that the media would ignore him, also seemed part of his strategy: to preserve the church from the superficiality of the media culture. Even as papal aides launched YouTube and Twitter feeds and Facebook pages in the pope's name, Benedict kept his distance from the social networks and from computers in general. He still wrote out his documents longhand, with a pencil. He received thousands of personal e-mails but never answered them. While Vatican officials were lauding the idea that communication in the digital age was a two-way dialogue, the pope spoke in a permanent monologue. In public talks, his insistence on making almost no concession to current events made him immensely popular with a core group of conservative Catholics, but made him irrelevant to those he was theoretically trying to reach: the huge percentage of Catholics who no longer went to church or paid much attention to religion in general. Here was a man who, on any day of the year, could open his window above Saint Peter's Square and command the attention of the world, exploring the moral and ethical dimensions of any issue he chose: economic collapse, human trafficking, environmental disaster, the arms trade, global politics. Instead, he opted to speak of Saint Hildegard of Bingen and her mystical visions in the twelfth century.

When Benedict did stray into topical areas, it was never for very long. Some of his most interesting statements, for example, critiqued the prevailing capitalist-consumerist economic model as a self-centered trap: "Take everything we can get in this brief moment of life. Consumerism, selfishness and entertainment alone are worthwhile. This is life. This is how we must live. And once again, it seems absurd, impossible, to oppose this dominant mind-set with all its media and propagandist power." These are dramatic words to come from a pope, but they have been typically undermined by the familiar tone of futility and the lack of any follow-up. The pope has always hesitated to delve into the details, or suggest remedies, or illustrate his arguments with real-world examples—even when they could be found in his own backyard.

In 2012 Benedict appeared to be a passive observer of a rare case of financial whistle-blowing at the Vatican. When Archbishop Carlo Maria Viganò took over as secretary-general of Vatican City in 2009, one of the first things he noticed was that the Vatican was paying an Italian company 550,000 euros—roughly $750,000—to set up its annual Nativity scene at Christmas. Viganò, shocked, managed to reduce the cost by more than a third the following year. The Christmas crèche was only the beginning, however. He soon discovered that the awarding of inflated contracts was a common practice in Vatican City, which seemed to have imported Italy's tolerant attitude toward favoritism, nepotism and corruption. When Archbishop Viganò took steps to rein in such practices and cut costs, he found himself criticized by anonymous sources in Italian newspaper articles. Fearing that he might be transferred to another post, in the spring of 2011 he took the unusual step of writing to Pope Benedict, spelling out the situation and asking for the pope's moral support—in effect, pleading to keep his job. Six months later a dejected Viganò was cleaning out his desk: The pope had named him the new apostolic nuncio to the United States. He would be stationed forty-five hundred miles from financial decision making in the Vatican.

When all this was revealed in early 2012 on the Italian TV show *Gli*

Intoccabili—The Untouchables—the media focused on the fact that Viganò's letters had become public, signaling an internal Vatican war and a potentially endless stream of revelations. In coming weeks "Vatileaks" would indeed provide several more documents and some tantalizing glimpses of life behind the Vatican walls. Throughout the affair Pope Benedict remained remarkably silent. This was a pope who had many times condemned corruption in civil society, and who in 2010 had created a new agency to guarantee financial transparency in the Vatican. Yet faced with actual evidence of impropriety and infighting in his own city-state, he appeared uninterested.

When the pope finally did act, it was to plug leaks rather than root out disreputable economic practices. He named a panel of three elderly cardinals, empowering them to investigate not the substance of Viganò's complaints, but rather how they had been divulged to the press. The arrest of Paolo Gabriele, the pope's personal valet, came after Vatican police had searched Gabriele's apartment and found a large cache of confidential documents. In the past the Vatican might have handled the case quietly, but in the view of top officials at the Secretariat of State, the rash of leaks had placed its very sovereignty at risk, and a show of strength was required. The world was thus treated to a highly unusual spectacle: a public trial at the Vatican.

The trial, which was open to the press and included testimony from some of Pope Benedict's closest aides, was viewed by the Vatican as a groundbreaking demonstration of transparency. But in many ways, the proceedings against Paolo Gabriele illustrated a disconnect with the modern understanding of due process.

The evidence against Gabriele was overwhelming: Vatican police testified they had found in his possession about a thousand purloined documents, both photocopies and originals, including some bearing Benedict's handwritten order: "to be destroyed." A gold nugget and a check for 100,000 euros, both gifts to the pontiff, also turned up in his apartment. Gabriele admitted photocopying documents, saying he had done so during work hours in the small office he shared with the pope's two personal secretaries. Gabriele also acknowledged passing some of the documents to Italian journalist Gianluigi Nuzzi, who quickly spun the material into a bestselling book about the Vatican. The papal valet said he had been inspired by the Holy Spirit, and that he had acted because he feared Pope Benedict was being manipulated by other Vatican officials.

After his arrest, Vatican investigators had persistently questioned Gabriele about his motives, his potential accomplices and, above all, his presumed *mandanti*—the higher-ups pulling the strings. But when Gabriele took the stand at his trial, he said he had acted alone. When he tried to explain the reasons for his actions, the presiding judge cut him off. Nor did the judge want to hear about others who might have been in contact with Gabriele or about the findings of the three cardinals appointed by the pope to investigate the leaks. In keeping with legal custom in Italy, the judge repeatedly "edited" the transcript of testimony, entering into the record his own summation of what witnesses had said, at times removing remarks about Pope Benedict and other high Vatican officials. In short, the Vatican was putting on trial a single employee, one with delusions of grandeur (according to a court-appointed psychiatrist), and not holding a public hearing on the alleged resentments, conflict and backstabbing in the Roman Curia. As expected, the trial ended with a quick conviction, a reduced sentence and the expectation of a papal pardon, allowing Benedict to put the whole episode behind him and move on to the "real" work of the church.

This scandal was primarily an Italian affair, and, like other recent events at the Vatican, it pointed to a deeper level of discord. The polarizing figure appeared to be the Vatican secretary of state, Cardinal Bertone, who had his share of loyalists and enemies throughout the Roman Curia and the Italian hierarchy. But the battle lines were so convoluted that not even Italian journalists could figure out who was on whose side. Each day's newspapers carried fantastical scenarios of secret allegiances, blackmail, double dealings and false friends. The Roman Curia seemed to have degenerated into a dominion of ecclesial mafiosi.

Faced with such an internal mess, Pope Benedict consulted briefly with top Vatican officials and a small group of cardinals, but he showed no interest in personally refereeing Curia power struggles. As commentators derided the "intrigue and disarray" within the Vatican, church officials began speaking openly about the leadership vacuum. As one European cardinal quipped to a French reporter, "Is there a pilot on board?"

The pope read the newspapers, too—at least some of them. He continued to be convinced the Vatican's problems were being inflated by a malicious mass media, and he complained publicly about "gratuitous" coverage that "went far beyond the facts." But at a deeper level Benedict was not overly concerned about the bad reviews and the epidemic of anarchy-in-the-Vatican stories. He had long ago immunized himself against the sting of worldly criticism. In a revealing off-the-cuff talk to Rome seminarians in February of 2012, he said the power of public opinion was based on appearance, not truth, and that "Christian nonconformism" should involve "freeing ourselves from this need to please, to speak as the masses think we ought to." Benedict would never acquiesce to the language or mind-set imposed by popular culture.

That was true even when the pope made overtures to those outside the church. In late 2011 Benedict had convened yet another edition of the interreligious "prayer for peace" summit in the Italian hill town of Assisi. A popular event first introduced in 1986 by John Paul II, the gathering in earlier versions had had its critics—among them Cardinal Joseph Ratzinger—for giving the impression that the prayers of all religions had an equal hearing before God. Benedict's aides solved that conundrum by eliminating public prayer from the program in Assisi. Oddly, it seemed, the world's religious leaders had come to the birthplace of Saint Francis simply to give speeches.

As I sat in the Assisi press center, one speech in particular now demanded my attention. Julia Kristeva, a Bulgarian-born French philosopher, psychoanalyst and linguist, was one of four nonbelievers invited by Pope Benedict to the Assisi encounter. These were agnostics, not flame-throwing atheists, and they had been carefully vetted by the Vatican to avoid any possibility of public embarrassment. Nevertheless, their presence here was a true innovation, and seemed to open the possibility of a more open dialogue. As Kristeva wound up her speech, however, I realized that this would be yet another dialogue of scholars, Benedict-style. "There is no longer a Universe; scientific research continually discovers and investigates the multiverse," Kristeva declared. "Do not be afraid to be mortal. Capable of understanding the multiverse, humanism is called to face an epochal task: inscribing mortality in the multiverses of life and the cosmos."

I looked over at a table of Italian reporters and held up Kristeva's text. "Did anyone understand that?" I asked. "Not a word," someone shot back as he busily typed his story.

All hailed the Assisi event as groundbreaking, and it was clear that Benedict himself relished the moment, leaving the distinct impression that the pope would much rather converse with intellectual agnostics than with questioning Catholics. And his "new evangelization" campaign was headed in the same direction. The Vatican had just launched a program called Courtyard of the Gentiles to reach nonbelievers and fallen-away Christians. It took special aim at university communities and was so heavily academic that my colleague Robert Mickens, correspondent for the British Catholic magazine *The Tablet*, dubbed it "Courtyard of the Eggheads."

On the conservative end of the Catholic spectrum, the pope was seen as a quiet hero, a countercultural truth teller who used words and the power of reason to cut through wrongheaded conventional wisdom. Conservatives loved the fact that Benedict didn't play the media's game. Even among journalists, he had his admirers. At times, he could be insightful and eloquent and even down-to-earth—for example, explaining why a true sense of justice demanded a Judgment Day, or telling young people that the church would never pander to them, or downplaying papal infallibility with the line: "The pope is not an oracle."

To younger audiences in particular, Benedict made an effort to simplify the message without diluting the content. He has often spoken about "friendship with Jesus" as the source of true happiness in life. Given his own deep faith, the pope should be able to say, "Just look at me." But that's part of the problem: Whatever his inner peace and harmony, Benedict rarely looks as if he's having fun.

Someone once asked me: When have you ever seen Pope Benedict express joy? I had to think long and hard. The spectrum of his public emotions typically ran from detached to mildly amused. Joy, delight, elation—or anger or indignation, for that matter—were just not in his emotional repertoire. Then I remembered his final full day in Bavaria in 2006, at a brief stop in the Regensburg Alte Kapelle, a thousand-year-old church decked out in rococo splendor after an eight-year restoration. Benedict was there to dedicate a new organ. It was neither a solemn liturgical moment nor an occasion for high teaching, just a minor cultural duty—local Catholics had proudly named it the Papst Benedikt Orgel. The pope devised a little talk for the event and delivered it with relish. He declared without hesitation that the organ was "the king of all musical instruments" because it could give expression to the full range of human sentiments, "from joy to sadness, from praise to lamentation."

As I listened to the speech, it struck me that Benedict was not simply reading it. He truly believed every word, and the conviction was clear in his voice.

"The organ's great range of timbre, from *piano* through to a thundering *fortissimo*, makes it an instrument superior to all others. It is capable of echoing and expressing all the experiences of human life," he said. When the organ is played, it reminds us of the "immensity and the magnificence of God."

Then Benedict sat back and listened as the first familiar notes of Bach's Toccata and Fugue in D Minor blasted through the pipes. When I glanced at the pope, he appeared transported, the thrill was clear on his face. It was music that brought him joy. But what was it exactly about music? Surely not the emotional pull that was typical of rock, or the catchy melodies found in popular songs. No, his pleasure was more mathematical: For him, the beauty was in the music's structure. As a classical pianist, he knew the system well: It was pure, it was orderly, it never disappointed.

And now, here in Regensburg, I'd just heard the pope offer an analogy between the organ and the Catholic Church. When an organ is tuned and well played, he said, it produces wonderful music. Dissonant notes are a sign of problems. In both cases, he explained, "an expert hand must constantly bring disharmony back to consonance."

This was the real Benedict. A man who saw himself as maestro. Faith was the music that never disappointed. He knew this music well, and he knew the consolation and satisfaction it offered. For eighty years he had comforted himself with its certainties, its harmony. And now he was trying, against all odds, to make everyone understand what to him seemed so apparent: This was a beautiful way to live.

ACKNOWLEDGMENTS

THIS BOOK TOOK SHAPE during many years of covering the Vatican, and it owes much to different sets of people who offered expertise, advice and criticism along the way. I first want to acknowledge Catholic News Service for providing me with an opportunity to report freely and accurately on the Vatican for nearly three decades. In particular, I thank CNS director Tony Spence, as well as the editorial staff in Washington, D.C., and of course my colleagues in the Rome bureau. My position as CNS Rome bureau chief helped give me greater access to officials at the Vatican, a crucial advantage in the news business, and allowed me to travel to more than sixty countries and witness how popes and Vatican officials interact with local cultures. I alone am responsible for the content of this book, but I am indebted to the management and reporting teams at CNS for the resources they provided and the high level of professionalism they demonstrated.

Reporting on the Vatican is often a cooperative enterprise, and journalists build on one another's work. In that sense, I want to acknowledge the work of my fellow *vaticanisti*, many of whom have offered me a wealth of insights, direction and encouragement over the years. They are far too numerous to list here, but they should be aware of my gratitude.

This project would never have been completed without the cooperation of a small universe of Vatican sources, whose openness and honesty were at times surprising and always appreciated. I could not begin to name them all—and many would prefer not to be named—but one expression of thanks should go to Jesuit Father Federico Lombardi, the Vatican spokesman, and his capable staff at the Vatican press office, who have assisted me and many other journalists, in Rome and abroad, in a spirit of candor and fairness.

My work benefited from previous books about the Vatican, and in particular drew upon information provided by the authors Jason Berry, John

Cornwell, David Gibson, Jesuit Father Thomas Reese and Massimo Sanso-lini.

Many people helped me by providing feedback on the manuscript in the draft stages, including Jason Berry, Hope Klocker, Bridget McKeon, Te-resa Murphy and Cindy Wooden. A special word of appreciation goes to my wife, Lauren Thavis, and my father, Richard Thavis, for their valuable comments on the work in progress. I am grateful, too, to those who encour-aged me at the beginning of my book project, especially Peter Dwyer, Al Eisele, Phoebe Natanson and Alan Thavis.

To my agent, Kristine Dahl of International Creative Management, goes my deep thanks for her enthusiastic support and her expertise in navi-gating the waters of the publishing world. Finally, I want to thank Rick Kot, my editor at Viking Penguin, and his assistant, Nicholas Bromley, for their insight, their fine editing skills and their patience with the author.

INDEX